FORTY
AND A

Harper & Row, Publishers, San Francisco
Cambridge, Hagerstown, New York, Philadelphia, Washington
London, Mexico City, São Paulo, Singapore, Sydney

ACRES GOAT

a memoir by

Will D. Campbell

Title page illustration by Jim Hsieh

Hardcover edition published in 1986 by Peachtree Publishers, Ltd. First Harper & Row paperback edition published in 1988. Reprinted by arrangement with Peachtree Publishers, Ltd.

Library of Congress Cataloging-in-Publication Data

Campbell, Will D.
Forty acres and a goat.

Reprint. Originally published: Atlanta, Ga. : Peachtree Publishers, c1986.
1. Campbell, Will D. 2. Civil rights workers—United States—Biography. 3. Southern Baptist Convention—Clergy—Biography. 4. Baptists—United States—Clergy—Biography. 5. Afro-Americans—Civil rights—Southern States. 6. Southern States—Race relations. I. Title. E185.98.C36A3 1988 973.923'092'4 [B] 87-45691 ISBN 0-06-061301-7

---

88 89 90 91 92 RRD 10 9 8 7 6 5 4 3 2 1

For Sister, Paul and Betty

Just because T. J. Eaves exists in more than one body doesn't make him any less real.

I
Abide With Me

HIS UNCLE COOT used to tell him, "Boy, there ain't no use to go to school to learn how to do something they won't let you do nohow." Looking back, he wondered how Uncle Coot knew that. He wasn't an educated man. At least he hadn't been to school much. Just enough to learn how to read and write good. As the boy looked back, he knew that didn't mean his Uncle Coot wasn't educated.

Uncle Coot, like all the men in the family in 1933, was an ordinary cotton farmer in the hill country of south Mississippi. He seemed old to the boy, though at the time he was not much past forty. As for him, he was what they called a yearling boy, nine or so. His daddy called him a dry gourd because 1924, the year he was born, was the hottest and driest summer anyone could remember.

Uncle Coot always seemed to be sure of things. He didn't claim to know much. Said he really didn't know anything at all. Said he just suspected a lot of things. That was one of the things he suspected —

that if you learn too much, the folks you learned it for won't listen to you because they will think that *you* think you know more than they know.

He and Uncle Coot were lying in the shade at the end of the cotton rows one day, waiting for Aunt Ruth to bring them some water. She would bring it in a five-pound Jewel shortening bucket with most of the red lettering worn off. The water would taste like homemade hog lard, because that was what had been in the bucket after the shortening had been used up frying chicken and making biscuits or crusts for blackberry pies. The homemade hog lard that took the place of the store-bought Jewel shortening was used for the same things as long as it lasted. Then the container became a water bucket. He and Uncle Coot would not complain about the taste, because that was the way water brought to the field in a bucket tasted in 1933.

"What you gonna be when you grow up, boy?"

"B'lieve I'll be a preacher, Uncle Coot." He had decided on that when he was just turned seven, right after he had been baptized. At nine, he couldn't remember a time when he didn't want to be a preacher. Much later a Jungian analyst, who then was an Army surgeon in the Second World War, told him he wanted to be a preacher because his mamma had decided he would be one five months before he was conceived. The doctor told him that even though he hadn't asked. And even though he was an orderly in the hospital and not one of the doctor's patients. He thought he intended to be a preacher because he had been *called* to be one. And drawing on some other things Uncle Coot had told him, he suspected that the call could come in various forms. Like, in their community, the preacher, the school principal, and the RFD mail rider were the only people who had cars. And it gets hot picking cotton in Mississippi in August. He knew he didn't want to be a school principal or a mail rider. The cars weren't air conditioned. But he had watched womenfolk fanning the preacher with palmetto fans while he ate Sunday dinner, and the call seemed to be carried by that breeze. Uncle Coot told him it was all right to think like that, considering one of the Sunday School's memory verses about mysterious ways and wonders. He wanted to be one of God's mysterious ways, His wonders to perform. He knew that the Lord was not devious. But maybe clever.

So when Uncle Coot had asked him, he had answered, "B'lieve I'll be a preacher." He had not told anyone before. Probably because no one else had ever asked.

"That's real good, boy," Uncle Coot said. "But be a good one." It had not occurred to him that there were anything but good preachers. That was when Uncle Coot first told him there wasn't any use to go to school to learn how to do something they won't let you do nohow.

It was a long time before he knew that Uncle Coot was telling him that too much education could be a bad thing for a preacher. That if you get too much learning, it will cut you off from the very people you want to serve. Preacher Gardner and Preacher Lane were powerful preachers in the county, and they had never been farther from home than the railroad. "Going to the railroad" was an expression people used when they meant they were going to town.

Not only did the boy intend to be a preacher, he intended to go a lot farther from home than the railroad. And he did.

At first the consolidated country high school seemed big to him. He once counted the books in the library and there were almost two hundred. He wondered how it would be to know everything in all those books. Then one day one of the teachers drew a big circle on the blackboard. She made a tiny dot in the circle. She told them the circle was the world and that if they knew everything in every book in every library in the world, the little dot was how much they would know. He questioned how important books were after that. And he started listening more to Uncle Coot.

He remembered that one of the books in their library had to be removed when his daddy discovered it was by Charles Taze Russell, founder of the Jehovah's Witnesses. His discourse on the Battle of Armageddon was not in keeping with Baptist doctrine. As Baptists, they believed in a rigid and complete separation of church and state. Anything in the school which did not reflect Baptist doctrine, especially if it reflected "Russellite" doctrine, was a clear violation of that principle. The civics teacher agreed with his daddy that the book should not be there. And for the reasons his daddy gave. However, the teacher pointed out that also as Baptists they did not believe in burning books. The two agreed on a compromise. They would quietly remove the book from the shelves and place it in the agriculture teacher's compost pit. There, among the rotting leaves, grass clippings, and emptyings of the school wastepaper baskets, there would never be a single and sudden moment when it would cease to be a book. The boy was sure his daddy was right about the book and the teacher right about its disposal. But the library seemed much smaller after that.

From the consolidated high school he went to Louisiana College, a small Baptist school across the Red River from Alexandria. Though he was there for little more than a year, he learned a lot of things. More than he would learn at any other school. Maybe it was because he had a lot of things to learn. Later he would learn other things at Wake Forest, Tulane, and Yale University. And in between by correspondence from the Armed Forces Institute during the Second World War. He was in the South Pacific, the courses were free, and he thought it would be a good way to get chemistry and calculus, two subjects he hated, on his college transcript.

All along he knew that it was a great distance from the shade of Uncle Coot's cotton rows to New England's Ivy League. What he did not know, but found out, was that it was a lot farther from New England's Ivy League *back* to the shade of Uncle Coot's cotton rows. That was the trip he had in mind but never made.

He tried. God knows he tried. After graduation, a gracious little village church in north Louisiana took a chance on him. Even then he was sure that the pulpit committee must have known that someone from the Baptist seminary in New Orleans, or Fort Worth, or no seminary at all, would be a better risk. He was glad they gambled, sorry that they lost. He lost too. It just didn't work out. Some were glad it didn't work out, but most helped him in the trying. A saintly old saw sharpener at the sawmill, the village nestor, discreetly suggested that he was saying what needed to be said, but maybe he could say it with more force. He knew the old man was telling him that he should pound the pulpit, raise his voice, hold an open Bible in one hand and gesture wildly with the other, leaving the typed manuscript at the parsonage. But he simply couldn't do it.

When he left the village, he thought he was going because he was not free to share all he had learned during eight years of higher education. As Director of Religious Life at a state university, he knew things there would be different. It was 1954 and the Supreme Court had recently ruled that public school segregation was unconstitutional. He could be an invaluable ally to the university which, he was sure, would draw on his enlightenment and liberalism as it moved to full equality.

Somehow that was not the case. So by middle 1956, he was seeking fuller fields of service. Having been thwarted in his maneuver to deliver the university's young from the shackles of racial bigotry and their elders from constitutional ignorance, he moved on.

A less stalwart pilgrim would have been dispirited in his quest for freedom. Two jobs in two years. Later on he reckoned that what he really was looking for was someone to pay him to do and say what he wanted to do and say. Slowly he learned that that isn't freedom, that freedom is not something you find or someone gives you. It is something you assume. And then you wait for someone to come and take it away from you. The amount of resistance you put up is the amount of freedom you will have. But that lesson was not yet. Now he was going to work for the most free and fearless agency of the nation's religious apparatus.

Because of his modest efforts to emancipate white minds and black bodies in Louisiana and Mississippi, and because the moral fervor (or naiveté) with which he had approached the task had attracted some national attention, he was offered the job of Race Relations Specialist with the National Council of Churches. He was to involve himself in the Civil Rights Movement which, in 1956, was gaining momentum and promised to be the most exciting time in the nation's social history since women's suffrage. A missioner to the Confederacy, bridge between white and black, challenging the recalcitrant, exposing the gothic politics of the degenerate southland; prophet with a Bible in one hand and a well worn copy of W. J. Cash in the other. For this he was born to be called.

He basked in the warmness of this spiritual home. An ecumenical oasis in the desert of denominational strife and moral impotence. A medium of ministry standing above petty doctrinal irrelevancies to judge the nation with the eyes and voice of an Amos or Isaiah. It was the vehicle he needed.

Little by little he began to suspect that the ethical stilts which held this ark afloat were as fragile as those supporting the establishments of Baptistland and Academe. Underneath there was the same quagmire of unfreedom. Every cause and every system seemed to have a credo, a line one is expected to follow, a prescribed channel in which to swim. To assay the banks is to court disfellowship. To challenge the line outright leads directly to the unemployment line.

It was a sad and disillusioning lesson to learn. Why wasn't he told that in the first grade? Or the first day at the university? That *all* institutions, every last one of them — no matter the claim, no matter the purpose, no matter the stated goals — exist sooner or later for their own selves, are self-loving, self-concerned, self-regarding, self-preserving, and are lusting for the soul of all who come near them. His flight from local parish to the enlightenment of the academy to the promised land of an ecumenical council had been a journey to nowhere.

What was left?

He tried not to be afraid when it happened, when the stilts splintered and he found himself once again with a call but no steeple. He had never doubted or questioned that call. He still couldn't trace it to some bush on fire that wouldn't burn up. He had never been struck blind on the East Fork Road like Paul going to Damascus, and there was no heavenly voice setting forth the details of just what he was supposed to do. Yet he was as sure then as he was in the shade of the big sweet gum trees on the edge of Uncle Coot's cotton field that the vocation he had chosen was somehow or other the doings of a higher power.

One of his schoolmates at Yale Divinity School used to tease him with the saying: "It's a mighty poor God who'll call a man and then not qualify him." He wondered if God the jester might have done that. From the beginning he had known that God was not bound by Aristotelian logic, that He had His own way of doing things. It might be that He occasionally calls one to a life of failure, thus delivering the called one from the sin of pride. The same call might even serve to keep *God* humble, though he had never thought of humility as being an attribute of God. An American steeped in the cult of success has trouble dealing with the notion of failure as God's will, but perhaps it is another of His mysterious ways. Maybe the call was authentic all right, but the qualifying had been neglected for reasons he had no right to understand.

Or maybe, way down deep, he didn't really want to be a preacher.

Maybe he had a psychological allergy to things holy which he had submerged and disguised in the raiment of something else, something he didn't understand and didn't want to understand. His penchant for self-destruction in his brief professional career seemed to give credence to the notion.

He began to have doubts. Not about the call but about himself. "What's the matter with me?" he asked himself.

* * *

With *me*? *Me* as antecedent to *himself*?

* * *

What *is* the matter with me? Why have I sat at this typewriter all morning bandying around the third person singular pronoun when reality lies in the first person singular?

He is *I*. I am *he*. Except when *he* referred to Uncle Coot. And twice when *He* referred to God. And now when he is . . . I am old, they tell me that God is not a He. (The usage is still correct grammatically, but theologically unsound. One must choose between being a grammarian and a theologian.)

Why *he*? Why has it not been *I* from the beginning? In a few minutes I will go to the kitchen for lunch. As is her custom, my wife Brenda will say, "Well, Will, what have you been doing this morning?" I answer: "He has been giving some thought to a new book. In fact, he even sat down at his desk and wrote a few pages. Furthermore, he. . . ." Nothing happens immediately. She looks at him funny-like and changes the subject. But later in the afternoon she will place a conference call to the three issue we have. "Kids, I think we had best get a little more serious about what we were discussing when y'all were home Christmas. You know, about putting your father in one of those nice cheery homes for the golden years."

"But, Mom, we were just teasing," one of them will say.

"Yeah. We were. But now I'm not so sure. All through lunch he thought he was someone else."

Writing about oneself does have some hazards. But only if the accomplishments have been such that the report of them places the writer within the rank of the high-and-mighty. Nothing he is apt to write . . . *I* am apt to write . . . will be in that category. So why be embarrassed or afraid? Almost every novel is an embellished autobiography, so let it be I. To do otherwise is to imply that one's own words and deeds are of such magnitude that if they are not ascribed to another, the common bounds of modesty are violated.

So it was I lying in the shade with Uncle Coot. It was I who did not heed his warning that what one thinks is the best possible preparation can lead to separation. And it was I who, after three jobs, was left with a pulpitless, roofless, unpropertied and uncodified church. I must have a church because I was called to be a preacher.

But what was left to try for a *church* after defeat in three ministerial dimensions?

Forty acres and a goat! This is a partial account of how that worked out . . . in the unlikely event someone else wants to try it later on.

II
Through Cloud and Sunshine

SOME PEOPLE THOUGHT Jackson was a strange name for a goat, but I never did. Not because we live here in the shadow of the Hermitage, where some of almost everything is named Andrew Jackson, Rachel, Old Hickory, Hermitage, or Tulip Grove. I'm not sure why I felt it an appropriate name for him. I do know that Jackson is an important name today. From Jesse to Mahalia. Reggie to Michael. I also know that it has fallen our lot to reap the harvest of seeds sown in the age of Jackson . . . an age going on.

Appropriate or not, that was his name.

There are many things in the Bible I have never understood. Sometimes I have dealt with them through blind acceptance. Some I have chosen not to spend much time thinking about. A few I have taken to the scholars, those overreckoned but generally useful technicians trained in matters of exegesis, hermeneutics, higher criticism and all that. One approach is probably as good as another. In a universe which makes so little sense anyway, a few violations of logic and rationality, an occasional contradiction, or seeming impossibility within systems the human mind has established for purposes of its own do not strike me as being of any special importance in measuring the worth of Scripture. A fish swallowing a man and not gagging in revulsion for three days may say something about the tolerance of the whale but little else. Also, the report of Joshua that the sun did not move (never mind his physics) for almost an entire day and everything on earth was not burned to a crisp is no harder to believe than an informed and civilized society allowing a few political animals unrestrained access to something which can, and probably will, incinerate the planet and unsettle the universe.

My early conditioning makes it difficult for mc to take even the most tentative exception to anything the Scripture states, even the things which to me make no sense. But there is one question I have long harbored: *Jesus, what was it with you and goats?*

He never seemed to like them. Sheep were synonymous with good. Goats with evil. The sheep are on the right. Goats on the left. (The political implications of that used to bother me too, until I learned that such declensions are largely irrelevant to anything that really matters.) Sheep receive the blessing of the Father and are said to enter and possess the prepared realm of reward. Goats go to the eternal fire that is ready for the devil and his angels. Sheep are loving and compassionate. Goats leave people hungry, naked, and in prison and do not visit them. Face to face, I'm sure I'll see it clearly. But here and now, in this prisonhouse of the flesh, I don't. For I loved Jackson very much.

He was a Capricorn. When he was old, I told his doctor that he was a Capricorn. He said that was unusual.

"Why is it unusual for a goat to be a Capricorn?" I asked him.

"Because goats don't have air conditioning," he told me. He said it as if there was nothing else to say. A few days earlier, my three-year-old grandson had told me I couldn't hum the same song he was humming. "Big folks don't hum that song, Papa!" he declared, dropping my hand as we walked in the woods.

"They don't?" I said, a little surprised at his certainty. "Why not?"

"Because," he said, taking my hand again, patting it gently and speaking as though I were the child, "big folks eat Chinese food with sticks."

I was sure that the logic of what he said was so apparent I shouldn't question it. Later I remembered that a month earlier I had asked for chopsticks in a Chinese restaurant. When he wanted some too, I told him little folks ate with spoons and forks. It became clear. Big folks are the only ones who can eat with sticks, and little folks are the only ones who can hum "Rolling in My Sweet Baby's Arms."

I didn't press the veterinarian about Capricorns and air conditioning but simply moved on to something else. If not many goats are Capricorns because they don't have air conditioning, well, there must be a reason. Something else I couldn't understand: He had told me the gestation period for goats was 151 days.

"What about five months?"

"No, 151 days. February. Leap Year. Thirty days hath September, April, June, and November."

Counting back from his birthday, January 19, he would have been conceived on August 15. It's too hot for some things in South Georgia in August, but not for an unknown goat couple in Bibb County, flesh and blood of Jackson. For whatever reason, their issue was a Capricorn. By sign and by being.

Rolling in My Sweet Baby's Arms. Indeed.

Jackson is dead now. He lived with us for almost two decades, just a few miles from where the Jackson for whom he was named lived and is buried.

One of the things I learned from him was that in many ways his days were an extension of the days of Andrew. And that he and the many other animals who came and went here were reflections of the human culture. And of what was happening in their time. And of what was happening in Andrew's time.

The age of the Jacksons. Many of the policies of Andrew's Age had to be reckoned with by the Age of the Capricorn Goat. And many of them are still not rectified. Most of our Jackson's friends were in the alleged liberal and democratic tradition of Andrew. Whether their activities will leave the world in any better shape than those of Andrew is yet to be recorded. They were times of uncertainty. Times of turbulence. The sixties. Then the seventies. But they were good times too. Maybe better times than the world will ever know again. The powers and principalities against which we wrestled seem now to have perfected their system so completely as to preclude the wrestling itself. At least there were clear issues then. Room and reason to struggle. A time between the Enfield Rifle and the black box. Jackson's people saw it all. His generation might have seen the last of struggle for a long time. Maybe in another millennium or so, when the world shall have partially recovered from a few minutes of nationalistic madness in the dark ages they will call "the crazy Twentieth" and has a clearer understanding of humanity's propensity for badness, there will be another chance. As for now, those dibblers of history who lived with Jackson the Capricorn goat will go on planting whatever seeds they have and play out the drama in their heroic, if sometimes pathetic, effort to stem the tide of apocalyptic mischief. It is not easy now to resist the powers and principalities. (Who among us can even identify them?) And if all we can do is record the efforts of Jackson's people and creatures, well, we will do that. For they were times which should not be forgotten. They were people, and other creatures, who tried.

"The Sixties." For some a term synonymous with social activism and reform. To others a cliché, an insert in American history, chaos sandwiched between two eras of order, the sowing of discord by the discordant. But for all a day of change, a time when nothing slept.

There was political exertion among black Americans and the young of all colors not known before. Days of Civil Rights. Days of Vietnam. "The Yanks are Coming," gave way to, "Hell No, we won't go!" Joan Baez was George M. Cohan in refinement. Or retrograde. Love for one's country was often expressed in open and sometimes violent defiance. "Friendly cop on the block" was translated "pig," and "American way of life" was "The Establishment." "I Wonder if Canada's Cold" became a foreign place of refuge, a song of evasion and desertion.

Old Black Joe lost his manners, and "Yassah boss" became "We demand!" Gentle voices calling were screams of protest and mass meetings in country church houses. Old times not forgotten had not to do with sweet magnolias and cotton fields, but with sitting at the back of the bus and Mamma washing white folk's clothes. "Look away" was not to Dixieland but to Supreme Court justices and massive civil rights marches.

Behavior which would have been seen as disgraceful in other times became acceptable and courageous within the age group which traditionally fights the nation's wars. Those who had expected and required it of them over the centuries were caught between cerebral respect and gut hostility and resentment, knowing in their hearts that they were sending their children on a mission of shame.

It was into this era that Jackson the Capricorn goat was born. And we were part of it all when he came to live with us. I as a bootleg preacher and freelance civil rights activist. Brenda as farmwife, mother of three children, coadjutor to a Baptist preacher with no parish save forty acres and a goat, administrator of an income of modest proportions.

* * *

Mahalia. A Scorpio. Symbol of death and rebirth, whose songs of grace and sovereignty — "He's Got the Whole World in His Hands," "His Eye Is on the Sparrow" — certainly certified her as a catechist of anarchy. If the Lord God Jehovah has all the power, Caesar is nothing and is to be neither feared nor trusted.

And George. He died as a self-proclaimed and verified revolutionary in San Quentin. *Soledad Brothers*, *Blood in My Eye*. Born August 21, barely within, but very much of, the sign of the Lion. Leo: just has to "shine," never giving up hope, urging himself and others onward when things are darkest. Self-assured, big brother to all, outgoing and outgiving; impulsive but expansive. The sort that "die with their boots on," never quiet nor still.

Reginald. Taurus the Bull. Ah, yes. Stubborn, unyielding, and "bull-headed." (Ask Billy Martin.) Bombastic and a hoarder, physical instincts over-emphasized. Taurus will listen but seldom agree. A candy bar named for him, and three home runs in one World Series game.

Jesse. Libra. Battling now — some think exploiting — the scars of an ancient wrong. Libra. A cardinal sign. A sign of air and balances. Can act as impulsively as a small child, thoughtlessly, without regard for anything other than seeking physical, mental, and emotional thrills. Or can be sane and serene, the master of one most difficult to rule — the self.

Michael. And his brothers. Bistro stuff in the sixties. Dominating the eighties. Singing, dancing, disporting his way to victory. Victory over the devils of poverty. Victory too over their own Witnesses of Jehovah, who peddle their *Watchtowers* from door to door on Saturday mornings and talk of Armageddon — no longer a quaint notion.

I don't mean to suggest that I take any stock at all in astrology. When I was a child, we planted certain crops when the Moon was waxing, chopped the weeds out when it was on the wane. We tried to get our hair cut as soon after New Moon as possible, because hair grew slower then and the two-bit haircut would last longer. We didn't call it astrology, though, and we knew nothing about natal charts, transits, trends, and aspects. It was just something we knew to do. Something passed on to us by our grandparents the way it had been passed on to them. If the credibility of it had been challenged, we would have settled it the way we settled the truth of the Bible. The Bible is true because the Bible says it's true.

I made fun of folks who took astrology seriously. Once a woman was talking with me about a problem threatening to destroy her family. As she was leaving I playfully, yet earnestly, made a sign of the cross on her forehead. "And if you don't mind," she said quite sternly, "I don't believe in your voodoo."

"Oh?"

Later, in a more relaxed setting, she asked my wife what our Zodiac signs were. Then told both us of more than we wanted to know, when she discovered that I was a Cancer and Brenda was an Aries.

Still, after Jackson the Capricorn came to Tennessee to live with us and a neighbor did a chart on him, I didn't *not* believe in astrology as fiercely as before.

From Andrew and "Stonewall," shot by his own Confederate troops in the Shenandoah Valley, to Jackson the Capricorn Goat who died quietly of old age in Tennessee, far from the land of his birth. Jacksons all. With signs of their own. All in their own way expressed, reacted to, or have been a protraction of what historians have called the revolutionary age of Jackson, seventh President of the United States.

Humans keep the census. So far as we know, other animals do not. We do not know that for sure, however, because we know so little about other animals. Far less, I suspect, than they know about us. And, until now, humans have conquered the other animals, though we don't know how long that will hold either. Who knows what will emerge supreme when this present era of law and government has wreaked its final havoc and a new epoch beyond epochs shall have begun? And who's to say that what we have thus far called human history was no more than a gossamer interlude in Creation's aeonic evolution, making its way back to some pre-Edenic perfection? (Love thy gnu!) Whatever. So far, humans have done the conquering. And the naming, giving first and last names to ourselves but not to those we call lower.

Jackson, a goat, was just named Jackson, first and last. It seemed enough. When something was needed to distinguish him from other Jacksons, the surname A'Goat was used. But it seldom seemed appropriate. The letter A with an apostrophe is Eastern. Jackson was American. Without boasting. Without apology. He lived in a revolutionary world like the other Jacksons. And left his own mark upon it. A world of less ambitious boundaries, but one he appropriated and savored.

* * *

We brought him to Tennessee from Georgia. From whence he had been in bondage. To this land.

We of the Great Depression were told that land was the only sensible investment. Its value goes up and down with the times. And, unlike stocks and bonds, you can walk and spit on it.

"Clear and unencumbered. We have a clear title to this little piece of ground." We heard it often as children. Words not so much of pride as of assurance. Certification that we would still be there next year and the year after that. No bank to foreclose and move us on. No landlord to evict. Our own land. Some of it passed down from an earlier generation. Some acquired on the stamina and gritty determination of a daddy and mamma whose labors knew no bounds and who never responded to the occasional seductive overtures of the city: a regular pay check. Lightbread and canned salmon from the store on weekdays.

Brenda was of the land also. Her parents were Louisiana rice farmers, that class between yeomanry and landed gentry. Mississippi hill cotton farmers, my people, were of the former. For reasons I don't understand, those who grew up in modest circumstances seem more inclined to regard the land with extravagance than do those who knew the comfort of the manor. It was so with us. Brenda was not at all pleased with the notion of moving into a rundown, two-hundred-year-old farmhouse. Made originally of logs, the big hand-hewn timbers in the attic still witnessing to its sturdy essence, it was later covered with poplar clapboard, edge lapping over edge like fallen dominoes. Eventually, before we came, the comfortable dog-fashion clapboard gave way to aluminum siding; durable, tasteless, one more testament to cultural deterioration in the name of industrial progress. There were also sound and understandable objections for her beyond the aesthetic. Three children in a drafty, barnlike house. They could freeze to death, fall in the old dug well in the yard, get snake bitten. Country schools of unknown quality. Rural mores may not tolerate an alleged radical, a white man who goes on civil rights marches, a preacher who has no place to preach. And it's a long way to the store.

Granddaughter of a country preacher and child of a farmer, she had vowed at a young age to marry neither. The one she chose aspired to be both. Maybe it was because of that early resolve, the subtle and unintended ascendancy of one person's will over another, that her choice of spouse never quite made it as either. As making it is measured. But she weighed the things favoring the move as well, things as practical as low mortgage payments and as quixotic as the now quaint and generally discredited covenant, "Whither thou goest I will go."

Perhaps it was no more than instinct that brought us to these Tennessee acres. Certainly it was not with the notion of farming for profit. It was, I think, the call of the land, the congenital passion for footing and space. The valley still exudes old man Oscar Bass's being and bears his name. A fourth generation black neighbor described him as "a redheaded, bearded, Irish-looking fellow, who would pepper you with buckshot for stealing his corn one day and make a batch of moonshine whiskey with you the next." He never married and was something of a recluse. He felt no need for modern conveniences, spurning the use of electricity, telephone, and automobile. Not long before he died, one of the worst ice storms ever to hit middle Tennessee paralyzed the area. Telephone and electric lines were down, and numerous lives were lost in the sub-zero cold. (Some of them could have been saved in the rural areas if families had not sealed in the "messy old fireplaces" when they installed the much touted cheap electric heat of the TVA.) Hundreds huddled together in church houses, schools, and other public places. Mr. Oscar was not seen throughout the crisis, and when a concerned neighbor finally knocked on his door, he found him by the fire, surrounded by his vast assortment of dogs, safe and warm.

"What storm?" he asked.

In amused disbelief, the man described the two-week siege, the death and destruction left in its wake.

"Now, since you mention it, I did notice that it was a tad slippery 'round the barn for a day or two there." Losing something you never had doesn't change your life at all.

Oscar Bass. One of many blood heirs of Humphry Basse and Mary Buschier, he a haberdasher on High Street, London, in the sixteenth century. And of their son, Nathaniel, who arrived in Jamestown, Virginia, in 1619 and settled at "Basse's Choice" nearby. A son, John, married Keziah Elizabeth Tucker, daughter of the Chief, or Elder, of the Nansemond tribe. Their son, William, also married a Nansemond woman and, when the occasion arose, chose to be certified a Nansemond Indian. *(Norfolk County, Virginia. — This certifies that William Bass, the bearer, tall, swarthy, dark eyes, weight about 13 stone, scar on the back of the left hand, is of English and Indian descent . . . and is numbered as a Nansemond by his own choosing, the said Bass dwells in this county & hath a good name for his industry & honesty. Given this day of the 20th of Sept, 1742.)* He was later Elder of the tribe but did not suffer the fate of John Ross, who was also Indian and Chief by choice. Their grandson, John Bass, came to the land of the Cherokees, to this county, as a white man. When he came, it was still a hunting ground, pure and undefiled. Unmolested oaks, ash, hickory, cherry, beech, black walnut, elm, maple, and red cedars formed a giant canopy for buffalo, bear, panther, otter, raccoon, rabbit, and squirrels aplenty. When Oscar was born just half a century later, the Canaan quality was gone. Gone too were the buffalo, panthers, and bears, all dispensable to the takers of this promised land. Oscar would have been content to leave the land as his people found it. And as far as he could he did. But he was the last of the line. No car, telephone, electricity, to keep him in constant touch with what he refused to acknowledge as progress.

Such was Old Man Oscar Bass. I wish I had known him. His RFD mailbox, which somehow escaped the estate auction after his death, long lines of rock walls, watering troughs he or the Cherokees made by chiseling deep cavities in huge sandstones, occasional scraps of antiquated farm tools, and bits of what I take to be from an illegal (though not uncommon at the time) artifact — the moonshine still — all tell me something about him. I wish I knew more.

It was to his land we came. And soon after brought Jackson. Though buffered by two city families between Mr. Bass's time and ours, there was still a mild wilderness quality remaining. The bucolic presence of the Old Man, though faint, was here.

But the barn? There was an untended, free-standing tool shed and an equally neglected chicken house nearby, but no barn. Going through an old barn produces various moods in grown-up offsprings of the land. To some, a pleasant reminiscence. In others, depression, euphoria or measurable variations between. More than a few, male and female, have told me it evokes libidinous urges; in some cases, urges long outlived or repressed. All that aside, a homestead of this vintage without a structure to keep livestock, store hay and grain, cure tobacco, or shelter newborn lambs and pigs is unusual. But there was not one here. There was one just down the road, though. Not the sort to attract Norman Rockwell, but charming and adequate. Sharply pitched roof, massive gables with stoutly hinged doors opening to a spacious hayloft. A drive-through hallway, lined with horse and milking stalls, and a ceiled-off area the more fancy would call a tack room but which working farmers called the corn crib or feed room. The sides, rough red, went from the roof to the ground all around. Some people covet their neighbor's house, wealth, spouse, or fancy car. I coveted his barn.

In my untidy envy, I began asking my neighbor about his barn one day. It was, he said, about sixty-five years old. It had been built for his father at a community barn raising — those delightful social occasions of earlier days when friends, kinfolk, and neighbors gathered en masse and built a barn, sometimes in one day. This one took longer because it was larger than most. He described the felling of the trees, how they were hauled to a wildcat sawmill on a wagon pulled by five Percheron mares. Each step. He referred to himself as a shirt-tail, yearling boy, and said he remembered it so well because his daddy let him ride the lead mare to the sawmill and back.

I listened as he lived again the marking of the trees to be cut, their shape and size and kind, amazed that he named among them cherry, walnut, chestnut, and cedar. I watched with him as the community of his father laid the foundation with twelve-by-twelve timbers, stood clear as they hoisted the heavy beams to the high places, sometimes by a team of smaller built men standing on the backs or shoulders of the stockier ones in a three-tier pyramid formation. I heard the last roofing nail driven in place by his father and tasted the corn whiskey, hidden from the womenfolks who were not yet summoned, as the workmen passed it round and round.

"The next winter they built one on your place," he told me when he finished describing the barn raising on his father's place. "They built one for Mr. Oscar."

"They built one for Mr. Oscar? Where is it?" I asked, not sure I wanted him to answer.

"Oh, they burned it down." He said it matter-of-factly. "That first family that bought the place, they burned it down." He curled his lips and shrugged his shoulders, holding the upward shrug and starting to chuckle under his breath; waiting, I suppose, for me to lead him on. When I didn't respond, just sat there looking at him, feeling like my birthright had been snatched from me, he dropped his shoulders and went on.

"Yeah. And I don't mean no harm. I know you've just moved out here from town and all. But town people are funny." He waited again. He knew that he had a comical and preposterous tale, but he wanted some encouragement, wanted me to ask him to use it all up. I asked him to tell me exactly what had happened.

He sighed lightly, leaned against the shady side of his daddy's barn and began. I could tell he had told it many times before, yet it was fresh and gripping. Like an inspired actor who has said the same lines a thousand times, but whose audience feels they are hearing something never spoken before. I was entertained, at times laughing when he laughed; at times infuriated, hoping throughout that in the end it would all be a joke, that he would lead me into the deep woods and show me the twin to the handsome structure in whose shadow we sat. I would open my eyes and there it would be. My barn!

"Yeah, like I say. Town people are funny. Not that I have anything against them, you understand. I've lived in town myself. But when they moved up there in the house where you live, they said they had a lot of trouble with rats. And I saw some of them. They really did have trouble with rats. Old Man Oscar lived there by hisself and I reckon he wasn't always the cleanest with things around the house. Every kind from tiny little mice to them big, long-tailed devils you see in alleys — Norway rats. I got three cats living in this barn for that very reason. Still I've seen rats in there that look like possums. Well, they got the Orkin people out there. I ought not to say Orkin. I don't really know what company it was."

I knew how his story was going to end, but he was enjoying the performance and I was enjoying watching him enjoy it.

"And they tried everything. So they told me. Different kinds of poison baits, traps, everything. As you know, them professional companies, they have to get results or you don't have to pay them. At least, that's what I've heard. So every time the people called and told them they still had rats, here they'd come again. Finally they told them all the rats were coming out of that old barn and that they'd have to get rid of it."

"So they burned it down," I said.

"It was quite a fire," he said, shaking his head the way one does when he hates to tell you something but can't wait to do it.

I had heard the cliché, but here it was in reality. They actually had burned down the barn to get rid of the rats. Town people *are* funny. Jackson could have had a nice barn.

* * *

The Dolan family lived a few hundred yards to the south of us, through a thick grove. Mr. Dolan was a Mescalero Indian, one of less than a thousand to survive the oppression of the Spanish, Comanches, and Americans, pushed from the Sierra Blanca to California to Texas, herded and interned finally on a forty-mile-square tract of semi-arid land in southern New Mexico. They were described by early observers as being the most passive of all Apaches, as being happy and gregarious. Intervening history changed that. Eddie Dolan was not happy. I never saw him laugh, not even the faintest smile. His wife, Kathleen, was a local woman, not an Indian. I don't know how to say that she was a native and he was not. I learned to say "native American" like good liberals did. But in time it seemed that was no more than further denial of what we did to those whose country we took. It is true that we gave them the name Indian, the explorers being lost at the time and thinking they were on the other side of the world. That seems to argue against using the term. But it is also true that we gave their land the name America, and to refer to those earlier owners as native *Americans* seems no more appropriate and speaks no more of justice than to call them *Indians*. Both are our designations.

Mr. Dolan was a man trouble and hard times continued to stalk in the same merciless and unrelenting fashion it had stalked his people since the European intrusion upon their land nearly five hundred years earlier. He missed the reservation and often returned. He made their meager living as a groomsman, and that meant following the horses from Chicago to Florida and being away most of the year. Sometimes he got local jobs, but if it snowed when he was a telephone lineman, he saw no sense in going to the office just to punch the time clock. He seldom held a job for long.

And Mrs. Dolan was a kind and good neighbor, but the same foreboding shadow seemed to haunt her as well. Like some calamitous specter, an unknowing arrogation of connubial contagion, the adversity was shared. She had been married before and had adult children. Not long after we came, one of her sons returned home from the Navy, bringing with him his young bride from California. It was a week of celebration. Old friends, kinfolk. We could hear the music, talking, and laughter through the trees. The fun ended one day when Jason and two of his cousins were coming home from town in the little sports car he had driven from California. Another car pulled out of a side road, forcing them onto a bridge railing and down a steep embankment. All three were killed. After the funeral, the bride went back West and Mrs. Dolan retreated into the deepest recesses of mourning.

At the earliest budding of solace she was struck again. It was Bonnie and Penny's birthday celebration and we had been out to eat. (They, our daughters, were born two years apart.) As we topped the hill and started the descent into our valley, we saw flames leaping into the sky. It was our house, or it was the Dolan house. Brenda raced the curves of the country dirt road and I tried feebly to prepare the children for a scene they could handle better than I. Penny, firstborn, was concerned that Goddie, her imaginary friend, might be trapped inside the burning building. By the time we made the turn down the long drive leading to our place, we could see that it was not ours.

The wife of another of Mrs. Dolan's sons had gone into premature labor and was inside our house, scared and crying. Her three small children were trying instinctively but pathetically to comfort her. Brenda stayed with her, and I made my way through the trees to the burning house. Little had been saved. Mrs. Dolan, standing alone close to the fire, closer than anyone else could stand, would not move and would not answer our pleas, a statue of despair and hurt put on hurt. She was not crying or making any sound at all. Just standing, staring as the ashes settled around the outlines of iron bedsteads, kitchen furniture and whatever the wretched conflagration could not reduce to unrecognizable nothing, the rock chimney towering over it all like a giant gravestone.

"Two lives was lost in that fire," Joel, her surviving son, said. "Edwina's parakeet and that white mouse." And a woman's spirit, I thought.

It must have been two hours from the time we arrived and darkness returned to the area as the smoldering embers gave way to gray ash. All that time Mrs. Dolan had not moved. Suddenly, and still without making a sound, she turned and walked through her field and into the pitch-black woods on the hillside.

"Where's she going?" I asked her son, who watched her with me but made no effort to stop her.

"She does that sometimes. She can't cry when there's somebody around. She always comes back."

It was a cold January night. I never knew where she spent the remaining hours of it. We banked the fireplace in our house and left the doors unlocked, but she was too proud or too wasted by this ruthless and ineffable visitation to come in.

It was mid-morning when I saw her again. A heavy fog, almost a mist, wet the air, and as I approached I could see a moving figure outlined against their old barn, which was far enough from the house to survive the fire. When I got close I could see that she was carrying some bedding and dragging an army canvas cot, half unfolded. "I really appreciate all you and Mrs. Campbell did for us last night." She said it over and over. I couldn't explain our helplessness, so I told her the baby, a seven-pound girl, had been born about four-thirty that morning. She smiled weakly, said she hoped they would be all right, and went about setting the cot up inside the feed room. I told her we would be glad to have her and Edwina stay with us until they could get settled somewhere. She thanked me, said we had done enough, that she had a kerosene heater and that they would be fine there for the time being, at least until Eddie got home from Hialeah.

We had known it was her house or ours on fire. How does one be glad it was *not* his house without being glad, if it had to be either, that it *was* hers? He tries not to think about it. Without success.

They made brave starts to rebuild that year. They found an abandoned house in another county, dismantled it piece by piece, and hauled it in. They got the foundation footing poured, the superstructure and roof built. But it was hardly more than a holding operation. The bold commencings seemed always to meet defeat. There was quarreling over whether they should sell the land and move on, maybe get a mobile home and put it on a relative's place, move to town, or go to New Mexico. Mr. Dolan continued to make frequent trips to the reservation. Sometimes she would go and bring him back, sometimes wait for him to come back on his own. Because Edwina was half Mescalero, she was entitled to a share of tribal income from the sale of horses, the same share as her father. Mrs. Dolan counted on it, waited for it so she could buy more supplies for the new house.

One Saturday Eddie left for good. "He just put his hammer down and walked off," she said. Why she thought this going away was final, I never knew. She continued the rueful efforts of building, often alone, but there was an air of resignation about her after that, and it did not go away.

Early one afternoon she came to our door, said she was too dirty to come in and said she had come to take care of some business. I knew what it would be and wished I didn't.

"Mr. Campbell, do you and Mrs. Campbell want to buy our place?" She said it as if speaking of the most ordinary thing. I offered to help her get a loan to finish the house, and she silently shook her head. It was the same when I asked if she didn't think Eddie would come back the way he always had. After a long pause, she added that the reservation had never really turned him loose. "And I don't reckon Eddie ever really turned it loose."

We didn't need the land, couldn't afford it, and with fifteen acres felt like land barons already. We were, after all, fresh from the subdivision. Yet if she sold it to one of the developers active in the area, we would be back in a subdivision. And they wouldn't give her what it was worth. She needed the money to survive. Those were the facts — facts which seemed weighted on our side, and were. But alongside facts was the gnawing of history: The Indians always lose the land. The record of Manifest Destiny kept pestering whatever trace of honor the success of that ignoble doctrine had left in the white soul, making further rationalization cumbersome. I didn't want to deal with it, and in vain I sought some Pilate basin of deliverance.

All of that was interspersed with light flurries of anger: Dammit, Eddie Dolan, you might as well have stayed in that cottonwood grove where General Carlton and the territorial militia placed your people more than a hundred years ago! You're back there anyway and have left behind a bequest of aggravation! . . . sins of the father . . . sour grapes . . . children's teeth set on edge! White man's burden . . . goddam!

There was, of course, no evil intent on anyone's part. No replay of Andrew Jackson's schemes. No scalping for bounty, nor carnage like Sand Creek, Wounded Knee, or Arizona Apache. No broken treaty, forced removal, trail of tears. No deceptive legislation with troops to compel a conquered people. No Babylonian captivity such as Eddie Dolan's mescal people had known at Bosque Redondo under Kit Carson. Yet it was another muster and roll call in microcosm. An asterisk no one intended but was there. One more faint echo on the record of national culpability.

The white folks got the land.

Mr. Dolan signed the document on the reservation in New Mexico, conveying to some white people living in the shadow of Andrew Jackson's Hermitage, and to their heirs in perpetuity, a parcel of land.

The man at the title company said his signature was worthless, that reservation Indians can't own land. He recorded the deed with the wife's signature.

The passing of time, and some slightly more exemplary behavior in later years, have assigned much of our truculent past to footnotes and sometimes to no mention at all. Schlesinger's *The Age of Jackson*, generally accepted as the definitive accounting of that era, says not one word concerning Andrew Jackson's Indian removal policy. And to remember it on the occasion of the transfer of title to a few acres in Tennessee sounds affected and masochistic. After all, we gave the Dolans twice what the land developer offered. Still and yet. . . .

Their land became our land, part of the Campbell place.

And Jackson A'Goat spent his first night as part of our family there.

Living to the west of the Oscar Bass place when we came was an elderly black couple, Mr. and Mrs. Young. Hezekiah and Kate. An earlier Hezekiah, the twelfth king of Judah, had long been my favorite king of that special land, despite some difficulties with my favorite prophet, Isaiah. I was pleased to have land joining that of his namesake. I was also pleased that he was a black Hezekiah.

It was a time of violent resistance in many urban and suburban areas when black families, no matter how literate and genteel, tried to move into white neighborhoods. In Levittown, Pennsylvania, a few years earlier, there had been weeks of rioting, firebombing, and general misbehaving when the William Myers family decided to move into what had been designed, built, and advertised as "the most perfectly planned community in America." There were schools, churches in balance of cross section, shopping centers, parks. Nothing had been left out in planning for wholesome family living. The Myers family might have been the prototype for the authors of the Levittown idea — family oriented, young, educated professionals, employment stability. Only one flaw: They were not white. Perfection in community planning had not reckoned with the greatest enemy of life in community — bigotry. When we came, we took pride in living peacefully in a setting of black, white, and brown in rural Tennessee.

Unlike their next door neighbor, Oscar Bass, the Youngs availed themselves of every modern convenience they could afford. Their car was old but adequate. The house and yard were largely carbons of many others belonging to poor but proud black families in the deep South. It was a small, six-room structure, well built. All the inside walls and ceilings were of heart pine, which had been covered with several layers of newspaper sheets for insulation. Though no doubt chosen at random, one could imagine important dates etched forever on the minds of the children raised there from seeing them every day stuck on the walls. Stories of the Graf Zeppelin, the kidnapping of the Lindberg baby, and a march on Washington by World War veterans, broken up by General Douglas MacArthur, were all on one wall. In another room, I learned that the passage of the Social Security Act and the death of Will Rogers came on consecutive days in August, 1935.

The yard was bordered with crepe myrtle bushes, once so common in the South that the sign of them said poor folks live nearby. Now they are promoted in seed catalogs as a rare oriental specimen of beauty. Closer around the house was a solid line of privet hedge, thickened by so many crew-cut trimmings as to make passage through it impossible. In the area between the crepe myrtle and privet hedge were several tall and scraggly cedar trees, with automobile tires cut in the shape of baskets hanging from the lower limbs and filled with a variety of petunias. Underneath a small shed was the water well with a neatly kept pulley, windlass, and a long, narrow water bucket with more than a hundred feet of cotton rope, replaced each year, to draw the water out. Near the well were two stocky peony plants, both white, which Mrs. Young said were planted by Hezekiah's mother more than seventy-five years ago. For winter color there was the inevitable bottle tree — dozens of brightly colored bottles, always dominated by the deep blue of Milk of Magnesia bottles, arranged in a neat pattern of cross pieces fastened to a center pole, the bottle on the end of each limb combining to produce a garish, though pleasing, campestral mosaic.

When we came to this valley, it might have been the paradigm for the Civil Rights Movement . . . the beloved community. But destiny, manifest to none in the movement, would not have it so for long. Mr. Hezekiah died. And there was no Manasseh to reign in his stead as with Hezekiah, King of Judah. His widow moved in with a daughter, and the old house was left to the mischief of all who knew that it was there. And to the wrack and ruin of time. Legends already existed about the place being haunted. The stories attracted the thrill seekers and Halloween revelers. A young girl, murdered during the Civil War and thrown into an abandoned well, still cried out for vengeance. Organized groups gathered to hear her wails and moans. A small cemetery, nothing more than sunken and unmarked graves containing the remains of some of Hezekiah's ancestors, added to the mythology. Professional soothsayers held late night seances, and amateurs convened with playing cards, Ouija boards, and a diversity of tools and equipment for conjury and witchcraft. Some of the gatherings were innocent. Others were fronts for thievery.

Mrs. Young had intended for everything to remain exactly as it was the day her husband died. Sheets, pillows, and handmade quilts were left on the same iron bed they had shared for half a century, a porcelain night jar nearby. Family pictures remained in place. A large, round oak table was set for two; silverware, saucers, and coffee cups. All of Mr. Young's clothes and most of hers hung in the closet. Kindling and firewood were neatly stacked near the Warm Morning potbelly stove. Piece by piece, everything in and around the house began to disappear. Eventually, even the heavy oak table was gone, carried through a mile of thick woods.

When everything was gone, even pages of the old newspapers on the walls, and only piles of rubbish scattered on the floors remained, Mrs. Young still resisted the pressures of her children and stepchildren to sell the land. But at last her sad day came. A daughter from Chicago called and asked if I would come and visit the family before she had to leave. Again, there was no evil intent. No guns and chains to hold black bodies in ships' holds. No white man standing with lighted match at the mouth of the cannon, lest the captives mutiny. No one ravaged by disease from lying for months in the bowels of cattle ships, they and their progeny bound for centuries of dispossession. No reneging on Sherman's Field Order 15, promising land to black people, and no breach of the Homestead Act. But before that February day ended, the Hezekiah and Kate Young place was part of the Will and Brenda Campbell place.

We were not, of course, the first to revere the land. Two hundred years earlier, ancestors of Hezekiah and Kate Young had scooped up and eaten handfuls of the African land from which they were being dragged in chains so that it might be forever a part of them.

The Mescaleros are back on the reservations. Black heirs are in Chicago and Detroit, Gary and Dayton, places of promise.

No one has done anything bad. But to some, no good has come.

* * *

Black people and white people almost never went to church together. Some lamented the fact that eleven o'clock Sunday morning was the most segregated hour of the week. But most assumed that was simply the way it was and the way it should remain. Back then, the separation was largely mandated by white people. Today the practice continues but is more by choice of both races.

It has not always been that way. When it was established by the finest theological minds of the day that black slaves had souls and were apt subjects for conversion and enlistment within the various established churches of the masters, no thought was given to forming separate congregations. For reasons of security, clandestine worship was generally discouraged. While in no way could the arrangement be considered an egalitarian one, at least they were under one roof, facing one altar, hearing the same sermon and the same words read from the lectionary, fearing one God. It is too much to retroactively expect those held so long in bondage to be content seated in slave balconies, their names an addendum to the church rolls. Zacharias, a slave belonging to T. L. McEwen. Jeremiah, a slave belonging to W. O. Elliot. (Interesting that so very many of them were given choice Biblical names even before they were adjudged to have souls.) When manumission had come and they were politically free, the effrontery by the people of Jesus continued: Elisabeth, F.W.C. (free woman of color), Joshua, F.M.C.

When that practice ended and former slaves took last names, often surnames of those who had owned them, several methods were used to effect the change to racial congregations and denominations. In some cases, routine by-laws did it. One could not miss a Sunday gathering without explanation. Women may be allowed two consecutive ones for childbearing purposes. Men none at all. If there were three in a row, fellowship was withdrawn and the member had to appear before the congregation and ask for restitution or be permanently expelled. Freed men and women who preferred to attend the newly formed Brown's Chapel simply did not show up and were soon dropped from the rolls. White consciences were clear. "We didn't kick them out, they left."

At other times, colored members left as a body or petitioned the parent congregation to permit them to form their own church. In 1865, the colored members of the First Baptist Church in Nashville, Tennessee, presented such a petition which, of course, was granted. They formed the First Colored Baptist Church of Nashville. Later the name was changed to First Baptist Church, Capitol Hill. Exactly one hundred years later, both congregations, five blocks apart, were about to begin massive building programs. The pastor of the black church, a brilliant preacher and scholar named Kelly Miller Smith, wrote an open letter to the two groups, reminding them of their common history and suggesting that they begin serious discussion of merger, conversations which would ". . . speak eloquently and convincingly to a world whose faith and interest in that which we call the Church is seriously waning." The response from the white pastor was brief and cryptic: "We believe there are too few good churches in downtown Nashville, not too many." The new buildings have long since been completed. No one even speaks of possible merger anymore. *Never on Sunday.*

Of course, since inhumanity was inherent in the institution of slavery, black people began pressing for their own churches almost as soon as the process of evangelism began among them. Those who were free, seeing that even whites who considered slavery wrong (humanitarians such as Thomas Jefferson and the great New England preacher, Lyman Beecher) were apt to be more concerned with the sensitivity of the slaveholders than with the suffering of the slaves, formed independent churches in the early nineteenth century.

It would be foolish to pass judgment now, to say that black people should have swallowed their pride, endured the insults and subservient roles until such time as the slave balconies were dismantled and the ambivalence cleared up within the souls of former masters. The idea of racial supremacy ran too deep within the breast of white American Christianity. And in the highest circles. Still, we can speculate. What if? What if the blacks had refused to leave the white dominated congregations, had resisted even violent expulsion? Is it unreasonable to think that one day, for reasons no more noble or Christian than economics, some wealthy planter or industrialist, weary of the burden of taxes for two school systems, might have said, "If the little black children are good enough to go to Sunday School with our children and learn about God, they are good enough to go to weekday school with them to learn about arithmetic"? And May 17, 1954, would have been another routine day in the U.S. Supreme Court, and these thirty years of litigation and strife would never have been?

But it didn't happen that way, and now we'll never know. What we do know is that in the sixties white people and black people seldom went to church together. Some of us who were dedicated to the notion of an integrated society proposed to change that. Now I can't remember why. I can recall our outrage at individual Christians being divided over something as trivial as skin color, something which should have been settled for them at Pentecost, the birthday of the Church, when peoples of all tribes, nations, races, and tongues were all together, in one place. But since most of us were in agreement that the poison red berries of institutional narcissism hung so ponderously on the branches of white Christendom as to be beyond the pale of radical reform, I can't recall why we didn't simply ignore them as a factor in achieving elementary justice for all people. Why bother?

But we did bother. And the bothering led us to Jackson. A group of Union Theological Seminary students in New York had started a program called the Student Interracial Ministry and had asked us to help. The idea was a summer intern project in which black seminarians would spend a summer in white congregations and white students in black ones. Finding cooperation among black churches came easy. White ones, almost impossible.

Joseph Millard Hendricks, a hybrid of rube and patrician egghead, pulpwood hauler one day and capstone of erudition the next, was on the faculty of Mercer University and part of a little organization called The Committee of Southern Churchmen, of which I was the sometimes-paid Director. Mercer is a Georgia Baptist school, not publicly notorious for its social liberalism but for many years a burrow for a few Southern radicals. Joe had asked us to meet him in Talbot County, his ancestral home place. He had several black churches which had agreed to take a student, and Joe wanted to screen the list.

Talbot County, Georgia, is one of the most remote and unravaged spots I know of in this country. Despite being ninety miles from Atlanta, forty from Fort Benning, and eighteen from Franklin Roosevelt's resort and place to die, it has escaped the countryphiles in search of trolls as well as the Atlanta guns of autumn. That is partly due to the presence of the Hendricks dynasty, owners of a goodly portion of the county. Their place includes where the Little Lazer River meets the Big Lazer, and the Ginhole, a spot of intrigue, ceremonials, and late night visitations where the Little Lazer hesitates, then races fiercely but good-naturedly over a sequence of crevices and giant river rocks to form an enchanting and invigorating pool of crystal clear water, unpolluted; a place which, if franchised without promotion or profit, might well solve most of the world's problems.

Mr. Charlie Hendricks was Joe's father. He was not the first of the Hendricks race but is believed to be the last in the line of genuine Mr. Charlies. The one you had to check with before making any changes in the county — building roads, stringing telephone or rural electric lines, or participation in any of the initialed New Deal programs. See Mr. Charlie if you need commodities or a WPA job. Chairman of the Draft Board during both World Wars.

"Mr. Charlie, Punkin' in jail for selling whiskey." "I'll go get him first thing Monday."

"Mr. Charlie, Freeman been messing with my little girl." "Tell him I want to talk to him."

Stories of Mr. Charlie abound still in Talbot County. And of Punkin', Freeman, and many others. Dramas which would be crude and in poor taste today, but in the context of the time, and alternative relationships considered, were benign.

Stories like:

You remember the time Joe brought one of his friends, Tom Trimble, down from Mercer to go fishing? B'lieve they said he taught philosophy. Or maybe it was psychology. Anyway, he was a real supereducated fellow but didn't take it seriously. Had all kind of funny accents. Just made fun of everything. Well, he kept hearing them talking about how Punkin' was coming over to dig them some worms.

"And who, may I ask, is this chap you call Punkin'?" he asked in his finest Oxford intonation.

"Punkin'?" Mr. Charlie said. "O, he's a colored fellow. Been here a long time."

"I gather then that he is a gentleman of some advanced years," Professor Trimble said. When Mr. Charlie ignored him, he continued. "I shall refrain from referring to a fellow human being by such an opprobrious designation. I ask, therefore, by what appellation was he christened?" Mr. Charlie still did not answer but looked at Joe, who stood in consummate amusement, knowing that the whole thing was a caricature, a mockery, of their more pompous colleagues back at school.

"What you going to call him, Professor?" Joe asked, long skilled in playing straight man for his friend.

"I shall address him as *Mis*ter *Pump*-kin."

"Joe, go dig the worms," Mr. Charlie said, shaking his head, "'cause Punkin' won't know who he's talking about and he'll go home."

Or: Mr. Charlie was driving out of the yard in his pickup truck, Punkin' sitting on the passenger side. A feisty dog ran after them, barking and snapping at the tires.

"Punkin', tell that dog to go back to the house!"

He rolled the window down and stuck his head and half his body out, yelling down at the dog. "Mr. Charlie say fo' you to go back to duh house!"

That story is as good a summary of race relations in the South in the mid-twentieth century as any. Neither man in the truck knew how rapidly it would change. And both would have had problems with some of the changes. Yet Mr. Charlie was not a latter-day Simon Legree. He lived within a system he did not personally create and did his best to make it as humane as possible.

Like the time, toward the end of his life, when a young social worker came out to see him about an alleged case of peonage on a nearby farm. She was accompanied by an agent of the Georgia Bureau of Investigation.

"We know, Mr. Hendricks, that you don't approve of that sort of thing any more than we do," she began. "You know, I was raised around here. Went to school with two of your boys. Never heard any black person who worked for you say you did him wrong. We want you to help us with that black man over on the Lawson place. You know who I'm talking about. He wouldn't even talk to us. Too scared, I suppose. Just sat on the steps of that little lean-to beside their house and stared at us. And we've heard they make him work all the time. Plowing, hoeing, hanging out the wash. Everything. When we were there he was shelling butterbeans. Two bushels of butterbeans. A grown man shelling butterbeans. And you know what they call him? Sure you do. Dummy. That's what they all call him. Dummy! Those days are gone, Mr. Hendricks. That sort of thing won't do anymore in this county. We need your cooperation. Your testimony."

"Did you talk to the Lawsons?" Mr. Charlie asked, motioning them to a bench under a giant pecan tree behind his house.

"Yes, sir. We did. Or tried to. All they would say was that he had been in their family for forty years. Like he's a piece of antique furniture. We're going to put him in a home in Atlanta."

Mr. Charlie spoke in his usual calm fashion. "Well, it's true that he's been in their family for forty years. Sleeps in that lean-to by their house like you say. And, yessum, he does work hard. Like we all do around here. Have to, to get by. And yeah, well, they do call him Dummy 'cause that's what his mamma called him. You know he can't hear. And he can't talk. Born deaf, so they tell me. His mamma had him over in another county. He was a grown boy when she moved over to the Lawson place. She died during that bad pneumonia winter — 'course, you weren't even born then — and after she was buried the boy disappeared." The man with the social worker had turned on a little tape recorder. Mr. Charlie asked him to turn it off and he did.

"He didn't have any kin. Leastwise, none that cared anything about him. And never had a daddy, if you know what I mean. Some hunters found him way over in the Flint River swamps. Said he was eating beech mash. Like the hogs do. It middle of winter. Old man Lawson heard about it and went over there and brought him back here. Then when he died and his grandnephew took over the farm, Dummy just sort of went with the place. That might not sound right to you, but that's just the way it was. He just went with the place. If I was you, I think I'd leave him alone. Too late for him."

"No, Mr. Hendricks. We can't do that. It isn't too late. They can teach him sign language at the home in Atlanta. It was built for people like him."

"Yessum. I know about the home. It's been there a long time. They wouldn't take him in the home back then though. Wouldn't take colored children. And he didn't know the folks who built the home. Never even been to Woodland, far as I know. Atlanta's awful big, young lady. And a long way off. You said you wanted me to help you. Far as I can tell, best leave him where he is."

They said the social worker and the GBI man never came back. Mr. Charlie had a lot of influence.

When we drove in, Joe was building a campfire beside a handsome and stout lodge his family had built above two large fish ponds. The lodge, which he called a cabin, was nestled a few hundred yards off the macadamite road running by his parents' house. Everyone in the family had come, because we all loved Joe and his "cabin."

After the yells of greetings and hugs all round, Brenda and the children scattered with their bags to their favorite rooms in the dormitory-like upstairs area.

"Who's that?" I asked, pointing to a medium-sized goat who stood about ten feet away, seemingly absorbed in the campfire-building.

"That's Jackson," Joe said, piling some half-rotten fence rails on the fire. "He'll be going back with you."

"Jackson," I said. "Of course. I should have known."

I knew he wouldn't be going back with us, but there was something unusual about him. His off-white hair had a soft, silky quality, unlike the coarse, individually textured hair most goats wear. His hoofs were only slightly cloven. Generally, ruminant animals have distinctly cloven feet. All four of his hoofs were glossy. The two front ones had a pinkish hue, looking manicured. His horns, delicately curved and short for his size, matched the front hoofs in color and texture, the match effeminate. The forehead protruded like half a softball, meaning superior intelligence, Joe told me later. Usually a blaze on an animal's head is darker than the rest of the body. This one, shaped like a small hen egg, was snow white and made the off-white seem darker than it was.

"He has no beard," I said. Joe had banked the fire and was sitting on the back of a pulpwood truck. As the flames settled down, the goat moved closer, then backed away again, apparently searching for a spot just close enough for the warmth to balance the evening chill of early winter. "Billy goats have beards," I added.

"Jacksons don't have beards," Joe said, feigning seriousness. "Now, you think about it. From Andrew to Mahalia. Has there ever been one with a beard?"

"What about Stonewall?" I said.

"He's old enough though," Joe said, ignoring Stonewall.

"Old enough for what?"

"Old enough to have a beard, goose. What were we talking about?"

"I'm not too sure any more," I said, feeling both amused and muddled.

It seems always to be the eyes that captivate and hold. From hummingbirds to elephants. Jackson's eyes were two large agates, too large for the rest of his head, with a dominance of yellow. There was little white around the irises, and the pupils looked like tiny insects jumping and dancing when he blinked. I first saw the eyes when he jumped on the truck and kneeled on his front legs beside Joe, facing me. I had never really looked at a goat before. And even more certainly I had never felt that I was being looked at, actually being *seen*, by a goat.

It was a curious moment. I had grown up with animals. And dogs, cats, hamsters, goldfish, horses, and chickens were plentiful at our homestead. Dogs were somehow of special importance, closer to being family members than the other animals. They were always around. Some taken for granted. Some serving a particular function. Some doted on as favorite pets. Each one was important. I remembered that when I was growing up I had early observed that there were two things sure to start a fight with another boy. No matter how big the offender. No matter how small the offended. One was to grab his cap off his head and run with it. The other was to kick his dog. Being a runt and not given to fighting, it was an observation of merit.

But this was not a dog. This was a goat. One with marks of refinement which set him apart. Something about him — maybe it was just his eyes — was reminiscent of some words Martin Buber, the esteemed theologian and philosopher I had admired, had written in his book, *I And Thou*. I asked Joe if he remembered the quote. We tried to reconstruct it, got the essence, and later looked it up.

> An animal's eyes have the power to speak a great language. Independently, without needing cooperation of sounds and gestures, most forcible when they rely wholly on their glance, the eyes express the mystery in its natural prison, the anxiety of becoming. This condition of the mystery is known only by the animal, it alone can disclose it to us — and this condition only lets itself be disclosed, not fully revealed. The language in which it is uttered is what it says — anxiety, the movement of the creature between the realms of vegetable security and spiritual venture. This language is the stammering of nature at the first touch of spirit, before it yields to spirit's cosmic venture that we call man. But no speech will ever repeat what that stammering knows and can proclaim.

"H'mmm." I mumbled it a lot as Joe Hendricks and I sat by the fire talking about the heretical disgrace of color consciousness in Jesus' name, of Negroes and whites not going to church together. How might we find one or two congregations willing to accept a black assistant for two months.

"H'mmm." Not about what we were discussing.

I hadn't thought about freckles for years. Used to be every *Collier's* magazine and *Saturday Evening Post*, and every issue of *Grit* newspaper had advertisements for freckle-removing cream. Fill in the coupon, send it in and get a free sample. We did it often just to receive something in the mail. Freckles were considered unsightly for reasons I still don't understand. They appeared before pimples, and every fair skinned farm boy and girl had them at some time. Here they were again. On the dainty little nose of a goat in Talbot County, Georgia. Beautiful, well-becoming freckles.

"He's a Capricorn," Joe said, when he caught my fixed gaze on Jackson.

"Maybe he's *the* Capricorn," I said, looking quickly away.

"I doubt if he's *the* Capricorn," Joe said. "But he is *a* Capricorn. Born January 19. Barely made it. Can you imagine a goat being an Aquarius?"

"Joe, are you putting me on? What the hell's coming down here? Some kind of Gaslight game? You trying to drive me crazy?"

"Naw, Will Davis. That'd be too short a drive," he laughed. "I'm just telling you about Jackson. Since he's going home with you."

"Do you know what a doreen is?" I asked, ignoring what he had just said.

"A what? A Florine? That's a friend's wife."

"No, no. A *do*reen," I said.

"How do you spell it?" Joe asked.

"Well, I never saw it written down. I reckon d-o-r-i-n-e, since you mention *Flo*rine. I had thought d-o-r-e-e-n. Or maybe d-o-r-e-n-e. But I don't know. Doesn't matter. Anyway, a doreen is a little round-shaped vanity. You know, like women carry in their purse with a mirror on the lid, and a powder puff and powder on the inside. That's all we ever called them at home. Now I can't find anybody who ever heard of one, except down home. I'll be damned. I hadn't thought of a doreen in years."

"You hadn't thought of it until you needed to change the subject," Joe said, still laughing. "Well, ole boy, you'll have to do better than doreen. No, to answer your question, I never heard of one, and I doubt if you have either."

"Now, Joe, we've been through a lot of stuff together. You've done a lot for me and I've been known to do you a favor or two. But I might as well tell you something before Brenda becomes my *first* wife. When we leave here Sunday, there'll be five people in that little car going back to Tennessee. But there won't be a goat."

"Jesus was a Capricorn, too," Joe said, still laughing.

The others had come outside and were standing by the fire. Joe began to talk in earnest about what he knew of the goat's history. Catherine, his ten-year-old daughter, had seen it tied in a cluster of cattails behind the Kappa Alpha fraternity house. All her life she had been fond of animals. She went to see the goat every day, took it food, and talked to some of the students about it. That was how she knew its birthday, though she suspected they made it up to make her think they were really fond of him. They claimed to have bought him from a black family on the edge of Macon. But the woman who cleaned the fraternity house told her they stole him and his twin sister from one of her neighbors. The sister had been barbequed one drunken evening by the fraternity boys. Whether part of some ancient fraternal rite which cannot be revealed to the uninitiated or an act of undiluted devilment, the male goat had been castrated following the barbeque of his sister. Surely the Freudians would do much with both the events and the sequence. Catherine was outraged and told the fraternity boys she was going to tell her daddy, who was the dean.

"It's your kind of story, Will Davis," Joe said. "Kismet. No question about it. A Capricorn, stolen from a poor darkie, gelded by an Old South fraternal order, and held captive, his female twin roasted on a spit, he delivered from the bulrushes by a fair young damsel."

"Your melodrama is entertaining, Joe," Brenda said. When she saw Joe wink at me, she quickly added, "But not convincing."

"Whoops!" Joe said.

"H'mmm." Familiar and far away.

Joe made a new start. "He's epiphanal, Will Davis. Lordy, read the signs."

Brenda tried to get the children to go inside, uneasy that they had climbed up onto the truck bed with Joe, and all three were rubbing and patting Jackson.

"Early one Sunday morning, while all the brothers were asleep, Catherine brought him home," Joe went on. "Just untied the leash and led him to our house. Trouble was, in Macon, Georgia, they have codes. Dogs, cats, parakeets, and lions are okay. But no horses, cows, or goats. You can have a mynah bird but not a chicken, even if the chicken is a bantam and smaller than the mynah bird."

"That doesn't make any sense," I said, joining the children in patting the goat.

"Codes seldom do," Joe said, jumping up and playing roughhouse with Jackson and the children, watching Brenda's reaction out of the corner of his eye, not wanting to overdo the strategy. "So we brought him down here to Talbot County. Problem is, when we go back to Macon there's no one here for him to talk to." Seeing that Brenda was about to speak again and fearing, I assumed, an irreversible commitment, he jumped quickly from the truck, Jackson right behind him. "But enough of all that. Let's fix some supper."

Jackson was a gentleman all weekend. We took long walks in the woods and he went along, politely waiting until everyone else had scaled the footlogs across the rivers and always last to pass through the gates. On Saturday night we sat around a campfire at the Ginhole, played the guitar, and sang country love songs. He took his place in the circle, discreetly chewing his cud, confident and comfortable in our company.

On Sunday night I had to be in Atlanta to help install one of the white interns in a black church. We had to leave in early afternoon. When the car was packed, everyone in place, and the good-byes all said, Joe, who had held Jackson in his arms for several minutes, placed him at Brenda's feet and closed the door. He offered no resistance, no protest at all, just lay calmly on the floor as I quickly wrestled the rutted dirt road and made it to the highway, trying to act casual.

The prevailing silence in the car was not equivalent to unanimity of agreement. It was simmering rage, mercifully capped by an unspeakable and unmeasurable incredulity. A family previously lenient in limitations they set for the father's behavior had just watched him cross those limits in an act so unbelievable as to defy verbal expression. Three hundred and fifty miles to go. An overnight stop in Atlanta. Five people and a goat shut up in a car with the heater going. Had it been less outrageous, something their collective mind could appropriate, believe was actually happening, it might have been different. But it was this act of lunacy. Locked in a hot car with a goat.

"There is always patricide," I said, trying to soften the tension. No one answered.

After several miles on the state road moving north, I heard a muted giggle. I wasn't sure what it meant, but the troubling silence had been broken. At first I thought it was a snicker. A snicker is hostile. A giggle can be hostile but it can also be a tentative bid for reconciliation. No, it's a giggle. Definitely a giggle. And it was Penny giggling. That's good, I thought. Penny, the oldest, the one most apt to set the tone, to influence the others, including the mother. I was encouraged but didn't risk another comment. The giggle became steady, and then I heard another one. Webb was starting to pick it up. Now Bonnie. All three were bouncing up and down, poking each other, acting delightfully silly, just . . . giggling.

Brenda was still uncommitted. I strained to see her face without turning my head. I could see her lips clenched tightly and I suspected, hoped, she was suppressing a deep down belly laugh. When she caught me looking at her, she couldn't hold it. The sounds from the back became immediately the up-graded giggles of laughter and the whole world was laughing. To me, a sound of sweet acquittal.

Just as suddenly, the quiet returned. And with it my uneasiness. Penny began to speak in the tone and manner of a first-grade school teacher. "Now, boys and girls, we all know that what you think is happening right now is not really happening. It's all make-believe. Of course, we have seen our daddy do some crazy things. We have seen him go barefooted in the snow and hunt mice in the house with a bow and arrow. We remember the time he auditioned for the symphony with a ukulele. And the letter he wrote my first-grade teacher about what she could do with her bomb shelter drill. And chewing tobacco at a church wedding. Some pret-teee goofy things this fellow has done. But we all know that he would nevvver, nevvver, at no time, shut us up in a car from Georgia to Tennessee with a goat. So if you think there's a goat in this car with us, just you put it right out of your little head. Our daddy wouldn't do that."

"And what do you think we're going to do with it when we get to the motel?" Brenda asked, not responding to Penny's bit of oratory. I wanted to go back to the laughing. Maybe we laughed too soon, I thought.

"He's a Capricorn," I said, trying to regain the levity.

"I'll cap-your-corn," she retorted.

Webb began humming, then singing the words to one of his favorite nursery songs. I joined him at first, then decided it wasn't a good idea and let him sing his song alone.

A Highland goat was feeling fine.
Ate six red shirts from off Sal's line.

Sal took a rail and broke his back,
And tied him to the railroad track.

And when the train was drawing nigh,
Bill thought it was his time to die.

He gave three awful shrieks of pain,
Coughed up the shirts and flagged the train.

I was touched by his efforts at restoration but saw it wasn't working.

Brenda said, "Well?" The reprieve was over and I was back in trouble.

Jackson, flatulent from eating fall cabbage, was adding to my weak standing. As Webb started to sing his song again, Jackson was in a shoving match with Brenda for the right to stand on the seat so he could see out.

A few years earlier I had bought a little Mercedes-Benz car, one of the first sold in Nashville. It cost $3,800, a lot of money for us to spend on an automobile, but I paid for it at nine cents a mile on my travels. There weren't many of them on the road, and other travelers would sometimes notice us. Now every car that came close honked, slowed down, or drove along beside us. I suppose, looking back, that there was something a bit unusual about a Mercedes-Benz with an out-of-state license driving up the road on a Sunday afternoon with a goat staring out the window.

"We're trash," Brenda sighed, trying to mask the still mounting temper. "Damned poor white trash. Riding a Georgia highway with a stupid goat."

"Yeah. Well, I'm looking for Flannery O'Conner. She liked trash," I said, feeling that a little assertion might be indicated.

"Be cute, Will!" she said. "We're hillbilly trash."

"No, we're not trash," I said, making sure the children could hear. "Trash don't haul goats in a Mercedes-Benz. Now, if we were in a 1949 Studebaker with a 'See Rock City' bumper sticker, a squirrel tail flying from the aerial, mud guards on the back fenders, baby shoes hanging from the rear-view mirror, and a goat looking out the window, then we'd be trash."

"Be cute!" she said again. Silence followed.

Today something as tame as the Student Interracial Ministry would go unnoticed. But in the early sixties it had attracted considerable attention and press coverage. Some of the organized anti-integration groups had posted warnings and veiled threats. All of us were asked to take sensible precautions. We had been told to go to a small, black-owned motel near the church which would allow black and white together. But they wouldn't have a kennel. And Brenda's question was in need of an answer: What are we going to do with him when we get to the motel?

I stopped at a Holiday Inn and asked the desk clerk if they had a kennel. He said they did but that it wasn't kept clean, said the boss was not there and that we could take our pet to the room. "I'm sure your pet is housebroke," he added. I told him we had just got him and I couldn't be a hundred percent sure that it was, not bothering to mention that I knew for sure that he wasn't car broke.

"It's a goat," Brenda said. I didn't know that she and Webb had moved in behind me.

"A goat?" he asked, looking again at my credit card.

"Well, it isn't exactly a goat," I said. "I mean, it is a goat all right, but it isn't your ordinary, run-of-the-mill, barnyard goat. He went to Mercer."

"To Mercer?" "To Mercer?" "To Mercer?" All three of the people behind the motel counter spoke at once.

"Yeah. . . . Well, he didn't exactly *go* there but. . . ."

"It's a goat," Brenda interrupted, as she went back to the car. Webb snuggled up beside me, the way children do when they sense conflict and want to breach it.

"I went to Mercer too," the desk clerk said; then, shaking his head and laughing, he corrected himself. "What I mean is, I went to Mercer. Period. I don't remember a goat."

"Never mind," I said.

"I tell you what," he said, still laughing. "Let's forget everything that's been said. I'll swear that I didn't register a goat if the boss catches us."

Several guests standing on the balcony watched with amused interest as we unloaded the car, Jackson making several trips in and out with us.

Webb and I had a ritual whenever we checked into a motel. The beds were our trampolines, and we would jump from bed to bed, to the floor, on the chairs, trying to dance like Ray Bolger did on television. Jackson joined in with vigor and excitement. He didn't, however, understand the boundaries, jumping not only onto the beds and chairs but on the dresser, into opened luggage, and on top of the television. I saw Brenda, Penny, and Bonnie quickly moving their things to the adjoining room. I had seen those quick and resolute triumvirates formed before and knew they were unbeatable. Webb, without question or protest, in the interest of harmony, or in his young mind perhaps in the interest of the prevention of the shedding of blood, joined me in finding the kennel.

There was no trouble at the interracial installation service. My sermon on reconciliation had an added dimension for those of us who had experienced the fairish estrangement of the afternoon. Brenda had winked at the appropriate points, and I felt pleasantly absolved as she drove us back to the motel. In violation of a Pauline admonition, the sun had gone down on her wrath. But in the spirit of one of the Proverbs — the forcing of wrath bringeth forth strife — all vexation was put away before the hour of slumber.

The trip to Mt. Juliet was predictably fractious. On balance, though, a tolerable journey with no major contests. Bonnie brought two rolls of toilet paper from the motel and fashioned a holder from a coat hanger. Jackson fed and entertained himself by grazing directly from the roller. An added blessing was that the tissue seemed to abate the flatulence. Glorious relief!

At a restaurant near Chattanooga, we had him staked in the grassy median. A tourist, not able to see him closely, asked Penny what breed our dog was.

"Oh, he's a Goatian," she said.

"A Croatian?" the man asked.

"No, no. Goatian. They have four ears, you know." Later we heard him explaning to his wife, sometimes impatiently when she doubted him, sometimes patronizingly when she didn't understand, that yes, some dogs do have two sets of ears, that he had seen a lot of them in Yugoslavia after World War II.

It was almost dark when we got home. The first winter storm had blown in and it was ten degrees outside. Clarise DeQuasie, a young friend and neighbor who worked at Vanderbilt University Library during the week, and on weekends drove her truck, tractor, or whatever was needed on her small chicken farm, wearing cowboy boots and blue jeans on both occasions, had house sat for us. She was one of the most authentically free people I ever knew. Despite eight years of higher education in liberal arts, Divinity School, and Library Science, she often assumed the role of the composed, unflappable person of the West Virginia mountains where she grew up. While most people, seeing a goat jump out of a car at the end of a long trip, would make some comment or inquiry, Clarise did not even acknowledge his presence. At least not until properly introduced. Then she was kind and friendly.

With her to greet us was Charles McCullin, a friend from college days who had been moved on as pastor of a Baptist Church because of a mild, but in context courageous, stand on the school desegregation controversy in Baton Rouge. As one of the hill country, he said, "Well, I see the family has grown since I've seen you." With them were Leon and Dottie.

Leon was a little spitz who had tetanus when he was two months old. He was saved from euthanasia by the daily wails and pleadings of three children in the veterinarian's office. He went on to have a long and successful life. He was named for Leon Walker, an ardent segregationist friend in Louisiana, and Leon McCrea, a black man I grew up with in Mississippi. Leon the spitz had an insatiate libido. As soon as Jackson jumped from the car, he was there to inquire by sight and smell if we had brought a girl or boy home with us, assuming with the tourist that it was for sure a big dog. And his own color. Jackson was cordial, returning the looks and smells, growing formal only when he felt that personal violation was imminent.

Dottie, an obese Dalmatian, middle-aged and cordial but also given to moments of violence when excited, approached Jackson for other reasons. She was convinced that he, whoever and whatever he was, was there on a hostile mission. She began circling him, snarling, lunging, and snapping. Jackson, seeking at first to dissuade her by maneuvers of charm, soon realized that some early guidelines must be established and that some exertion was in order. He bounced back into the car, stood still and silent for a moment, waiting for her broad side to be toward him. With perfect timing, he sprang out like a cobra, head down, and struck Dottie squarely in the rib cage. "Ouf!" The sound was more human than canine as the air was knocked from her lungs and she hit the ground. They were never especially close, but she never questioned his right to territory again.

Jackson was home.

Since our experience with him in Georgia had been that he seldom strayed far from where the people were, I assumed that he would stay close while we unloaded the car and got settled. There was the delicate matter of where he would stay until we could make permanent arrangements. Bonnie and Webb had pulled me aside and asked if I thought Mamma would agree to let him spend the night inside, just this once, because it was so cold. I told them no.

Just as we were settling down for a drink by the fireplace with Clarise and Charles, Webb announced that Jackson was gone. A quick look around didn't find him. "Aw, he's around here somewhere close," I said, not convincing anyone. We honked the horn, a signal he had responded to in Georgia because it meant a walk in the woods or ride on the truck to the store. None of our calls brought him. It had started to snow and the temperature was still dropping. While we bundled up for a thorough search, Bonnie composed two lines of a poem,

His fleece was white as snow,
because it was,

sure that we would find a little frozen statue when morning came.

After almost an hour of scouring the place — under vehicles, in the chicken house, tool shed, a little cabin I used as an office and writing studio — someone suggested that we try the Dolan House. We had completed the structure they had started, named it for them, and used it as a guest house. Suddenly we saw two little diamonds caught in the heavy beam of the flashlight. Jackson was nestled in some leaves which had blown against the cinder block foundation, the blocks still warm from the afternoon sun. He appeared comfortable, secure, and unafraid. He had chosen his own place. The Dolan House. And he presided over it from that night until his life's end.

III

Change and Decay

THE ROLE OF white liberal Southerner in the upheavals of the sixties and winding down of the seventies was a cross between fifth column and dewclaw. Neither is a comfortable stance. Fifth column has a traitorous ring to it. The dewclaw, that vestige of a toe on the hind feet of many dogs which does not touch the ground, is totally worthless.

Accepting the function of fifth column carries the burden of betrayal of one's own people. It is not lightly carried. Not even in the pursuit of an ideal as noble as the rectification of human owning human. There was no question where the cause of justice lay as the fledgling Civil Rights Movement of the late fifties feathered out in the sixties. Yet, as itinerant missioners such as I moved from place to place encouraging white participation in the struggle, acting as propagandist to friendly and unfriendly media, occasionally infiltrating the established structures of power, offering solace and sanction to black victims of bigotry, there was a gnawing and indefinable phantom riding along: "You weren't raised like this. You are betraying your kind."

The covert aspect of the mission was but one troubling piece of his predicament. In his head there was no quarrel. But in the gut there was the fencing with numerous cultural considerations: family ties, regional loyalties, generations of things being the way things were, tendons and sinews, blood and bones reeking with unspoken notions of class, caste, and clan. A minor victory from an effort which took months to achieve might be felt as a major incursion on his soul when it was done. The social psychologists sometimes explained the violence of the recalcitrant South as long-repressed guilt. Delta planters and Virginia aristrocrats, they told us, had their first sexual experience with a colored servant and must now destroy her to be pure. Perhaps so. But the same teachers told us that guilt resulted from violation of the behavioral norm. If that be so, it was the liberal white who stood in transgression, not the fulminating editors and legislators. Even the night-riding White Knights, who did what they did in defense of "the Southern way of life," were behaving according to their raising. We of the liberal persuasion were not.

But dewclaw? Uselessness? For the first time in Southern history, white support was not essential for the success of a movement for racial justice. The time had come. The Supreme Court decision of May 17, 1954, declaring segregation by race in public schools to be unconstitutional was inevitable, affected more by world opinion than by torts, briefs, and the testimony of expert witnesses. Much of culture and commerce stood in the doorway of the inevitable and had to be moved aside. But the outcome had been settled by the wave of emerging and developing peoples and nations, the vast majority being of color. So if we, those strange creatures called white liberals, held in contempt by the right from the outset and later by the left as well, chose to participate, it had to be for reasons and needs of our own. Some of the reasons were as lofty as humanistic or religious commitment. Some of the needs probably deep-seated psychological scars. If reasons and needs were recognized, the alliance could work. Otherwise, it was a delusion. (Or so it all seemed to me.)

I think, hope, I accepted the role of fifth column in the Movement because of long ago congenital religious values. I think, hope, that I did it without developing a chemical dependency upon it, as some seemed to do. The major symptom of those addicted was the certainty that the Movement would not move without one's self in the vanguard. Maybe the reason I never had such feeling was lack of courage. I don't know. Actually, I was seldom referred to as being a "liberal" by those who thought of themselves as being truly that. But the detractors, in need of easy labels, lumped us all together.

Without the inebriation of vainglory and the resulting dependency, there were sometimes serious doubts and sometimes loneliness. In the fall of 1956 I had gone to Clinton, Tennessee, a small, mountain-edge town which was under a court order to admit a few blacks to its previously all-white school. John Kasper, a native of New Jersey and a self-styled champion of white supremacy and constitutional government, had agitated and organized during the summer months, and when the school opened it was greeted by demonstrations, riots, and physical acts of disapproval. My purpose in going was to talk with the white clergy. Until then they had done little to restore the town to social sanity and civility. All of them were cordial but felt helpless. The one who stood out as the most singularly hopeless to inspire was Dr. Paul Turner, pastor of the First Baptist Church, a large and prestigious congregation in the center of town. He said nothing to suggest that he had any intention of becoming involved at any level, talking mainly about his good church, with good people, who had been good to him and his family. I came away convinced that I had been in the company of a spineless, success oriented captive of the status quo, who would see the black children slaughtered rather than chance the loss of one tithing member of his club. Two days later I was driving to Alabama and heard on radio news that Dr. Paul Turner had walked to school with the Negro children, and that a part of the mob, which had continued to gather each day as the children descended the long hill leading to the schoolhouse, had attacked and savagely beaten him.

His congregation was supportive of his action at first. Later disharmony developed, ostensibly unrelated to the issue of race, and he moved on. Trouble seemed to move with him. In not many years, he killed himself with a pistol. I have no reason to believe that there was the slightest nexus between my visit and his decision to take a stand for human decency. And none to think that the stand he took and the progression of controversy and defeats he met were related and led eventually to his taking his own life.

But one wonders. For one fugacious moment, he ponders what it is he is about.

Leaving Clinton in shambles, Mr. Kasper moved on to Nashville for a repeat performance. All through the summer of 1957, concerned whites and involved blacks had met to discuss plans for a smooth implementation of the then-celebrated "Nashville Plan." Yielding to legal pressure, the school board had proposed and the Court accepted a plan whereby children in the first grade would be admitted to formerly all-white schools. The following year, they would advance to the second grade and others would take their place. On and on, adding one grade each year, until the entire system was desegregated. Looking back, our efforts, and the plan itself, must have brought laughter from the gods and demons alike. I recall the Superintendent of Education, an aging professional basking in the short-lived glory of his "Nashville Plan," giving us its history and evolution. He told of the first meeting of the school board when Negro parents attended to present their demands. He described the night and events of the meeting in pictorial detail, including a fierce rain that was falling at the time. He concluded by saying, "You have all heard the old saying. Well, that night it was really happening. It was literally raining little nigger babies with their tails tied together!" Blacks, angry at him, whites, embarrassed for him, filed silently and dispiritedly from the room.

The efforts of the liberals to discredit Kasper were as racist as his advocates. We circulated pictures of him dancing with his black girlfriend in New York to suggest that he wasn't serious about racial segregation. He countered that the pictures proved that he was acting as a strict constitutionalist, trying to preserve state's rights, and was not a bigot.

In those early days of desegregating attempts, the figure always seemed to be nine. Nine in Clinton. Nine little six-year-olds in Nashville. Nine high-schoolers in Little Rock. Perhaps it was some sort of sardonic Southern symbolism directed at the "nine old men in Washington" who had done this to us.

When school began in Nashville, we watched with fear and sorrow the effectiveness of Mr. Kasper's community organizing. Rioters gathered each day at the schools where the nine black children were enrolled. Hundreds of screaming, irrational, sometimes armed men and women, on one occasion pulling cobblestones from the sidewalk and hurling them at the building. One school was destroyed by a dynamite blast in a nocturnal act of defiance. Nine days after the first black child crossed its portal.

One of the children was the daughter of Pastor Kelly Miller Smith. Late one night I sat with him in his study, peeking often through the window in a vigil against threats to the building. After a long period of comfortable silence, I asked, "Kelly, what if something happens to little Joy?" He moved the candle, the only light we had risked, closer to him and opened his study Bible and began to read about Abraham being told by the Lord to take his only little boy up on a mountain, tie him on a pile of wood, cut his throat, and burn him. He read a sentence and then talked about it.

> Take now thy son, thine only son Isaac, whom thou lovest, and get thee into the land of Moriah; and offer him there for a burnt offering upon one of the mountains which I will tell thee of.

"You see, my brother, we don't even get to choose the mountain," he said. "God chooses the mountain. All we're asked to do is obey."

> . . . and Abraham built an altar there, and laid the wood in order, and bound Isaac his son, and laid him on the altar upon the wood. And Abraham stretched forth his hand, and took the knife to slay his son.

I thought he was going to cry as he half-closed the book. Instead he began to laugh.

"Will, we're talking about some hard sayings. We're talking about faithfulness to Almighty God. The God of Abraham, Isaac, and Jacob. The God of my black mamma and daddy in Mississippi and your white mamma and daddy in Mississippi. If that God says we've got to do it, well, we've got to do it."

I sat silent, a little sorry I had asked the question but grateful for the preaching. He put the Bible down, cast a quick glance out the window, then looked straight at me and quoted the rest of the Scripture from memory:

> And Abraham lifted up his eyes, and looked and behold behind him a ram caught in a thicket by his horns.

He leaned back, shoved the candle between us and bent his head in prayer. "Lord, make the thicket tight. And the ram's horns long. Amen."

It was well past midnight when a young couple came to relieve us in the vigil. The picture of little Joy, walking through the angry mob, her hand thrust trustingly and lovingly in the hand of her father, would not go away as I drove home. What are we doing to the children? The dear, sweet, innocent little children.

I don't know about your thickets and rams' horns, Kelly. We both came out of Mississippi, but you brought something out with you that I don't have. Are you sure you would sacrifice your child on the altar of integration, the altar of black and white together? My God, Kelly! I know white people. I've lived with us all my life. Are you sure this is the right altar?

No, Will. Not the altar of integration. The altar of faithfulness.

I went directly to the children's room when I got home. I stood for a long time, looking down at our sleeping six-year-old. I felt like I wanted to pray and started to kneel down beside her bed. When I realized what the prayer already forming on my lips would be, I straightened up quickly and self-consciously and left the room.

Lord, I am thankful that my little girl is white.

I fixed a drink and sat alone for a long time on the back steps of a quiet and peaceful house.

Years later, when little Joy Smith was all grown up, an actress in New York City, she explained why she wasn't afraid. "I had heard the talk," she said. "At home, in church, on the news. I knew that there was something special about my going to that particular school." Because she had always been so secure in the love of those close to her, she assumed that the crowds had turned out in her honor. She even remembered wanting to go back to the door one morning, when the mob was especially noisy outside her classroom, and do a curtain call. So are actresses born. Even after all those years, it made me feel better.

What we were seeing was not, of course, the beginning of racial uneasiness in America, nor the first stirring of black determination to be free. That began when African men and women scampered to safety from slave stalkers while others were led, yoked and chained, down the Congo to the ships waiting off the shore. Loaded on ships bearing such names as Justice, Jesus, Brotherhood, Liberty, and Gift of God, many of them hurled themselves and each other overboard rather than face the suffering and ignomy of unindentured servanthood. The uneasiness continued as the human cargo sought to stay the hand of torment by stealth and open mutiny as the captains, most of them longtime wearers of the sign of the Christ, moved them nearer to a land they would inhabit but have not even yet possessed. Because they were not the simple and undomesticated primitives much of American sixth-grade civics has taught, but often trained and skilled potters and weavers, miners, workers of gold and bronze, farmers and shepherds, artisans of various sorts, people steeped in the tradition and history of an ancient land replete with kings and kingdoms, stories and mythology, it was assured from the beginning that the struggle would go on until the country of which they soon would be unwilling vassals became what it claimed already to be. The bloody admonition of Nat Turner, scholarly prophecy of Frederick Douglass, raw fortitude of Harriet Tubman and Sojourner Truth, revolutionary fervor of Denmark Vesey, unnumbered blacks fighting against Andrew Jackson alongside the Seminoles — all of those and thousands more were a surety that the stirrings would not cease.

What we were seeing was the prologue to still another chapter in the continuation of the inevitable struggle. Many thought it would be the last chapter, that by these stirrings it would be finally and firmly established that we are, in fact, all created equal. We know now that there must be others. Unless history itself has no chapters left to write.

The chapter to which we were party began in the guise of comedy but moved quickly to tragedy. In 1946 a black man named Herman Marion Sweatt applied to the University of Texas Law School, the most heavily endowed state school in America. In response to a District Court order that they establish separate but equal legal education within six months, this great state set up a makeshift law school especially for him. What was there to do but laugh? A one-student law school. Laugh and go back to court. In 1948 South Carolina still excluded Negroes from voting in primary elections on the grounds that the democratic primary was a private club. Judge J. W. Waring laughed the notion out of his court and out of existence. (In exchange, he was laughed and scorned out of his position of status in the social circles of Charleston.) In that same year, Oklahoma, a state for less than half a century, virtually given to the Indians by Andrew Jackson when it was thought to be a feckless wilderness, taken back when its potential was discovered, responded to a lawsuit by G. W. McLaurin and admitted him to the University Law School. Having seen Texas fail at racial separatism when they built a law school especially for Mr. Sweatt, they constructed a little anteroom just outside the room where Mr. McLaurin's classmates sat. More laughter. And more court. But the laughter would not last. Soon children were being murdered at their prayers, leaders assassinated, churches and synagogues dynamited.

By the time Dr. Martin Luther King, Jr., and others formed the Southern Christian Leadership Conference in 1957, the prologue was finished. A suit in Clarendon County, South Carolina, challenging segregated and unequal education, had been won, and on May 17, 1954, the United States Supreme Court issued its most celebrated and maligned opinion. In opposition to that decision, and any other effort to change the pattern of a segregated society, the powerful White Citizens Council had been formed in Mississippi and spread rapidly to the other Southern states. But support and subsidy of the decision came on many fronts and in many forms. One of the more important ones was the flinging of the gauntlet in Montgomery, Alabama, declaring that black riders of public buses would no longer tolerate sitting on the back seats. After a year of boycott, demonstrations, mass meetings, counter lawsuits and violence, the high Court ruled that racial segregation on public transportation was illegal. The organization which had served as the vehicle for the protest, the Montgomery Improvement Association, with Dr. King as President, became the inspiration and model for a Southwide movement to encourage and coordinate activities in other cities.

I was on my way to the initial meeting of that organization when, by accident, I met someone who would change my life. It was not quite daylight as I pulled onto Highway 41 outside Nashville heading south. I struggled to get the defroster lever in position. As the headlights barely cut through the heavy ground fog, I saw a figure on the edge of the pavement just in time to swerve and miss him. Shaken, I stopped and backed up to ask if he wanted a ride. He was a young black man who looked to be in his early twenties. He was neatly but inexpensively dressed in a dark blue jacket and equally dark trousers. You may be free, I thought, but you're free to get yourself killed standing on a dark road dressed like that. He said he was waiting for the bus, but he grabbed a battered Gladstone bag, threw it onto the back seat and started to crawl in beside it. There was a solid white, leather-bound Bible fastened to the side with adhesive tape, probably the reflection I saw in time to miss him. Having recently moved from Mississippi, I was accustomed to Negro workers riding in the back seat when white people were driving them to or from work, but I had not noticed that being the custom in Tennessee.

"Why don't you sit up here with me?" I said, opening the door on his side.

"Yes, suh. Yes, suh." He untaped the Bible, put the bag on the floor and got in the front seat, sitting as close to the window as he could and rolling it down as I pulled back onto the highway. He had a small jar of Vicks Vap-O-Rub in his hand. He opened it, stuffed a small amount into each nostril, breathed deeply through his nose, and leaned back. The Vicks smell had a slight exhilarating effect.

"You a Christian?" he asked, dropping the Vicks jar and clutching the Bible close to his chest. I had never been asked that question by a Negro before, and for a moment it seemed inappropriate to my Mississippi breeding.

"My name is Campbell, Will Campbell," I said, extending my hand and not answering his question. "By the way, I'm a liberal." He placed his right hand in mine but did not return the grip. The salve on his fingers stuck to my hand. When I was growing up, white people seldom shook hands with Negroes. The few times I did as a boy, generally when grown-ups weren't around, I was more conscious of my right hand than of the left for several minutes. I remembered that that always bothered me.

"Yes, suh, Mr. Campbell. Yes, suh. Pleased to make ya 'quaintance."

"What's yours?" I asked.

"Oh. T.J. Mine's T.J." He seemed surprised that I had asked.

"T.J.? What's your other name?"

"Oh. Yes, suh, Mr. Campbell. Yes, suh. My other name Eaves. T.J. Eaves. Yes, suh. That's what tis. T.J. Eaves."

"It's a pleasure to know you, Mr. Eaves," I said, offering my hand again. He took it in the same fashion as before. He shifted even closer to the door, obviously uncomfortable.

"They just calls me T.J. Yes, suh, Mr. Campbell. They just calls me T.J."

Though I had grown up with such obsequiousness, it had been a long time since I had been with it. I was annoyed that he had not recognized my hard-won enlightenment or had not accepted it. I remembered a time, a few years earlier, when I was in my only church parish. An old man who kept the grounds for the church house told me one day that he was a nigger and asked me not to call him Mister. I brought him inside, talked with him about racial pride, why he should look upon himself as a man and not refer to himself by such an opprobrious term. When I finished and he still had not touched the coffee and cookies I had fixed for us both, he looked me straight in the eyes, something black people seldom did with whites, and said, "Reverend Campbell, you a white man. But you don't see what I tole you. You call me Mister Green. That all right fo' you. Other white folks heah you. Pretty soon you be gone. Like all them other preachers. You be gone on to some big church. Willie Green still be heah. You be jus' some brashy, young Yankee that didn't know no better. Willie be a uppity nigger what thinks everybody s'posed to call him Mister. Reverend Campbell, I'se a nigger. But I'se a seventy-odd-year-old nigger. A live nigger. I'd druther be a live nigger than a daid Mister."

They hadn't taught us that in Social Ethics. I thought about Willie Green as I rode along with T. J. Eaves. He was a young man. In Tennessee. And a new day had dawned. Yet I was uncomfortable. And embarrassed. Why was he acting this way? I remembered that I still had a Mississippi accent. Maybe that was it.

"What you do, Mr. Campbell?" he asked after a long silence.

I told him that I was a farmer, but that I also worked for a Christian organization, and that my job was to involve myself in the racial conflict in the South and to promote the freedom movement. He placed the Bible on the seat between us, and I thought I heard him try to stifle a deep sigh.

"Then you a Christian," he said. He said it like a pleasant announcement, laughing softly as he spoke.

"I try to be," I said. "Sometimes, I think, I don't do so hot."

"Jesus done the hot part," he said, laughing louder now. "We got the cool part. He done did the hot part. We just sort of follow along. And try not to complain."

We talked freely after that. About Jesus. And Jackson. He knew a lot about both. He had grown up on a farm in Alabama, came to Nashville to go to school but had to drop out to work. He was pastor of a small rural church in Cheatham County and worked as a yard man for a wealthy Nashville family during the week. As he talked, I noticed that the dialect speech was largely affected. He moved in and out from perfect grammar to the backwoods vernacular of Alabama with ease. There was something special about him. Something different. Something I liked and trusted. And something I had the feeling white folks weren't going to believe.

We talked about the young Montgomery preacher, Martin Luther King, Jr. He had never met him but had heard him speak several times. Spent two weeks with a cousin in Montgomery during the bus boycott and drove maids to and from work. I told him I was on my way to an Atlanta meeting of Negro leaders from around the South who would be discussing an organization to coordinate other boycotts and protests as they developed, and I asked him to go on with me. He said he was going to Alabama to see his daddy and had to be back in three days.

Before we got to Chattanooga he said he knew a nice little place where we could get something to eat. Rigid segregation was still the rubric in the South, and Negro travelers had to plan ahead for places to eat, use a bathroom, or find lodging. He directed me to a place called Nanny's Shanty.

"Okay if I go in?" I asked as he opened his door.

"Sure," he said. "Don't nobody care."

He ordered two barbeque sandwiches and a quart of Falstaff beer. The White Citizens Council had organized an effective boycott of Falstaff because they had heard the company gave some money to the

NAACP. I wasn't surprised at the brand he ordered but had not expected him to be a beer drinker. Sensing that, I suppose, he took a long pull from the tall bottle, winked and said, "You remember what St. Paul say. A little toddy fo de body. And sometime my stomach sho do hurt." He poured a small amount in a glass the waitress had brought and pushed it across the table to me. When I tasted it, like a diner testing fine wine, he filled the glass, letting the foam run onto the table. "See yo stomach give you trouble too," he said, winking again and calling to the woman behind the counter for another Falstaff. "Mr. Falstaff need the business," he laughed.

"Say, man. Why don't you go on to Alabama with me? You ain't going to learn anything about colored people in Atlanta. Dr. King don't know nothing 'bout being colored. He silver spoon raised." He told me his daddy had written him to come home, that some young people from Montgomery were coming up to ask their congregation to help them with their civil rights work. Said he thought his daddy was scared and that he wanted to be with him. The Atlanta meeting was scheduled for the next day, but I decided to go with him. "You won't be sorry," he told me.

Instead of continuing toward Atlanta, we drove back north to South Pittsburg. When we turned off the main road there and headed due south, I asked him why he hadn't stopped me there before if that was the way to his daddy's place. "Well, I figured you would go with me," he said. He was more jovial, more relaxed than he had been since we met five hours earlier.

We traveled in the direction of Scottsboro, a town which in forty years had not lost the onus of the case of the "Scottsboro Boys," nine Negroes, some of them children, who were tried and convicted of raping two white women on a southbound freight train, sentenced to death in the electric chair, and after years of appeals, legal maneuvers, and political exploitation, and a total of 130 years spent in prison, the last one released. We crossed the Tennessee River before we got to Scottsboro and headed back toward the Georgia line. When we did, he said it might be best if he drove. Though I was new to the field of race relations, I was familiar with southern mores and knew that in rural Alabama in 1956 it was more acceptable for him to be driving me than for me to be driving him. He didn't say that though. Just said he knew the roads. We made several turns, the roads getting more narrow with each turn onto a different one. When we stopped, about fifteen miles from the last little town we had gone through, he said we were at the church. But it was dark, misting rain, and I couldn't see. "Let's wait a minute," he said. "Let our eyes get used to the dark."

"You think it's all right if I go in with you?" I asked, knowing what it would be like if the two of us were about to enter a white country church.

"Yeah. It'll be okay. We'll sit down toward the back at first. Then I'll inch on up toward the front. They'll know you're not from the man if I'm with you."

"You're not with me," I whispered. "I'm with you."

"Whatever."

He hadn't told me what kind of a meeting we were going to. I expected it to be the usual rural, black Baptist service and wondered why we couldn't hear the noise as we got closer to the building. "Be careful where you walk," he chuckled. "We're in the middle of a cow pasture." I could see thin strips of subdued yellow light coming from the edges of loose fitting shutters. Not shutters with moveable slats that close and meet in the middle of the window; these were the solid wooden kind, homemade out of wide boards and hinged like doors.

The building, a small, rectangular, one-room structure, seemed as indigenous as the small hackberry, post oak, and sweet gum trees which extended from the house to the clearing all around. Huge stumps indicated that all the timber-sized trees had been recently cut. The smell inside was a mixture of kerosene lamps placed at intervals on little shelves along the wall, the tarnished reflectors doing little to help, and a pine knot fire burning in the stove. The stove was not the traditional pot-belly kind, generally used for heating, but a cook stove, a wrought iron range with a water reservoir on the side and a warming oven extending above the entire width of the cooking surface. It looked new, and I wondered why they had a cook stove instead of a more efficient heater. T.J. told me later that a white lady had given it to them, that her family had used it only one year before a TVA co-op had been formed and they got electricity. The same white lady, he said, collected and gave to them the old Sunday School Quarterlies from the white Baptist Church. "I grew up confusing April Fool's Day with New

Year's," he said. "We were always a quarter behind."

It was a small crowd inside the church, not more than fifty, mostly men. "They're students come up from Alabama State College in Montgomery," T.J. whispered, nodding toward the front where five young men sat on a bench directly in front of the pulpit. They seemed restless, shuffling their feet, clearing their throats, which I supposed meant they didn't like what the old man speaking was saying.

"We just a bunch of Christian people up here," I heard him say as we sat down about a fourth of the way down, out of the direct light of the nearest lamp. "I know you boys been to college. Know you worked with Dr. King in Montgomery. Know you got some things done down there. Know we got to get some things done up here too. Know someday we gon' go down to the courthouse and register to vote. Know we gon' get on the Greyhound someday and sit right up front. Know someday our young people gon' go to the high school without ridin' all way cross the county."

Each time the old man said "someday," one of the students would echo, "Now!" He seemed not even to hear them.

"But like I say, we just Christian people up here. Mr. Folsom done won that election fair and square. He the governor now. Fair and square, he the governor now."

"He's not our governor," one of the students said, the others laughing and jostling one another. The old man still did not acknowledge their heckling.

"Romans 13 say, 'Let every soul be subject unto the higher powers. For there is no power but of God.' Whosoever resists the power, he be resisting God."

"Let's go," the youngest looking of the students said. "Pop don't understand. Pop won't ever understand!" He motioned for the others to follow him out of the building.

"Let him finish," said one of the church members, a woman about forty who had been sitting beside where the old man stood. I thought she might be his daughter. As she spoke, she made her way to the front, sat on the far end of the same bench as the students, facing the congregation.

"Mr Folsom the governor now. Mr. Folsom the power. Fair and square, he the power."

"Fol-som. Fol-som. Fol-som." The students were chanting in unison, slapping their hands with the chant.

"Folsom ain't nothing but a California jailhouse where they lock our people up," one of them shouted as the chanting stopped.

"Fol-som. Fol-som. Fol-som," the chant began again.

"I said let him finish," the woman said, standing up, facing the students with her hands on her hips. The others sat silently, seeming to know that they didn't have to take sides, that something important was going on.

"Mr. Folsom a good man. But he just a man. Mr. Folsom a high power. But he ain't the highest power. Mr. Folsom the law. Big Jim the law. But what you talk about!"

"Is he the preacher?" I whispered. T.J. shook his head no and started to move forward, like he knew what was coming and didn't want to miss any of it. I watched alone from the shadows.

The old man did not move from where he stood. He spoke as calmly and dispassionately as he had from the beginning. "In Romans 7 it say we are delivered from the law. The law ain't no count no more. We dead to law. We married to another. To Jesus. Raised up. Now we got to bring forth good fruit. Folks married . . . they chillun goin' look like 'um. We married to Jesus now."

The students looked at one another, shrugged, understanding a lot less of what the old man was saying to them than he had understood of what they said to him. For he had understood it all.

"Big Jim just a man. A good man. But just a man. Big Jim a high power. But they's a higher power. Big Jim a pole bean body with a half-runner heart." The church shook with laughter, applause and approval. The students facing them sat mute, not understanding. They were of the cities. Birmingham, Selma, Montgomery, Mobile. A generation separated them from the world of pole beans and half-runners. Those they faced knew of such things, knew that the pole bean grows tall and produces well, but only if it grows on something other than itself — a pole or trellis. And that the half-runner needs no support outside itself but is not as productive, is generally inferior to the high yielding pole bean, planted by those too lazy or too busy to supply the trellis.

The old man, pleased, repeated it. "Big Jim a pole bean body with a half-runner heart." The small gathering came to its feet, yelling

"Preach! Preach!" and "Well? Well?" Egging him on. He seemed unaffected by their response and continued to speak in the same hushed but secure way.

"Mr. Folsom just need to take his buggy wheel to the river." The noise from the crowd was far in excess of its number. Again the students did not understand, had never watched their daddy or granddaddy remove a buggy wheel, its spokes loose on the hub and rim from sun and wear and years, take it to the river where the cold running water would swell the wooden parts to a fit as tight as new in a few days of soaking, and the buggy could roll on. Renewed.

I thought the old man was about to sit down but the enthusiasm of the group cheered him on. "You know," he started anew, "if'n you got a big enough chock you can stop most any wagon from rolling. What I'm sayin' is, if'n there ain't no twenty-mule team a-pullin' the wagon over the chock. Then the lead mule, he'll git down, he'll strain and pull 'til the hames 'bout to split and the traces 'bout to snap. And the other mules, they pull right 'long behindst him. And they pull the wagon right over the top of that chock. I'm tellin' ya' now. And I don't care how big a chock it tis 'cause they gon' pull it right over it."

The people were on their feet again. "Yeah! Preach now! Tell us! Yeah!" They yelled the words in unison as if they had been rehearsed. A few of the older men had not stood, but they were with him. "Well? Well?" they called from where they sat. Said like a question, "Well," as they used it in antiphonal fashion, was a verb. It meant, "We agree. We hear you. Go on."

And their neighbor went on. "What I'm tellin' you is, Governor Folsom got a big chock. A mighty big chock. Ain't no question 'bout it. But we the mules. Aw, we ready mules." His voice dropped to a whisper and everyone strained to hear him, knowing he was almost through. "And when the one what trained us say 'Giddy-up,' ain't no chock ever been made big enough to stop the wagon."

The old man sat down, and after a long applause the room was quiet. The young men drove back to Montgomery. Feeling, perhaps, but not comprehending. And I went into the night knowing something I had not known before.

* * *

"Goddamit, where you been?" the skinny one said, holding the bulb he had removed from the dome light so it wouldn't come on. "We been settin' here since midnight."

"Well, big deal. It ain't but 12:30. And you better watch your mouth. You know Wiley don't go for that kind of talk."

"And Wiley can kiss my ass. What'd you bring him for?"

"Because he's the best demolition man ever to screw a slope-headed whore in Korea, that's why," the fat one said. "You bring the caps?"

"Caps? I thought he wasn't using dynamite. Thought he was using plastic. Like they used on the gooks. But, yeah. I brought the caps."

"We're using it all. You know the plan. That's why four people come in four cars. One got the caps, one got the sticks, one got the plastic, and one got the fuses. Anybody get picked up, well, he ain't got a thing that'll go off."

"Who's bringing the diesel? You got the diesel?" the skinny one asked, closing the door by the handle so it wouldn't slam.

"Wiley said don't bring no diesel. Said it was too slow. And looks suspicious riding around with a can of diesel in the trunk of a gasoline car. Said we'd siphon some gas out. Said for us to make sure there ain't no pilot lights on. Said to make sure the niggers didn't leave no heaters going. You sure they all gone?"

"They didn't meet last night. Rupert stayed at his post till quarter of. No coming or going either way."

"Where's Rupert?"

"Gone home. Like he was supposed to. Supposed to give me the report and get the hell home. He'll be sound asleep side his old lady when the fun starts. Or not asleep one. You got any whiskey?"

"You crazy?" the fat one asked. "Wiley don't put up with no drinking. Said if anybody was drinking we could get ourselves another boy."

"What time the other one coming?" the skinny one asked, reaching through the window and opening the glove compartment.

"The other one'll be here at ten after one. That's what Wiley said. And said he'd be here eight minutes later. Said don't do nothing on the hour, half hour, or quarter hour. That Wiley knows his stuff." He reached out and took the bottle, an almost full pint of Four Roses. He tore the Alabama state liquor stamp off, chewed on it for a minute, then

washed it down with two gulps of the whiskey. "Here. Have a pull. Then we'll put it up. Don't want Wiley mad at us."

At exactly ten minutes after one, a car pulled off the road and into the grove where the two were standing. The driver turned the lights off but didn't get out. "That's the other one," the skinny one said. "He's supposed to stay in his car until Wiley gets here. They met two hours ago in Wiggins. Wiley put a strip of tape on his car doors and windows. Wiley don't trust him. Afraid he'd call the cops or somebody at the last minute. Or back out. Wiley'll know if he's been out of the car since he left him."

"Wiley shore takes the sport out of a good coon hunt," the fat one said. "Jesus. Adhesive tape on your car door. And don't forget to watch your mouth when he gets here. Don't breathe on him either. Jesus."

"Seems like a lot of trouble for one little nigger church."

When Wiley arrived, he walked slowly around the other one's car, shining a small pen light along each door and window, then tapped gently on the driver's side. The two men who had been waiting saw a small white-gloved hand, holding what was clearly a woman's purse, reach through the window. Wiley took the purse and looked inside, then opened the door. A tall, medium built, blonde woman got out.

"Goddam," the skinny one said. "You didn't tell me the other one was a woman."

"Watch it!" the fat one snapped. "I didn't know it. The skipper just said there would be four of us."

"You brought yours?" Wiley said to each of them when he was close enough for them to hear his whisper. Each one handed him a package a little bigger than a shoe box. They were wrapped in white tissue paper with identical red ribbons. He began to walk back to the road, in the direction of the little churchhouse.

"What about gasoline?" one of the men asked.

"Never mind." Wiley said. "There won't be enough left to burn."

The Monday issue of the Birmingham *News* reported that the Mt. Sinai Baptist Church had been destroyed by what the Sheriff said "appeared to be a dynamite blast." It said the building had been used for civil rights meetings. Two years had passed since the meeting with the students.

"Was the old man we saw that night still living?" I asked T.J. Eaves.

"Daddy was teaching the classes," he said.

"Why didn't you tell me that was your daddy?" I said. "How is he?"

"You didn't ask me. Daddy's all right. He lived long enough to see a new day dawning. I think."

"Did the Governor ever take his buggy wheel to the river?" I asked.

"Well, you know, Folsom's wheel wasn't all that dry. But you ought to see Wallace's."

* * *

"You know why they call this Missionary Ridge?" I asked T.J. We were in Chattanooga again, this time with Jim Lawson, a young black Methodist preacher. He was pious, tough, stubborn, and very bright. Despite his youth, he had already been a missionary twice — first as a federal prisoner for refusing, as a pacifist, to register for the draft during the Korean War; and later, two years as a Methodist missionary in India. Now he was working for the Fellowship of Reconciliation, was a student at Vanderbilt Divinity School (the first black person admitted), and was about to marry my secretary. It was he, more than any other individual, who was responsible for the non-violent direction the student sit-in movement took during the sixties. By way of thanks, Vanderbilt University expelled him. He lectured, drilled and trained the students, night after night, in the philosophy and technique of non-violent resistance. He liked my friend, T.J. Eaves, but sometimes grew impatient when T.J. asked a lot of questions. He also found it strange that T.J. was a storehouse of information when he had not gone to school much. Sometimes I felt that they competed as to who knew the most. Jim grew up in an academic atmosphere in Ohio, attended fine schools, and had cultural advantages neither T.J. nor I enjoyed. T.J. learned what he knew by asking questions of everyone he met. And by reading books. When he was a child in Alabama and the Bookmobile wouldn't stop at colored folk's houses, he got a job on weekends keeping the vehicles clean. He would slip books out one Saturday and return them the next.

"Sure, I know why they call this Missionary Ridge," Jim Lawson said. "Because white missionaries used to tell the Indians about the lowly Gallilean up here."

"I didn't ask you," I said. "You're supposed to know. You used to *be* a missionary."

"I know too," T.J. said. "But I wonder what happened to that hotbed of missionary activity." He laughed, gesturing all around at white churches we were passing. We were there trying to encourage the leadership in this city of continuing racial unrest. They were visiting black ministers, while I called on white ones I knew or knew about.

"Let's go to Rossville," T.J. said, indicating with his hand that I should turn left at the next street.

"Rossville? What's in Rossville?" Jim Lawson asked. "I don't think there are many of our people in Rossville, Georgia."

"I want to see how much Will knows about the noble savages he took to Oklahoma," T.J. said.

"Oklahoma? Man, I've never been to Oklahoma but once, and I went by myself."

"How much do you know about John Ross?" he asked, motioning a south turn.

"Probably not as much as you do," I said, following his direction.

"John Ross was a freedom fighter." It was a term many of the civil rights activists used to describe themselves. ("What do you do?" "I'm a freedom fighter.") "He wasn't but one-eighth Cherokee, you know. He didn't have to go through all he did. He could have stayed right on his big plantation, worked his slaves, and had a good life." He stopped talking for a minute or so, switched the radio on, then off again when he heard the news going off. "Well, not a *good* life," he continued. "Easy life, I guess, is what I'm saying."

"John Ross owned slaves?" Jim asked. "I didn't know Indians owned slaves."

"That's because white folks taught you history, too," he said, laughing. "Like Will. Black folks taught me history. Bet you thought the Indians the white man herded up and transported to Oklahoma were nomadic savages, living in teepees and running through the woods yelling, 'Woo, woo, woo, woo,'" he said, raising his voice to an affected falsetto, slapping his mouth repeatedly with his open hand to exaggerate the silliness of the sound.

Jim looked at me and winked. "You sure know a lot of big words, T.J."

"You mean, for an Alabama field nigger, right?"

T.J. began to relate story after story about the removal of the Indians to the West, his tone and manner that of a classroom lecturer. He told of trick after trick, recited names, dates, and places of treaty after broken treaty, described in gripping and graphic detail the concerted oppression of the Cherokees, their brave but hopeless defense of their tribal existence, and the tragic migration.

In my limited study of American history, Andrew Jackson was a folk hero. I was never exposed to his blemishes. But as I drove the streets of Rossville, Georgia, with two black men, on a mission somehow related to things he left undone, I was hearing facts I had known before but had not digested.

T.J. painted a gripping picture of a Cherokee farm family much like my own family. They are seated at the supper table on the place they had worked hard to pay for. Suddenly soldiers surround the house and appear at doors and windows, bayonets unsheathed and gleaming in the light of the coal oil lamp. The mother goes out and calls the chickens and feeds them one last time, takes the youngest child on her back and two little girls by the hand, then follows her husband and the soldiers into the night. Before they are out of hearing distance, the plunderers are there, following the soldiers like hungry wolves, taking from the house every item of any value, rounding up the cattle, taking food from the pantry and grain from the barn. The soldiers gave the family no time to bring anything except the clothes they wore. The father and one of the children will die before they reach Oklahoma.

"How'd you know all that, T.J. Eaves?" Jim asked when he paused.

"That's the trouble with you Yankee Negro gentlemen," he answered, half-teasing, exaggerating Neeee-gro. "You think pulpwood darkies stay ignorant forever. But since you asked, I learned it from my grandma. And she learned it from her mamma. My great grandma was a Cherokee. Her mamma, that would be my great, great grandma, gave her to a slave man who was helping load the Indians on barges. She was three years old. Grandma said her mother remembered it. Said the man lived on a giant plantation, and when he took her home she just sort of mixed in with the other little slaves. She married one of them after emancipation, then faded into the woodwork."

"Sure," Jim said, laughing. "And no doubt Mee-maw was a princess. Why does everyone in the South want to be a descendant of Indian royalty?"

"Nope," T.J. said. "She was just an ordinary little papoose. And after that an ordinary little slave child."

He went on with his grandma's stories. An elderly Cherokee neighbor, finding the soldiers at his door, calmly calls his children and grandchildren around him, kneels down and asks them to pray with him. He was baptized a Christian at birth. The dumbfounded soldiers look on. Rising up, he leads the way into exile. He will die before the flatboat he is loaded onto leaves the Tennessee River.

Not far from Little Rock I watch as John Ross buries his wife, Wuatie. I feel the emotion and pathos of the scene as the indomitable freedom fighter covers the woman who has borne them six children. The soldiers give him time to mark, but not mourn, her passing before they ride on, leaving her halfway between a place none of them wanted to leave and a place none of them wanted to go to.

"Are you sure you're the same fellow I picked up in the fog that morning?" I asked him when he stopped. I had been entertained, moved, and impressed with his history lesson.

"I think so," he said. "But sometimes I ain't so sure." He patted Jim Lawson on the shoulder. "By the way, sir. I also learned to read."

"I'm sorry I asked you that . . . how you knew all that," Jim said. "I guess I do have Yankee manners sometimes. But you taught me something. You really did."

"What?"

"That the Movement didn't start in Nashville or Montgomery."

When I got home I began to read up on John Ross and Andrew Jackson's Indian removal. I found a quote from John Ross that jolted me: "The perpetrator of a wrong never forgives his victims." Is that what makes white folks behave like white folks? We can't forgive them for what we've done to them? But that gets complicated too. Jim Lawson told me later that his ancestors were never slaves, and I told him that none of my ancestors ever owned any.

"By the accident of birth, I can't forgive you for a wrong I never did to you," I told him. "And you have to forgive me for not forgiving you for something you don't need forgiving for."

"There's more to the wrong than slavery," he said. And I knew that he was right. Knew that I'm stuck forever with this incurable skin disease.

* * *

"Why do they call you Booker T.?" I asked T.J. Eaves as we stood in front of the Clark Memorial Methodist Church in Nashville, waiting for Jim Lawson to begin another training session on non-violent resistance.

"I reckon they think I'm an Uncle Tom," he said, apparently not disturbed by the comparison.

"They think Booker T. Washington was an Uncle Tom?" I asked.

"They do now. But heroes come and go. He'll be back. Just you mark my word. Yessir, Mr. Will, he be back. Shore as you born." I marveled again at how he could switch back and forth from good grammar to bad, wondering at his criteria for each one.

"You don't have to call me Mister," I said. "Didn't we establish that already?"

"You extablish hit. I never. You older than me. My mamma tell me some manners. Ain't got nothing to do wid color." I let him go.

"Well, why do they think you're an Uncle Tom? It seems to me you carry your end of the stick."

"In the Movement you aren't supposed to complicate things," he said. "It's all right to ask certain questions, but some others aren't welcome."

"Like what?" I asked.

"Like, 'What we do if we demonstratin' in somebody's store and the manager have a heart attack?' I mean, how 'sponsible are we for that cat we calling brother?"

"I guess being our brother's keeper does get out of hand sometimes," I said.

"And the second commandment is like unto it. Thou shalt love thy neighbor as thyself." His enunciation was perfect.

The session had already started. Several students were seated facing the wall, pretending they were at a lunch counter. John Lewis, only seventeen but already a leader, was the manager who refused to serve them. Another group stood behind the demonstrators. They were playing the role of white hecklers. They taunted the seated students with an assortment of insults, pulled their hair, blew cigarette smoke in their faces. The students sat silent, absorbing the abuse.

"Okay, Bennie, you be the waiter now. Come tell these people why they can't be served in a white restaurant," John Lewis said.

Bennie was a medical student at Meharry Medical Center, a school which, at the time, trained the majority of all Negro physicians. He was tall, light-skinned, bullnecked, and slightly overweight. "Bennie's from New Jersey," someone in the crowd of observers yelled. "He doesn't know anything about crackers." Almost everyone laughed. John Lewis held up his hands to stop the laughter, walked quickly to the crowd, and led a young man out. He wrote something down on his note pad, tore the sheet off and handed it to him. "Say that word out loud. Loud enough for everyone in the room to hear it."

"I don't say that word," the embarrassed young man replied.

"Say it anyway," Lewis said. "Everyone here has heard it. And when we go down to Woolworth's and McClellan's and Grant's next week to sit in, they'll hear it a lot more. Go ahead. Say it. It's 'nigger.' N-i-g-g-e-r. Nigger! And when you say c-r-a-c-k-e-r, you're saying the same thing. There aren't any niggers in this Movement. And there aren't any crackers on the other side. That's a hate word. We're talking about the beloved community. We don't hate people. People aren't our enemy. We hate segregation. Systems are our enemy. We're talking about unconditional love. We keep loving them no matter what they do to us. And if you love somebody, you don't fight back. You take it. We're talking about non-violence. We're talking about *satyagraha*, as Gandhi called it. We're talking about the passive resistance of Martin Luther King, Jr. And if you can't understand that, remember this: That's the only weapon we have. White folks make all the guns. White folks make all the razors. White folks make all the jails. But all the guns, knives, and jails in the world can't put love down. Nobody makes love. God makes love. We *do* love. Go ahead, Bennie."

Everyone was still and quiet when he finished. It was as though the full import of what they were about had sunk in for the first time. He had made it clear that when the sit-ins (as the demonstrations at segregated eating places had come to be called) began, they would be subjected to behavior they would not have believed one human being could direct toward another. Sacrificial lambs on the altar of intolerance.

"That part about weapons bothers me," T.J. said, as we walked toward the parking lot when it was over. "I mean, if they have weapons and we have weapons and in the end our weapon is the strongest . . . well, I just wonder."

The basic training was over, and this was not the first day of combat. But it was the first time these non-violent soldiers would be taken prisoners of war. Although it was a snowy February day in Nashville, the storm was not enough to keep the Saturday crowd at home. And not enough to keep the black students, assembled since early morning at Kelly Miller Smith's First Baptist Church, from their intentions — to send a delegation to all the variety and department store lunch counters in the downtown area. My job had been to find out what the mayor and police department planned to do. I knew the demonstrators would be arrested, and I passed that word. Their plan, meanwhile, was to send a small group of students at first. As soon as one group was arrested and hauled to jail in the paddy wagons, another group would be summoned to come from the church and take their seats at the counters and tables. Again and again. And so it went. As white officers armed with pistols, billy clubs, and handcuffs made arrest after arrest, they seemed irritated that there was no occasion to use force. Their experience of the past, and their present expectation, was of drunken, unruly Jefferson Street Negroes in Saturday night fights — sullen, resisting arrests, having to be subdued with blackjacks and handcuffs, physical exertion as routine as the night court arraignment. But these law-breakers were sober, quiet, clean, and well mannered. When told that they were under arrest, they offered no resistance. They arose as a body and moved to the waiting paddy wagons, a phalanx of sacrifice, an oblation as foreign as Martians to men trained in the use of physical might. They were witnessing a power they had not seen before.

I edged along beside each group, whispering encouragement, noting the number packed into each wagon, feeling guilt and complicity for not hurling my white body into their ranks screaming, "If you're taking them, you're taking me." A police lieutenant I recognized as being also a Sears sales clerk on his off-time eyed me talking to Diane Nash, having to lean directly to her ear to be heard above the roar of the hostile crowd. She had emerged as a pivotal leader, and I was trying to ask her if she wanted to be bailed out immediately so she could return to her command post.

"Who the hell are you?" the lieutenant asked as the door of the last paddy wagon was slammed shut, the sirens and lights punctuating the clamor of the multitude as the vehicles sped away. "Who are you?" he asked again when I didn't answer immediately.

"I'm nobody," I said, pretending to scribble a note on the pad I was holding. "I'm a reporter." It was only half a lie.

"Well, you better stick to your job and let us do ours," he grumbled. Then, perhaps remembering the public relations aspect of his job, he chuckled and added, "Where are all these damn nig . . . uh . . . Negroes coming from?" I thought it best not to answer. Instead I pondered the implications of his question as I waited outside the store for the next wave of demonstrators to arrive from the church. He had asked the most pertinent question of all: Where are they coming from? If all the store owners and managers, the mayors and governors and squires and legislators could ask and answer it, the crisis would end.

I thought of a colony of black ants I had tried to destroy, or at least control, on the edge of my asparagus bed. Because asparagus grows in extremely rich soil, it provides a perfect home for ants. When I first discovered them, I flooded the nest with a garden hose, watching the workers floating, floundering, washing down the gulley the heavy stream created. "I'll drown the rascals," I thought. (In the years to follow I would see firemen direct high pressure water hoses at demonstrating men, women, and little children with a force that would send them tumbling down sidewalks, hurled against buildings like seashells at high tide.) The next morning the nest was back in order. They had pulled the kernels of barley seeds stored as feed deep inside the tunnels outside to dry in the sun. A few days later I shoveled deep into the ground, turning the nest, inhabitants and stored food upside down. When I returned an hour later the workers were recreating it, some carrying larvae and pupae back into the pile of dirt, others digging new tunnels for still others to drag the barley seeds into the storage area. Several of the workers, sterile females, were guarding the queen, waiting until an appropriate chamber was built in which she could continue her procreating chores. I watched the long column moving in, each one pulling a seed many times heavier than itself. "Lift that barge. Tote that bale," I sang. I saw that the ants were not all alike. The line was sprinkled with hundreds of brown ants, much smaller than the others. Our science teacher had told us once about slave ants. "But they aren't really slaves," she told us. One species of ants would sometimes steal the eggs from another colony for food. When some of them went through the stages to maturity, they simply went about the work that was going on, treated no differently from the others. I wondered if she considered telling us, little white seventh-graders in rigidly segregated Mississippi, that we who stole the babies of other nations might have learned a lesson from the lowly insects all about us.

An alcoholic country musician who was staying with us at the time was taking antabuse. He suggested that I mix some of his antabuse with honey, then pour some beer on them. He said if the combination affected the ants the way it did him, they would all vomit themselves to death. I tried chlordane instead. It left thousands of them dead. But in a few days the dead ones had been moved out and the colony was as active as before. "Where are all these damn ants coming from?" Then someone told me that the ants did not hurt the asparagus, actually helped it by loosening the soil.

"Where are all these damn nig . . . uh . . . Negroes coming from?"

From African villages and the bowels of slave ships. From cotton plantations and city slums. Ole Miss's kitchen and Massa's fields. Bwana's betrayal and Charleston auctions. Coming, coming, coming. The fathers have eaten a sour grape and the children's teeth are set on edge; white teeth now become fangs. Where all these Negroes were coming from was easy: They are the issue of Nat Turner and Frederick Douglass, sons and daughters of Harriet Tubman, Sojourner Truth, David Walker, Denmark Vesey, and millions of unnamed women riding the back seats of buses on their way to nurse, feed, and raise white babies, their own babies roaming the streets or looking after each other, their menfolk still stripped of the title *man* by Dred Scott's defeat. The question the lieutenant, and I, should have been asking was, "Where are all these damn, or damned, whitefolks coming from?" Did they choose a mission of bigotry when they reached their majority, when it was time to make lifetime decisions and commitments? Did they plan this outing of violence and hate with a mind as free and uncluttered by the things of history and culture as the buffalo that grazed this meadow now called Fifth and Church? Or did the historical and societal implants decree that they would, on this occasion, behave exactly as they are behaving? How would the sliderule of Andrew Jackson's Manifest Destiny measure them on this day of dishonor?

You, lad, who just screamed, "Fuck you, nigger!" at that young woman who neither asks nor expects more of the world than you and I. You, who told me ten minutes ago that you and your brother came to town today to get your hair cut at the Barber College because they will do it for a quarter. Do you know why you are here? Do you care? *Can* you care? Or are you singing the same canticle of hurt as she, an antiphonal response to seeds you did not plant, furrows you did not till but whose harvest is now imposed upon us all?

And you, heritors of Messrs. Woolworth, Kress, McClellan, Walgreen, and W.T. Grant. Can you see us from your Aspen slopes, your secured Connecticut estates, your frozen lakes of Saranac, your lofty perch on the East Side? Do you care? Can you care? We are the children of washer-women and pulpwood haulers — darky slaves and indentured rednecks, warriors today against each other in an ageless war neither chose, congregated here on this frigid twenty-seventh day of February in the leap year of 1960. Must we forever fight your battles? Battles in which we have so little stake? From Plymouth Rock to Fort Sumter and Appomattox, bondage and alleged Reconstruction, World Wars I and II, and now Fifth and Church, we have sung the song of "we the people." Was it only a cruel hoax, a lie of nationalism? Have we always been props and pawns in a drama directed, orchestrated, and choreographed by some patrician deific force we can never hope to master? Are we, black and white here congregated, the nates of the body politic doomed to go on warring with each other over hamburgers and Coca-Colas with sirloin and champagne not even at issue?

I thought of things like that as I stood in the middle of a screaming mob of white people, my people, angry because the slave ants wanted a piece of our barley. Thought of it but said none of it. For I was scared most of the time it was happening.

There had been no serious incidents of violence, but the white hecklers had increased and could only be described as a mob. The city administration, confused and uninformed, seeing that they would not have enough jail space, decided to pull the police out of the stores and order them closed in the interest of public safety. No one on the streets was allowed to go inside, but the students were left at the mercy of the frustrated and increasingly angry mob which remained inside when the police left. Frustrated because none of their verbal or physical abuse seemed to faze the students, who continued to sit like statues. Angry because never before had they seen a Negro disobey or ignore an order from white authority.

In the Woolworth store, there was a lunch counter downstairs and a smaller one upstairs. I watched as the hecklers downstairs increased the things they were willing to do when the police were gone.

"You black bitch! Take this!" The speaker, a young man whose dress and demeanor bespoke his own cultural and economic status, had a bad head cold. He sucked a massive glob of stringy phlegm into his throat, hawked loudly, rolled it slowly and deliberately on the end of his tongue as his buddies cheered him on, then spit straight onto a young woman's neck. There was handclapping and laughter, the student not moving at all, leaving the meringue of hate sliding slowly down her spine.

I think it was the first time my spirit groaned for the perpetrator of an act of racial violence. Suddenly, the man who spat seemed to me the victim. The word "raca" kept reverberating through my bones. *Raca. Raca. Raca.* The word came originally from the noise in the throat of one preparing to spit. "You are nothing. You are dirt. I will *spit* on you! *Raca!*" Jesus said such a one would have to answer in the final judgment. Poor man. You poor, dear man. I really do love you. It was as if a heavy burden had been lifted. Yet it was replaced by an even heavier one.

A small, elderly white woman came slowly out of the crowd, leaned over and whispered something to the woman, then turned and faced the man squarely. She held an egg poacher she had purchased in one hand. She smiled slightly, at first I thought sympathetically, and said,

"Young man, I have a grandson about your age. And I'll bet you have a nice little sister at home. How would you feel if someone did that to her?" As the crowd laughed awkwardly, he dropped his head and, without answering, drifted into the milling throng. The woman, nonchalantly, moved as one of them.

For a few minutes, the hecklers drew back — waiting for another leader. Occasionally one person would jump in quickly, put a cigarette out on a student's back, thump an ear, or make some tentative effort to jerk someone from a stool. But randomly.

"You know what this is, girl?" asked a big man holding a glass half-filled with a clear liquid. He appeared older than most of the others. His face was leathery and wrinkled but not from age. Weathered from outside work, I supposed. I felt sick and afraid, the new burden grievous. The man looked like where I came from. But for geography, he could be an uncle or cousin. And except for something or other, in my fear I knew not what, he could be me. He had a commanding presence, and the crowd grew quiet to hear him.

"This heah is bat'try acid. Rite out o mah ole truck. Carbolic acid, ya mite say." He held it over her head, far enough forward for her to see it. The inflection and cadence of his voice, sprinkled by unintended diphthongs, was so overstepped as to make him suspicious. (That was long before we knew that the federal intelligence apparatus often infiltrated and adulterated whatever they wished to discredit. I cannot say that that was what we were seeing. But I wonder about it.)

"And if you don't git yo' black ass out of heah befo' I count to ten, I'm gon' pour it rite over yo' frizzly head."

The student still did not move, just sat staring directly ahead. "And come sunup, there won't be one hair left on top of that nigger-ass skull." He tilted the glass, almost letting the liquid drip onto her head, still holding it where she could sense that it was there. "You gon' look like a cue ball, bitch. A black-ass cue ball!"

A murmur of endorsement went up from the line of faces watching and listening. The male students seated on each side of her shifted nervously on the stools. The fingers of one of them curled back and forth into a hard fist. I had watched him at some of the training sessions, though I didn't know his name. He was well-built, like a trained athlete. The white man was heavier but flabby looking. I knew the student could beat him senseless.

The elderly white woman moved to the front again. She stood between the man and the student. Pretending he didn't see her, the big man began to count. She looked directly up into his face and said something I couldn't hear. When he reached eight in his count, he stopped and turned to face the crowd. They were still attentive, sensing danger. He faked a laugh, lowered the glass and began to address them.

"Naw. I tell ya what. Ain't no need to waste no good bat-try acid lik' that. I mean, she-itt. I ain't got nothin' 'gainst all them innocent lil' lice crawlin' in that filthy-ass head. I got a better idy." He turned to her again and with his free hand pushed her skirt almost to her thighs. "Les' jus pour this carbolic right in yo' nigger-ass lap." He wheeled back toward the crowd. "And next time she spread her legs for that jungle bunny sittin' next to 'er, well, she-itt. Ain't gon' be a kinky tail feather in sight."

The student sat with her hands on the counter, leaving the skirt where it was. The muscular built man beside her was breathing heavily, both hands clenched tightly, leaning almost off the stool. The elderly white woman jerked the student's skirt down with a motion almost too quick to see and then grabbed the tormentor with both arms in a tight embrace and began to cry. "Why? Why? Why? My God, why?" He gazed down at her for one ungainly moment, his face flushed red. She continued to weep, saying nothing. Suddenly the man gently wriggled free, backing away.

"Aw, lady, I didn't mean no harm. It ain't nothing but tap water nohow." As he moved into the crowd and away from the students at the counter, everyone moved with him. The woman, no longer crying, walked up and down the path they had left. Solidly in charge.

Upstairs the hecklers and students had been unaware of what was happening below. The potential for a violent eruption there had grown since the first students had sat down. There were fewer of them and they were all males. The leader of the antagonists was a thin, flamboyant, city-looking fellow with a Jerusalem cross around his neck. He wore a sharp-pointed Robin Hood hat with a tall, waffing peacock feather. His friends called him "Ole Greenhat" and constantly egged him on. He had singled out one student for special attention. With rabbit punches to the back of his neck, sharp chops to the clavicle muscles, and jabs to the kidney area, he seemed determined to goad him into a fight. It was obvious the student was on the verge of breaking. I considered trying the same tactic the old woman had tried downstairs. But my assignment from the Movement was to observe carefully, make notes, be as prepared as possible to be a credible witness in case of court trials. I wasn't sure that was why I didn't do what she did.

"It's open season, Green Hat. Get that coon!"

"Give him a peanut, Green Hat. Monkeys don't eat hamburgers nohow."

"Naw, peel him a 'nanner. He'll go back up the tree then."

Suddenly Green Hat, infuriated that he had not succeeded in provoking the student, lost control of himself. He grabbed the young black man around the neck with both hands and jerked him to the floor. The student, heaving with emotion, began rolling toward the stairs, Green Hat kicking, pawing, screaming obscenities.

Instantaneously and simultaneously there was the whoosh of a switchblade knife in Green Hat's hand and the appearance of a new face from the crowd. He was a collegiate type, handsome, neat, and well dressed — what today would be called a preppie. I had never seen him before. Never saw him again. As Green Hat was swinging downward with the knife, the young collegian caught him with a powerful blow to the face, knocking him to the floor. "You son-of-a-bitch! If you touch him one more time, I'll stomp the piss out of you!" He quickly kicked the opened knife, which the man had dropped, out of reach and stood over him.

"Here come the cops!" Green Hat yelled. "Let's get out of here." He made a hasty retreat down the stairs and out the door, his pals close behind. There were, of course, no cops. Green Hat had lost face.

I never bothered to try to understand which of the two, the old woman with the egg poacher or the young man with the fast knuckles, did the will of the Lord that cold and snowy day. But it was clear to everyone present that each was an instrument in the prevention of serious violence and the shedding of blood.

John Lewis was arrested that day. He was jailed forty-three more times after that, and his body bears the scars of many beatings. Nonetheless, he remained non-violent, never learned to hate white people, and never became embittered as many did. He is a councilman in Atlanta now. And still talks of the beloved community.

Diane Nash was there. A native of Chicago and a student at Fisk University, she emerged as spokeswoman for the Nashville Sit-in Movement. Of course, at that time she was known as "spokesman." Many considered her the Joan of Arc of the Movement. She was arrested that day and many times thereafter.

Bernard LaFayette of Tampa was there, too. A student at American Baptist, he later earned a doctor's degree at Harvard. He spent that night and many more in jail. Marian Barry, now mayor of Washington, D.C., was there, along with Angela Butler, beautiful daughter of a South Carolina preacher. Her black skin glowed purple. Student at Fisk. Hurled by two beefy police officers into a paddy wagon already overloaded.

Paul LaPrad was the first student to be arrested. Paul was white, an exchange student at Fisk. He was a pacifist, a member of the Church of the Brethren. As the only white student sitting in at the Woolworth lunch counter, he was singled out as the leader, the assumption being that Negroes were not intelligent enough to devise such a creative scheme. He was pried loose from the counter by several strong young whites and thrown to the floor. He absorbed their beating without striking back. Paul was arrested for disorderly conduct and was taken away. His attackers remained.

T.J. Eaves. And others. Eighty-one in all. Jailed for walking into a public business and ordering a hamburger and a Coca-Cola in February, 1960.

"Don't eat no yellow snow, Will," T.J. called out as the officer slammed the paddy wagon door. Late that night, safely at home, I figured out what he meant.

IV
Earth's Vain Shadows Flee

JUST BEFORE THE FIRE at Mrs. Dolan's house, her little daughter, Edwina, gave Bonnie a kitten. She named him Ralph. A few months later, Ralph, with a different idea of gender, gave birth to six little ones, beginning a feline dynasty which still goes on. She was a good mother; nursing, cleaning, protecting. We thought it a fine lesson in parental love for our children to observe.

One morning the kittens were gone. All of them. A few hours later they were back. No one knew where they had been. Two days later, they disappeared again. This time they were gone overnight. The children, more upset each time, could not understand their absences. I had to explain that Mother Ralph was having school. It was a plunge into the real world. Each time she took them into the woods and left them, they had to survive on their own until she returned. Eventually she taught them how to hunt — tear birds or small animals apart with their claws and teeth — how to climb trees when they were pursued, and other techniques of longevity.

It was a painful lesson for the children. I suppose it was our fault. We had led them to believe that our commitment to the realm of nature was based on the lovely pastoral scenes they could observe from the window of a warm house, upon the kindness and generosity of the lower animals to each other.

"You see that cow grazing on the hillside, seeming so at peace with the universe?" I asked the children.

"Yes, sir."

"Well, there is more happening there than you see. For in every drop of water in a cow's body there are a million little bugs being chased by a million bigger bugs trying to kill them. Nature is not just cruising down the river on a Sunday afternoon."

"Did you have to tell them that?" Brenda asked when the children were gone.

"It's the truth."

"You didn't make that up. Who said that first? That stuff about all the little bugs being chased by bigger bugs trying to kill them." I told her I didn't know who said it first. I heard it somewhere. Maybe one day I'll check it out.

But she wasn't happy that I had used "school" in the analogy. "They'll think the teacher is going to take them way off somewhere and leave them."

"Unfortunately, they'll do just that," I said. "They might as well learn."

Certainly no one who has ever watched a female cardinal sit on the edge of a bird feeder with her adolescent child, crack a seed and put it in the little one's beak, back away, repeat it and back away again until it has learned to eat alone, can doubt that the smaller creatures do have an educational system of their own. All of them do. It is not as complex, systematized, and prone to deception and deterioration as our fine tuned pedagogy. But it exists, basic and consistent. Their system turns around propagation and survival of their particular species and leads nowhere else. Ours seems now to lead toward destruction of our species and theirs.

It is not that they are concerned exclusively with their own kind. Jackson was not. On one important occasion he had to choose between what was his kind and what would be his kin. Because the education system of the animals is not grounded in reading, writing, and arithmetic, Jackson never read the story of Jesus' mother and brothers coming to get him because they had heard he was behaving in a peculiar fashion. That he was crazy. But he had a similar experience.

His best friend was Nell, the quintessential old black mare. At one time, every family had one. She was the symbol of virility and stability, of continuity, of ancestry. Reminder, too, that life is not easy, but that as the sun is setting, there is rest and reward. Nell was already old when she joined the family, yet she established herself. She had worked hard and continued to work, pulling the plows, the Amish hack, riding the children. And friend to Jackson. They played, ate, slept, roamed the fields and woods together. Surely they were neighbors of a variety seldom seen.

While one goat lived with us, at least a hundred lived with Mr. Bill Jenkins, a friend and farmer, who told me that in ninety years on this earth he had never been in a minute's trouble. "Except that time I killed my wife."

One foggy spring morning, Mr. Bill's goats approached our farm, apparently on a mission of rescue of one of their kind feared to be in captivity. At first I heard their bleating far over the hill. Mr. Jenkins kept his fences mended, and I wondered how they had gotten out. Nell and I were getting ready to plant beans and corn that day, and I was brushing and combing her while she ate a bucket of sweetfeed and oats. Jackson at times ate with her and at times nuzzled me with his horns to express his jealousy. The fog was thick, but I could tell by the sound that the goats were on our side of the hill. As they drew closer, Jackson seemed confused and agitated. He would bounce and dance in their direction, then run back and stand under Nell's belly. He did that whenever there was danger, and she would stand as solid refuge until it passed.

Suddenly, the sun burned through and I could see the herd of goats, not more than a hundred yards away. They had stopped their calling and were simply trodding along, slowly and deliberately. A phalanx. They had come to take Jackson away.

Nell left her breakfast and began walking in their direction. Jackson stayed a few steps in front, and she let him. "I will go with you as far as I can, but I won't try to stop you."

All the Jenkins goats stopped as one when they were a few feet from Nell and Jackson. A burly ram, with curled horns and long goatee, stepped to the front like a military commander. Jackson, who had taken his place under Nell again when she stopped, moved out to face him. I remembered the stories of battles to death for ascendancy among the passionate *Capra*. I stood with not even a stick to stop them. Nell stood watching.

The massive scrotum of the big billy, almost touching the grass, seemed a mocking boast of superiority. Jackson had been stripped of any such title by the patricians of Bibb County, Georgia. It seemed not to be a factor. It was he who made the first move. He gradually and tentatively stretched his neck to touch the nose of the early morning visitor, whose own nose moved out not quite halfway to meet him. When they touched, each one jerked back as if the other had been electrically wired. They backed away, ducked their heads, and bowed their necks in a charge position. Neither Nell nor the big goat's entourage moved. Suddenly, as if by prior agreement and on cue, they both turned. The big one began to move back in the direction of their home, all the others trailing along in single file, some bleating for Jackson to follow. Jackson did not flee to the sanctuary of Nell's underbelly, just stood beside her watching them. When the last of them fell in line and moved away, he began to follow. Nell still made no move to influence him. When they were almost out of sight, Jackson, the only one bleating now, stopped and looked back at Nell; bidding, I thought, farewell, or asking her to come with him. The line continued to move away from him as he stood in uneasy ambivalence, considering.

> "Who is my mother, or my brethren?"
>
> ". . . to set a man at variance against his father, and the daughter against her mother, and the daughter in law against her mother in law.
> He that findeth his life shall lose it: and he that loseth his life . . . shall find it."

When Jackson started his rabbit leaps back in her direction, covering the distance in less time than it took her to turn around, the old woman with the egg poacher ambled back to the barn, secure in the knowledge that she would never be alone.

* * *

If the Civil Rights Movement of black students was flawed, as all Movements made up of flawed human beings are, it was (in my white liberal, and thus flawed, judgment) in the inability of so many of them to appreciate the legacy of the old black mares of history. Not all of them were old at the time. Not all were female. And not all of them were black. Those who were black came to be known as Aunt Jemima or Uncle Tom. If white, they were moderates and often considered to be more of an impediment to the Movement than the Ku Klux Klan, because they represented more power. Finally, some of them were "white liberals," a category who became the most dishonored of all who tried.

This was not true of the Movement of the early Student Non-violent Coordinating Committee; people like John Lewis, Jim Lawson, Diane Nash, Bernard LaFayette, Ruby Doris Smith, Angela Butler, Joe Lewis Smith, and the thousands of other brave young men and women of the early sixties who suffered imprisonment but continued to believe in and talk of the beloved community. They gave honor where honor was due. At times, even when it wasn't. But by the time Stokely Carmichael and his compeers ousted the tough and loving originals, even people like Martin King, Thurgood Marshall, Roy Wilkins, and Whitney Young were seen as enemies, tools of white racism and American imperialism.

Because white credibility and white religion have continued to erode since the Puritan fathers thanked God for His cooperation and benevolence as they slaughtered the Indians, it was understandable that young black people of the sixties would look with suspicion upon anything done allegedly for their benefit by black and white together. Nevertheless, the old black mares, the liberal stand-bys, moderates, even the gradualists have played their roles in nudging America in the direction of the prayer of Langston Hughes. A little nearer to

> The land that never has been yet —
> and yet must be —

People like Leslie Dunbar, a brilliant, Lincolnesque Southerner who gave up a career in university teaching to devote his life to peaceful solutions to complex problems. Harold Fleming, a Harvard educated Georgia country boy who did the same. Each took his turn directing the important but generally unsung work of the Southern Regional Council. Later they and their kind presided over some of the old money of the Fields, Mellons, McCormicks, Fords, and Rockefellers in foundations bearing their names. Whether Marshall, Andrew, Cyrus, Henry, or John D. would have approved of the manner in which their leavings were spent is a different matter. I approved, for it was they who financed the work of the Committee of Southern Churchmen, the little organization which paid us a modest salary as often as it could during those years when what we were up to was not looked upon with great favor.

Big and little people, whose intended mission might have been the purchase of an egg poacher but who, along the way, heard the Lord's song and moved a mountain.

There were, of course, the big ones who continued to be esteemed by even the most revolutionary.

Harriet Tubman, born a slave. Born to escape despite a head injury by a plantation overseer at fifteen. Born to be the most famous conductor of the Underground Railroad, escorting her people to freedom. O, Freedom!

Sojourner Truth, freedom fighter as feminist, freedom fighter as abolitionist. Marching on.

Lillian Smith and Paula Snelling, evangelists of justice, opening with their words the curtains of a new dawning. *Strange Fruit.*

Josh White singing about it.

> Southern trees bear a strange fruit.
> Blood on the leaves, and blood on the root.
> Black bodies swinging in the Southern breeze,
> Strange fruit hanging from the poplar trees.

All the cantors of the blues, from Bessie Smith to Big Bill Broonzy to Huddie Ledbetter, joining the chorus.

And Jessie Daniel Ames, with her heroic army of Southern white women, the Association of Southern Women for the Prevention of

Lynching, interrupting the long winter of free killing, stilling the breeze, stunting the fruit from the poplar tree as they sought to remove the crown of chivalry which they said had been pressed like a crown of thorns upon their heads. Forty thousand of these old black mares, mostly white, respectable, church-going women, stepped from their pedestals the menfolk had put them on to approach county sheriffs and state governors, chase mobs and stand tight-lipped in courtrooms, putting the lie forever to the notion that mob murder was committed on their behalf, spreading the startling news that in more than seventy percent of lynchings the alleged crime had not to do with woman's honor but with economic greed. By 1962 the voice of that righteous army seemed irrelevant to black people seeking more than physical survival. The lynch noose was more subtle, but they had plowed the new ground. Their day had paved the way for the new pursuits. And many who had been poor and powerless Negro tenant farmers in 1932 remembered that the women's deeds had brought a glimmer of hope not known before.

Those and thousands upon thousands, unknown and unnamed in the history of the Movement. My grandma. In 1931 she wouldn't let the men whip a young black boy. A little thing. Unless you were the one about to be beaten with a gin belt.

They with the egg poachers. And they with the fast knuckles. The unsung but reliable and authentic old black mares who cracked the ice on the frozen pond of oppression. Not all old. Not all black. Not all women.

V
Ills Have No Weight

THE SHORES OF East Africa, where captive people scooped up and ate handfuls of dirt, and the lunch counters of the American South, where their issue would attempt to eat a sandwich, were pages of the same book. The struggle to be free would not die. But some of the people would die now as then.

The white blanket of snow which covered the earth in February when the first sit-ins took place gave way to the colors of spring. No settlement seemed in sight as the Negro students continued to demand that they be served by occupying the lunch counter stools until they were arrested or the stores closed. There were also marches, and mass meetings nightly in many Negro churches, and boycotts of the merchants cut heavily into the sale of Easter finery. A mayor's committee in Nashville recommended that lunch counters be divided into three sections: one for whites, one for Negroes, and one for those who did not object to integrated eating. The students saw it as nothing more than entertainment.

"Do you ever feel like St. Paul?" I asked T.J. Eaves as we drove away from the Nashville courthouse. He had misunderstood the instruction for the demonstration the previous Friday and had just stood trial. The student activists, knowing that the police had informers in their ranks, sometimes used a code when announcing plans for the next day's activities. Each target store or restaurant was assigned a number. The number and the name of the business to which it corresponded were posted on the bulletin board at the headquarters church. Those plans were made in advance of the mass meeting by the Central Committee. If the leader called out, "Code nine at one," those who knew only what was posted on the board assumed the demonstration would be at Langford's Restaurant at one o'clock. But those who knew the code would subtract two digits from the location number and add one to the announced time to convene. So "code nine at one" really meant "code seven at two o'clock." It was Cross Keys Restaurant, not Langford's.

T.J. had forgotten to do the adding and subtracting. I suspected that he did it on purpose, for sometimes he didn't do what everyone else did. He went to Langford's at one. When he walked in alone, he was met by the bevy of policemen who had the wrong information. Perhaps indignant that they had been tricked, knowing that a hundred Negro students were marching on another business while they, two dozen strong, were dealing with a lone disturber of the peace, they immediately arrested him. One of them had clubbed him inside the paddy wagon and again in the elevator as he was being taken to the booking room.

I felt partly responsible, because in my covert role I had tried to strike a deal which, if it had been successful, would have desegregated one of the leading restaurants without trouble of any kind. Mr. Langford was a successful restauranteur, with cafes and lunch counters in many cities. He had always followed local customs with regard to race but had no special feelings about segregation. Through his pastor, a kind and gentle little Episcopal priest, he had sent word to me that he had an idea. He would not meet with any of the students, only with Reverend Kelly Miller Smith. (White people could not believe that the movement was truly democratic at that time and not directed by an individual leader.) Kelly had some misgivings about meeting with him without some of the students present but agreed to do so as a favor to me.

Mr. Langford explained that he was willing to desegregate his downtown restaurant, located in the Life and Casualty Building, but that he had a problem with his white waitresses. Therefore, his wife, a stellar churchwoman, strong-willed Minnesotan who had met him as a waitress, said she would don an apron and serve the first Negroes admitted. He told us he was influential in the Restaurant Association, and that if that group voted to abolish the color bar, the escalating crisis in the city could be solved immediately. He asked to be exempted from demonstrations until Friday. When the lunch rush was over, two or three Negro students or ministers would enter and be seated. They were to order tea or coffee and his wife would serve them. The word would begin to get around town that his facility was open. He knew the white hecklers would be present on Monday. No Negroes should show up that day. He had an arrangement with a wrestling promoter to quietly remove anyone causing trouble. He didn't want the police in his business. His wife would continue to mingle with the other waitresses, setting the example, serving anyone seated at one of her tables. By the end of the week he thought his restaurant would be operating normally, and he could take the matter to the scheduled meeting of the Restaurant Association. Kelly said he thought he could work it out with the students.

When the police showed up in force the next day, followed by T.J., who knew nothing of the plan, Mr. Langford felt betrayed. I called him at home that night to try to explain, but he exploded. Despite his moderation in matters of bigotry, he had other excesses. It was obvious that he had indulged heavily in one of them. "Campbell! You let me down! You and Kelly Smith let me down. You said I could trust him, and I did. Now the deal is off." I tried to convince him that it was a mix-up. "The deal is off. I've hired every cauliflower-earred, worn-out ex-wrestler in Nashville. They're strong as bulls. And for five dollars a head they'll hang every nigger who sets foot in my business from the top of the Life and Casualty Building." He was screaming, and I could hear his wife in the background trying to calm him. It was plain that he did not intend to be calmed. "Just tell your lying, double-crossing nigger friends that if they come in my place, it might be the last place they'll ever come in." He slammed the phone dead.

I was left with an irate businessman, a friend in jail, a saintly priest who would understand but be disappointed, and a thoroughly foiled scheme. Working behind the scenes gets crowded. I decided not to try it again. Let the movement move.

T.J. was charged with trespassing and assaulting an officer. Even the bailiff chuckled when the charges were read. The scrawny, baby-faced little black man, with gentleness showing in his eyes, stood accused by a seasoned white officer two heads taller than he and out-weighing him by nearly a hundred pounds.

The courtroom had the air of a capital offense. T.J. was brought in handcuffed and looked more like a puppet, his wizened face outlined in the dim light, than one accused of what the prosecutor tried to develop as an atrocious crime.

He was being defended by Mr. Z. Alexander Looby, an elderly Haitian attorney and Lincoln Republican, who believed in both law and justice.

"T.J., will you tell this court what you were doing at one o'clock last Tuesday?" asked the prosecutor.

"I went to dinner," he said quietly. Before the prosecutor could speak again, Mr. Looby asked the judge to ask him to address his client with courtesy.

"*Mister* Eaves," he said mockingly, "will you tell this court why you went to Langford's Restaurant?"

"For dinner," he answered.

"Don't you mean lunch? Around here we have dinner in the evening."

"Yessir, I know that. But down home we eat dinner at dinnertime. And that's in the middle of the day. About twelve o'clock. Sometimes eleven-thirty. Then at night we eat supper."

At the mention of "down home" the prosecutor's eyebrows shot up. "Down home? Uh huh. I see. So you're an outsider? You're an outside agitator. Come in here to stir up trouble. Well, boy, you've come to the right place. If you want trouble, you couldn't have picked a better place. We've had just about enough of outside agitation." T.J., having heard that the prosecutor lived in New Jersey until coming to Vanderbilt Law School six years earlier, while he had lived in Alabama until coming to Nashville to attend American Baptist Seminary seven years earlier, smiled and said nothing. The questioning continued.

"Will you tell this court why you chose to go to Langford's?"

"Instead of where?"

"Instead of, well, let's say, Rita's Ribs and Other Things. My colored friends tell me that's a nice place. Why didn't you go there?"

"I don't like Rita's ribs," he said. "And I'm not into her 'other things.' I'm a preacher." Twenty or so students were in the courtroom. A ripple of laughter spread among them at his mention of Rita's "other things." The judge rapped for order and said if it happened again he would clear the courtroom.

"Have you ever had any of Rita's ribs?" the prosecutor asked.

"Yessir."

"Have you ever had any of Rita's other things?" T.J. did not answer. The prosecutor looked at the judge, nodding for him to instruct T.J. to answer. Mr. Looby objected to the frivolous and irrelevant question. The judge sustained him. It didn't matter to T.J. He would not have answered.

The questioning continued for more than an hour, some of it along technical and fine lines of law, some of it fatuous nonsense. The judge seemed bored and annoyed that something so inconsequential was taking so much of his time. He had been on the bench long enough to intuit that T.J. did not, and would not, hit the officer nor anyone else. The first time the prosecutor asked him to describe exactly how he had attacked the policeman, T.J. replied calmly, "I didn't." He gave no answer to further grilling on the subject, even when the judge threatened contempt if he didn't. When the questioning returned to why he went to Langford's, where he knew he would be violating the law, instead of going to Rita's Ribs and Other Things, where he knew he would be served, T.J., obviously weary of it all, grinned broadly, cocked his head and said, "Cause, suh, I'se just a dumb, trifling nigger."

At first a murmur of surprise and disapproval went up from the students. Then spontaneous laughter and applause. The judge, on the verge of laughter himself, said he was giving them one more chance to show respect for his court. Then he asked both sides to join him in his chambers. George Barrett, a young white man who would later become one of Nashville's most prestigious lawyers, was assisting Mr. Looby in the defense. He was one of the first white lawyers to join in defending a civil rights case in the South. He told me later what happened. The judge told the assistant district attorney that he resented the caricature of a trial and told both parties that if T.J. would plead guilty to the trespass charge he would dismiss the more serious charge of assault. T.J. said he would admit to being in the restaurant but not to trespass. Mr. Looby convinced the judge that since the state considered his presence a trespass, T.J.'s saying he was there was tantamount to a guilty plea. The judge fined him fifty dollars.

"Long live Hambone," T.J. said, as we walked toward the exit.

"Well, you beat that one," I said. "But I'm not sure your brothers were happy with your performance."

"Pole bean bodies. Half-runner minds," he said, trying to sound like his father did in Alabama that night.

"Is that why they call you Booker T.?" Then I asked him if he ever felt like St. Paul.

"Say do Booker T. ever feel like St. Paul?" he said, the mimic again.

"Yeah. Getting beat up by the law. Thrown in jail for your beliefs. Things like that. Don't you ever feel like Paul in Caesarea?"

"Caesarea? Who dat? Dat gonorrhea's sister?"

"Knock it off, T.J.," I said, a bit impatiently. "No wonder they call you Booker T. You're nothing but an Uncle Tom."

"Yeah. Maybe so," he said. "Yeah, maybe I'm just an Uncle Tom."

"No, you aren't," I said quickly with a voice of apology. "I know you aren't. And you know it. But why don't you answer my question? I'm not the district attorney, you know. Do you ever feel martyred? Suffering for your beliefs? Convictions?"

"My beliefs?" he said, dabbing the oozing abrasion on his forehead with a big, blue bandana. He repeated the two words, this time not as a question. "My beliefs."

"Yeah. Don't you believe in civil rights?"

"No." He answered, almost before I finished the question, as if he had been hoping, waiting for me to ask it.

"No?"

"You heard it. No. Like I told a deacon's wife one night when she asked me if I believed in prayer. No!"

"You told a deacon's wife you didn't believe in prayer? In a Baptist Church? I hope you had your bags packed."

"Well, she was after me anyhow. And, matter of fact, I did have my bags packed. And my last sermon ready on a text from that St. Paul you're talking about. 'Finally, brethren, farewell.' And the mistletoe pinned on my coattail. But as the Lord would have it, I'm still there. Turns out her old man, my deacon, didn't like her much more than she liked me."

He began to talk about something else, but watching me, knowing, I supposed, that I wanted to hear why he didn't believe in prayer. When I didn't ask him, he told me. "I don't believe in prayer because I believe in God. And He says you can't serve two masters."

I had driven him to the emergency room of the black hospital to get the wound on his head tended to properly. When he saw where we were, he waved me on. Said he'd rub a little spider web and soot in it when he got home. "Anyway," he said, "I've had it for awhile. Seems like it doesn't want to scab over. But it will. No big deal."

I protested mildly, but when I saw he wasn't going to get out of the car, I pulled away. He went on talking. "Prayer is something *I* do. And even then I might not do it right. Who knows? God is something God does. He doesn't have to pray. I don't believe in anything I do. Like I say."

"That why you say you don't believe in civil rights? Because that's something we do? Well, maybe God is helping us do it." I felt I was gaining on him. But not for long.

"Helping us? That's like saying He helps us make rain. He doesn't have to help us do something if He wants it done. Don't you reckon He'd just rare back and do it?"

"Maybe that's what He's doing," I said, not too sure of my ground.

"Maybe," he said. "And then again, maybe not. I'm in civil rights trying to get *my* civil rights. God didn't keep them away from me. Man does that. The government. Whoever. Whatever. There's a big difference between civil rights and God rights. God gave me the same rights He gave you. You take some of them away from me and that's your problem. That's between you and Him. But when you think about it, there's something pretty selfish about trying so hard to get *my* rights. Maybe the Christian thing to be doing is to be handing over the rights I already have. Jesus said don't resist evil. Said if you take away my sweater to give you my coat. That if that policeman hits me on one side of the head to turn the other side and let him hit that too. And if he makes me run a mile, run two." He cleared his throat lightly, leaned down and tied his shoe. I started to tell him that he *was* turning the other cheek, that he wasn't resisting evil, but decided against it.

"So maybe the only folks who can be in civil rights and it be Christian is white folks," he continued. "You see what I mean?"

I told him I wasn't sure I did. Wasn't even sure I wanted to see what he meant. "Are you sitting there telling me Dr. Martin Luther King, Jr., isn't a fine Christian leader?" I said.

"I'm sitting here telling you I don't know whether he's a fine Christian leader or not. I know he's a fine civil rights leader. I'm not one of his Church sheep. I'm one of his civil rights sheep. And I'll follow him to the shearing. That's where they take off all my clothes. Then on to the slaughter house where they make lamb chops out of me. But that's because I'm damned, damned, damned sick and tired of white folks shitting on me!"

He was yelling and he was angry. I had not heard him say many slang or angry words before, and I was a little frightened.

I tried to pick up on the bit about white folks being the only ones who could do civil rights as a Christian act. I called the names of several prominent white preachers in the South and asked him to tell me one thing they had done for civil rights. "Name *one* thing!" I demanded. "One word in a sermon. One march. One bond put up for a jailed protester. One *amicus* brief. One anydamnthing!" I realized that I, too, was yelling. He admitted that he couldn't but said that wasn't the point. "If the Movement is depending for its Christianity on fat steepled whites," I said, "The Movement is going to be famished for Jesus."

"I didn't say anything about fat and I didn't say anything about steeples," he said. "And it's kind of funny that you did."

I named some active black preachers. "Yeah, yeah, yeah," T.J. said over and over after each name. "They're tough. Got guts. All that. But what I'm telling you is that as I read the Book, Brother Jesus is asking us to *give up* power, not get more. All those white cats you named under the big steeples, yeah they got power to give up. They got influence. And what's it good for? Somebody told me one time that the quickest way to lose your influence is to use it. Go tell'um, Brother Will. Go tell'um to get rid of some of it."

I had stopped the car in front of Rita's Ribs and Other Things to get us something to eat. He said he wasn't hungry but I ordered two sandwiches and two Cokes anyway. He sat quietly as we waited for the carhop to return. He was calm but seemed sad, a blank stare on his face. He shook his head and whispered, "And when your folks drop their power, I'll tell mine to let it lie where it fell. Not to pick it up. Cause if they do they're in a peck of trouble."

When we finished eating and were waiting for the woman to come and get the trays, he suddenly sat up straight and started laughing. "Now I'm going to tell you something else, Brother Will," he began. I knew it was something he had been debating in his mind, trying to decide if he wanted to tell me or not.

"Tell me," I said. "I need a good laugh too."

"You're always bragging about the big Negro preacher heroes. So let me tell you why I decided to be a colored preacher, Mutharoe. Ever since the Civil War, nigger preachers have been the sorriest bunch of cheaters, greedy gougers, selfish bastards . . . riding the backs of poor folks, taking up special love offerings on the preacher's birthday, the preacher's third anniversary as pastor, the preacher's anniversary of being ordained, the preacher's wedding anniversary, the preacher's this, that, and the other, taking up a collection for a new car, new suit of clothes, paint his house, buy him a trip to Detroit, asking folks to tithe their nickels and dimes when they can't afford to feed their young'uns. Jesus! I'm telling you now, and I want you to listen. They've been worse than the boss man. Next to nigger undertakers, nigger preachers have been about the most corrupt bunch of thieves ever born." He opened the window and spat out. "So what do you think of your folk heroes now?" he said, spitting again.

"I think Senator Eastland couldn't have said it better," I said, paying the woman and driving away. "Good Lord, man, what the Sam Hill are you talking about?" I wondered what I would have said if he had been white and said those things. I had never heard him say "nigger" except when he was doing his act.

"What I'm talking about is if you ain't doing it for Jesus, don't do it," he said, handing me the exact change for his part of the tab. "And that's all I'm talking about. Ole T.J'll be all right."

"Well, maybe you're right about colored preachers," I said uneasily, ignoring his last remark. "But so far they have been the leaders in this thing. It's been on their shoulders. You'll have to admit that."

"Yeah. I'll admit that. Mister God is a weird one. He picks some strange hoe hands."

There was another long period of silence as I fought the going-home traffic. When he spoke again, his voice soft and gentle, I understood what he had been telling me. "Will Campbell." There was a pause. "I love you."

"I really believe you do," I said. "So will you do me a favor? Just stay away from white folks. 'Cause they ain't going to believe you."

"I'se jus' a pulpwood nigger," he said, laughing out loud. Then changing voices he exclaimed, "You're white! Do you believe me?"

"I guess I don't have much choice," I said.

I knew T.J. could make it on his own.

* * *

"Why don't you let me take you to the doctor?" I asked T.J. The wound on his head, right at the edge of his hairline, had become a chronic, ulcerated lesion. I had learned that it was not from the beating he got the day he wandered innocently into Langford's Restaurant. He had had it since the first day of demonstrations at Woolworth's on Fifth Avenue. That I had not noticed it right away said more to me than I wanted to know. Now he carefully shaved the semicircle of hair around it each morning with the same exactness and care he gave his mustache. He called it the tonsure of the Movement. Said he wished everybody had one. On hot days, the drainage from it gave off an offensive and lingering odor. Some of our mutual friends talked to me about it. "That's a pretty serious social handicap," one of them told me. "He won't ever keep a girlfriend."

We were on our way to Lebanon to get some chicken feed at the Farmer's Co-op. He hadn't answered my question about going to the doctor. "You know, I don't enjoy having a runny sore on my head any more than you would. It's no badge of honor for me. But what the heck!" He had the window down and was holding his head close to the outside, suggesting, I supposed, that he would protect me as best he could from the smell of his misfortune. He began telling me about a young woman in his congregation he thought he might marry, shifting the subject again.

But when we had the feed loaded and were back in the truck, he didn't seem to object when I started talking about his sore again. "Yeah, okay. If that's what you want to talk about."

"So you'll go to the doctor," I said quickly. Not as a question.

"No. I won't go. The truth is I've been to several doctors about it. They use some big words, give me some kind of salve, and that's all. What gets me is that y'all wound us and then cuss us when you smell the pus." He had rolled the window up. For emphasis I supposed.

"Y'all, hell," I countered. "I didn't hit you on the head. And an old Mississippi aristocrat put it better a long time ago. He said, 'We crippled the colored people and then criticized them for limping.' Or something like that. Is that what you're saying?"

"Mississippi aristocrat, huh? Now, Massa Will, what he know 'bout dat?"

"Sure, T.J. Go into your damned nigger act!" I said, feigning anger. "Every time I get a little close, that's your defense." I lit my pipe and blew gales of smoke in his direction. "I'm not Ross Barnett, you know. Neither was David Cohn. He was a Jew in Baptistland. Give us a break, for Christ's sake!"

I expected him to get mad, sulk, and say nothing. Instead he began to laugh. "Why are we riding along here half-fighting, good friends half-fighting? Because one of us is white and one of us is black?"

He began to ask about my own health. I had had colon surgery the year before. They thought it might be cancer but it wasn't. Nonetheless, it almost proved fatal. For some reason my heart stopped when the surgeon, a big ex-football player from Mississippi, cut me open. The night before the operation, Brenda had asked him where he left his politics when he went into surgery. He said he didn't have much politics but what he did have stayed in the scrub room. She told him that was a little close, that she would feel better if he left it in the parking lot, but she authorized him to go ahead.

"I knew I couldn't go out there and tell your wife you had died on us," he said when he told me about it a month later.

"Died?" I said. "That's a pretty permanent word you're using there, Doctor."

"Well, we call it cardiac arrest now. Used to be we'd just pull the sheet up." Lying there naked on that cold metal examining table, the conversation gave me modest pause. "There wasn't any damage done though," he went on. "I mean, that's what took us so long. We had to drag all that equipment in there, do an EKG, EEG, all that to see if there was too much heart or brain damage to go on." I told him I was glad the salvaging proved promising enough to be worth their while. "No damage at all," he said, looking at the new EKG reading the nurse had run.

I asked him how long I was gone. He said about three minutes all together. They would get the heart going and then it would stop again. I asked him if he would give me an affidavit saying that I had been dead for three days. He laughed, but it didn't seem a very funny laugh, so I got dressed.

T.J. knew the story, had visited me often in the hospital and had done most of the farm work while I recovered. But he still liked to tease me about my untimely death. "So you see," I said after we had rehashed the whole thing, "a fellow can get well from some pretty serious ailments. I'm good as new."

"Yeah, but you had to die before you got well," he said slowly. Neither of us said anything right away. I wasn't sure he had meant to say what he did. He seemed uncomfortable. I decided not to pursue it. Finally he did. "I reckon I just said the nigger in me has to die before my sore gets well."

"Or maybe the honky hate has to die before your sore gets well," I said.

We were pulling alongside the shed to unload the feed. He sat for a moment, sighed deeply, and as he opened the door said, "Getting integrated doesn't come easy, Brother Will."

We had planned to clean out the chicken house when we finished unloading the feed. "I guess shoveling chicken shit together is as good a place as any to start," I said.

VI
Earth's Joys Grow Dim

NINETEEN SIXTY-FIVE was one of the most violent years in the civil rights struggle. In many ways it was also the most promising. The year leading up to it had seen riots in Harlem, Brooklyn, Rochester, Jersey City, Chicago, Philadelphia, and many other cities in the North, where the passive resistance of Dr. King and others had little influence. Physical retaliation became commonplace there. In Harlem, when a white off-duty police officer shot a black teen-ager to death, rioting broke out and had it not been for the life-risking and brilliant street speeches of James Farmer, then national Director of CORE, there seems little doubt that many would have perished in the ruins of upper Manhattan. In the South black citizens continued to absorb the violence through ongoing massive demonstrations, boycotts, mass meetings, and community organizing. In Mississippi a few weeks after the Harlem riots, the bodies of three civil rights workers were discovered buried in a farm pond levee, but the resulting frustration and anger were channeled into even more constructive determination.

It was also the year that Martin Luther King, Jr., became the youngest man in history to receive the Nobel Peace Prize. And the year in which, in addition to the three men murdered in Mississippi, there were eighty physically assaulted, more than one thousand arrested, and thirty buildings bombed or burned in that state alone.

Then came "Bloody '65." Selma, Alabama. That was the year and that was the town which seemed to mark the most distinctive turning point. Gains had been made. But concurrent with the gains there had developed a schism between whites and blacks who had worked side by side for justice, and that schism soon would make a mockery of the notion of a beloved community. The label "white liberal," worn as a badge of honor for many years by white people sympathetic to what was considered the black cause, seemed overnight to become a term of scorn.

T.J., no more of an ideologue than I, had long made jokes about the liberals as a group, but I took it to be good-natured joshing. He divided us into categories: macrame, alfalfa sprout, and earth shoe. The macrame liberals were sanctimonious, hypocritical, and self-righteous. They wanted Negro children in white schools down South but became silent or hostile when a Negro family wanted to move next door in Scarsdale. They would join a civil rights march in Montgomery and go to jail but would not picket the federal courthouse in New Haven or Boston. Many years earlier there had been an elderly Negro man who presided over the door to the restaurant in the Atlanta airport. That was when the terminal was more like a bus station and the traffic was mainly two-engine propeller-type airplanes. The old man had the white hair, white beard, and clothes of Joel Chandler Harris's Uncle Remus. And that was what he was called. No Negro was allowed to eat in the restaurant, but Uncle Remus sat beside a cotton bale at the door with a string in his hand. He pulled the door open for customers and was paid by the tips of amused travelers. I told T.J. about being on my way home from a human relations session and seeing a woman who had been at the meeting sitting alone in the terminal eating dried apples from her handbag. When I asked her if she wanted to join me for lunch, she said she would never go through that door as long as the old man opening it for her couldn't go inside. We agreed that it was a high-minded gesture but I found it mildly incongruous that she saw no problem in living in Westchester County. And presiding over the altar guild in her suburban Episcopal Church.

The alfalfa sprout liberals were all talk and no do. They attended meetings, read books by James Baldwin, organized discussion groups in their recreation rooms, but seldom went public with their sentiments.

He reserved the most harsh treatment for the earth shoe liberals. "That's the ones," he would tell me, "who adopt Korean babies, strap them on their backs, and participate in civil rights marches." If I asked him what was wrong with adopting Korean orphans, he always said the same thing. "What's wrong with adopting black orphans? There are lots of them around." Sometimes he would add, "And some of them have white daddies who were on civil rights marches when the babies commenced."

Once I asked him what kind of a liberal I was. "Do you remember that time you picked me up in the fog, almost ran over me, and said, 'I'm a liberal,' when I gave you that lamprey eel handshake?"

I told him I remembered it well but wished I didn't.

"Well, what kind of a liberal were you talking about?" he asked.

"You're doing the rating, Brother T.J.," I said. "What would you say?"

"I'd say everything's cool, man," he laughed, slapping me on the back. "Everything's cool."

I also asked him once if there were any earth shoe black liberals. He said there were and reminded me of a time when we were in St. Augustine and several of the Movement leaders were planning to get arrested that afternoon. We were having lunch with some of them. One ordered two huge Porterhouse steaks with matching potatoes, salads, and desserts. When someone asked him if he always ate that much lunch, he said usually he didn't eat lunch at all, but that he was thinking about fasting in prison as part of his protest and wanted to be ready for it. "That," T.J. said, "is your basic earth shoe black liberal."

The attention of the nation, and much of the world, was focused on Selma, Alabama, as 1965 began. On the second day of the year, civil rights forces began a voter registration drive there. Dr. King, present to lead the new program, was attacked as he registered at a formerly all-white Selma hotel. By mid-month Dallas County law officers were arresting would-be black voters and those who encouraged and supported them. Even after a federal court issued a restraining order against those interfering with the right to vote, local whites in the town and county stiffened their resistance. On the first day of February more than seven hundred black people, Dr. King among them, were arrested. On February 26 Jimmie Lee Jackson, a young black demonstrator, died after being wounded by a state trooper in nearby Marion when he came to the aid of his mother who was being clubbed. It was my mother and my sister's birthday.

T.J. had resigned his pastorate, dropped out of school for the third time, and was working full-time in the Alabama voting rights movement. The draconic regime of Governor George Wallace was at its peak. The Gothic politics of the deep South was feeling the pressure of two successive liberal national administrations, but nothing struggles for life as fiercely as when it is in the throes of death. Legal segregation was not dead but was mortally wounded. During that winter and spring, it would show that it had power even as the end approached. A white minister from Boston, James Reeb, in Selma assisting in the voting rights drive, would die from wounds received at the hands of three white citizens. Viola Liuzzo, a white supporter from Detroit, would be shot dead as she drove black marchers who had participated in the biggest of the demonstrations. One of the men in the car from which the shot came later admitted that he was in the employ of the FBI as an informer at the time. Lethal rumors as to what would happen when the giant influx of "outsiders," pouring in from around the country, was complete gripped the white populace with the same intensity as those accompanying an invading army. Businesses and households armed themselves with shotguns and automatic weapons. One businessman told me later that he had been offered, but declined, the use of a Browning automatic rifle by the Army Reserve. I knew him as an honest, but scared, man.

The most massive and brutal assault came on March 7 when several hundred protesters attempted to march across the Edmund Pettus Bridge in Selma. T.J. was there and gave me a vivid and doleful account of what happened.

"All we wanted to do was walk across that bridge," he told me.

Apparently the white lawmen, many of them deputized that day for the occasion, were just as determined that they would move no farther than the bridge's edge. On motorcycles, in squad cars, on horseback, and on foot they blocked the roadway. When the marchers continued to move, the phalanx charged the unarmed citizens in violent and crazed defense of the Edmund Pettus Bridge and Alabama's sovereignty. With gas masks in place, giving them the appearance of extraterrestrial marauders, they stormed the ranks of protesters with bull whips, billy clubs, electric cattle prods, and gas canisters. Generations of hate, long held in escrow for just such an opportunity, was turned loose on their defenseless prey. Screaming invectives, they trampled young and old, men and women alike, popping the whips on exposed flesh, clubbing the fallen, chasing the blinded trying to escape the clouds of tear gas. In little more than a minute, what had been a compact and well-mannered formation seeking justice had become a scattered, bleeding, hysterical throng seeking physical survival.

T.J. was sitting in the door of my log cabin office as he told me about it. He had been injured but not seriously. The club which struck his skull had mercifully missed the unhealing sore. He had been treated and released. John Lewis, suffering from a concussion, was still in the hospital. "You ought to go down and see about John," he said. There was something different about T.J.'s countenance. Generally he looked me straight in the eyes when he talked. Now he stared at the ground, occasionally moving outside the door as he spoke. Jackson nuzzled his leg, hinting for a bite to eat. T.J. ignored him.

As I watched him and heard the uncharacteristic forlorn quality in his voice, I was overwhelmed by a deep sense of guilt that I had not been there. He said nothing to suggest that my absence had been a cause for disappointment. But I sensed it. I wanted to tell him that I was sorry I had not been there. I knew, however, that it would not be true. As I listened to the stark horror of the scene, another part of me was glad that I was not there. Knowing that, I wanted to ask him to forgive me for not being there and being glad that I wasn't. That didn't seem appropriate, was somehow strained and presumptuous. Who was I to assume that my meager efforts would be missed by this dynamic black Movement? Or wanted in the first place.

Perhaps I was also bothered that while others had been killed, jailed, or beaten, my participation in the Movement had been from a relatively safe distance. In fact, other than a few rejections by old friends and relatives, occasional threats and late night phone calls, I had not suffered at all. I rationalized that there were many roles to be played by many different individuals, and that my role was one of reporter, observer, liaison between black and white, negotiator between merchants, mayors, media, and Movement. But as I sat with my friend that windy March afternoon, heard the story of brutality told with a voice of dejection and loneliness, smelling the foul symbol of bigotry wafting from his head, the justification was cumbersome.

T.J. seemed to sense what I was feeling. "I think it was what they did to the horses that upset me the most," he said, looking far in the distance.

"The horses?" I asked, for the moment relieved. "What did they do to the horses? I thought it was all directed at y'all."

"They made the horses do it," he said. "They made them run over us, step on us, knock us down. Horses don't do that to people. Horses are kind. I saw one of them jump straight over a young girl lying on the ground, like jumping over a hurdle at the steeplechase. The man — he didn't even have a uniform on — wheeled the horse around, kept spurring and jerking on the reins, trying to make him step on the girl's head."

"Jesus God," I said. "I'm really sorry." The words sounded hollow and I wished I hadn't said anything at all. Then I said something equally as vacuous. "You know, sometimes I get tired of working behind the scenes."

"Yeah. I guess it does get kind of crowded back there sometimes," he said, chuckling for the first time. That was as close as he came to expressing what I suspected he was feeling, that white folks get the safe assignments.

As he continued to talk about the horses, I remembered something he had said in 1963 as we watched Police Commissioner Bull Conner's dogs in Birmingham. As they lunged and snarled, straining against the restraining harness, trying to get at school children demonstrating in front of a church house, T.J. said, "Bull Conner has given dogs a bad name." Later as we watched Reverend Fred Shuttlesworth knocked against the building with a fireman's high-pressure water hose, the stream rolling his unconscious body along the church parking lot, he added, "And now he's given water a bad name." I remembered a letter to the editor in Birmingham from a woman who claimed affiliation with the Society for the Prevention of Cruelty to Animals. She complained that the dogs had no protection from the tear gas used to break up demonstrations. But there was neither sarcasm nor cynicism in T.J.'s voice. He really was concerned for the horses which had been forced to do something he believed was not in keeping with their nature.

Selma was not the only outbreak of violence in 1965. Malcolm X was assassinated in New York City. Demonstrations, marked by massive arrests, took place in Jackson, Mississippi, Bogalusa, Louisiana, and many other places. In Bogalusa there were the first stirrings of blacks in the South defending themselves by other than non-violent means. The Deacons of Defense and Justice, organized when a strong unit of the Ku Klux Klan was terrorizing black communities, announced that they were armed and prepared to exert themselves in a retaliatory fashion if their streets were invaded. It was also the year of the Watts, Los Angeles, riots.

There came, though, a whisper of hope. With the urging of President Lyndon Johnson, a voting rights bill was passed by Congress. The bill brought an end to the poll tax as well as the literacy test, that wretched scheme which in the past had disqualified Negroes brave enough to try to register with such questions as, How many bubbles are there in a bar of soap?

But hand in hand with the gains and the pain, the suspicion and distrust of all whites by many black activists was increasing. At first it was vague and ill-defined. People like John Lewis and Dr. King saw it coming and tried to head it off. But it was a prairie fire which would not soon be quenched. It was inevitable that whenever blacks were free enough to speak the truth publicly they would. And they did. Hurt put on hurt doesn't heal. And matching hate with hate does not love make. It was understandable, but it was also tragic.

Within a year the loving and gentle John Lewis, proponent of the beloved community, champion of non-violence and perhaps the nation's most effective and influential young black leader as he labored and suffered as chairman of the Student Non-violent Coordinating Committee, was replaced by Stokely Carmichael, a West Indian-born, New York-reared young man who espoused a far more militant approach. His rhetoric was persuasive and volatile, and he made it clear that his intent was to achieve liberation and that he felt that could best be done by a separatist route. Many heard his words as a call for violence.

Within the year the wise and seasoned director of the Congress of Racial Equality, James Farmer, was replaced in similar fashion. While even the assertive Elijah Muhammad, founder and head of the Black Muslims in America, had trouble dubbing him an Uncle Tom, Mr. Farmer had given his life to racial justice by way of a truly integrated society and was therefore vulnerable before those who saw white as totally evil. The organization which he had helped to create, under the new leadership of Floyd McKissick, soon became almost all black and followed the path of separatism.

Several things must be said in defense of the rhetoric, if not the actions, of leaders like Carmichael, Huey Newton, and others of a more militant persuasion. When they warned that exerting a lot of effort to influence passage of so-called civil rights legislation was foolish because it would be appropriated and used against those it was designed to protect, they could not have known that the first person to be prosecuted under the Civil Rights Act of 1968 would be H. Rap Brown, then a leader in the Student Non-violent Coordinating Committee. Or, that a bit later it would be used against antiwar demonstrators in Chicago. But it happened just that way. They would also remind us, if we failed to remind ourselves, that intelligence operatives engaged in numerous reprehensible and illegal acts to destroy or discredit not only radical blacks but left-wing groups of all kinds, including individuals as tame and American as Martin King. They mailed forged letters, tapes, committed burglaries, opened mail, and even seem to have conspired in murder in the death of Fred Hampton, a Black Panther leader, as he lay sleeping at five o'clock in the morning in a Chicago apartment house. There were grounds for mistrust.

White fellow travelers were watching, wondering, and worrying. Have we done something wrong? Even, "What do they want now?"

from some. Others licked their wounds and regrouped as all white or lamely integrated organizations with the same goals and concerns. For example, when SNCC made it clear that the dedicated and hard working young whites who had worked within their organization from the beginning were neither trusted nor wanted, the outcasts formed the Southern Student Organizing Committee and went on doing what they could. Others kept their distance, dusted off old colored jokes, gradually found their way back into the mainstream of white society.

Of course, organizations like the NAACP, the Southern Regional Council in Atlanta, and a number of other old, established agencies continued in their pursuit of racial integration. But they were considered impotent and passé by millions of young black people who had become impatient and weary of waiting for a better day. Black caucuses became as routine as nominating committees in groups that contained both black and white.

Without meaning to, the Committee of Southern Churchmen, the only institutional vehicle a few of us had, fell into the trap. We were concerned that a lot of young Southerners went North for their theological training and then stayed up there in comfortable and liberal parishes. Though most of us were steeple drop-outs by then, we wanted our finest and brightest sons and daughters back home to help us. In whatever capacity. We decided to take a delegation of our folk to the seminaries in the East to confer with Southern students. It turned out to be pretty much a fiasco, in some ways a droll interlude in serious business, though not without a lesson learned.

The plan was to fly to New York, split up into ones and twos, and cover the area in three days. I went to Boston. Most of my time was spent trying to explain why our little group was against a civil suit against Thomas Coleman, an Alabama white citizen and sometime law officer. A few months earlier Coleman had shot and killed Jonathan Daniel, a student at the Episcopal Theological Seminary in Cambridge. Jonathan was in Lowndes County, Alabama, helping to organize and register black voters. Although Coleman acknowledged the killing, when he was tried the white Alabama jury acquitted him. Daniel's fellow students and the faculty were understandably enraged by the not-guilty verdict and were considering bringing a lawsuit in civil court. Our position was that in our understanding of the Gospel, the act of God in Christ had rendered the same verdict upon us all as the state of Alabama had in Thomas Coleman's case — not guilty. We conceded that the Alabama jury had freed him to go and kill again while the Lord had liberated us to go and sin no more. Nevertheless, the verdict was the same. Not only that, we argued, if they had sent Jonathan out as a prophet to Alabama, which we considered him to be, well . . . the prophets have always been stoned and killed, so what did we expect to happen to him? The notion that we really are free, reconciled, was difficult to peddle in Cambridge, Massachusetts, in the fall of 1965. Though I was grateful that the umbrage to the message I brought North manifested itself in a more genteel manner than the Southern opposition to Jonathan's message, it was met with scant enthusiasm. And I soon departed.

In New Haven, Elbert Jean and Joe Hendricks were faring little better. Elbert was a rustic Arkansas preacher who had abandoned his Methodist ways and joined the War on Poverty in Tennessee. He pronounced it "povertry." Joe was the Mercer University professor and displaced Baptist preacher who had given us Jackson. Though tough, brilliant, dedicated to justice, and sophisticated in their own ways, both were from the backwoods rural South and every mannerism and utterance projected it. And neither was above exaggerating their bucolic leanings to double-dog-dare the urbanity of the Ivy League to meet them on level ground, being sure that any covey encountered in an open field would be sorely scattered.

The Yale gathering listened to their pitch with patience and cordiality. But they had an agenda of their own. One of the faculty men present indicated that he was in sympathy with their mission but felt that our group could best serve the Movement by recruiting some bright, well-qualified black students to send to the Ivy League.

Elbert, sensing that what the professor was looking for was students with dark skin but white culture, grew more and more restless and finally motioned him to silence. "Well, Doctor, now I know what you're looking for, but they're in big demand and short supply right now. Everybody up here wants some of them. And we're fresh out. But I tell you what, Papa's got a few old blue-gums left on his place close to Shiloh, Arkansas, and if you're interested I can put you in a shipment of them mighty cheap." That, followed by a moderate but audible crepitation, ended the encounter.

In New York Charles Rice, an equally iconoclastic though outwardly refined Episcopal priest, and Andy Lipscomb, an Alabama Methodist preacher turned carpenter, were wreaking their own havoc. Charles, told by a black student at Union Seminary that as one Christian to another he could tell him how he should be involving himself in the Southern problem, retorted that as one Christian to another he could tell *him* that how he involved himself in the Southern problem was none of his damn business. And when a white student told him that he resented his attitude toward Southern preachers, that he had said he didn't like them as a class, he responded by saying that he had been misunderstood, that as a class he didn't like preachers of any region.

A few weeks later we reconvened to discuss the journey. T.J., who had wanted to go with us because he had never been to New York, said it was all the wrath of God upon what he called our "First Segregated Missionary Journey." Our strategy in making it all white was that we wanted to show the Southern students that they would not be alone if they chose to come back South after graduation, that there were whites active in civil rights.

Tom Trimble, the Mercer University philosophy teacher, clown, and mime, had not made the trip but was with us now. "I shall serve as facilitator during this period of debriefing and interfacing," he said in his exaggerated professorial style, taking his place in the circle. "Pedagogy, of course, is my métier, my mission as it were. Perhaps what you see now as a debacle may yet be perceived as your finest hour." His mouth was fixed in a cocksure half-grin, his dancing eyes looking from one to another, his smug shoulders and erect torso all combining to form the perfect caricature of an arrogant lecturer who had just made what was to him a profound and startling statement.

Joe Hendricks, knowing that when Tom was at his craziest he was on the verge of being serious, acknowledged the foolishness. "What'd we do wrong, Professor?" he asked.

"Wrong hub." He said it without hesitation and with no hint of nonsense. But just as quickly he returned to his world of buffoonery, mimicking a hellfire and damnation preacher with a sermon on the Tower of Babel. Joe sat watching him seriously while the rest of us laughed.

"Wrong hub?" he asked when Tom sat down.

He was serious again. "Yeah. Wrong hub. We've got the wrong hub. We went out on behalf of the Movement. In fact, we've been doing that all along. God is just one more spoke in the wheel. Everything turns around the Movement, around the hub. Unless the Movement is just another spoke we've put there, and a frail one at that, well, the tower will crumble."

"Let the Church say, 'Amen,'" Joe Hendricks said.

"Amen," we all said. All except T.J.

Suddenly Tom was the radio holiness preacher who punctuates his sentences with loud grunts or meaningless sounds. But we knew he meant for us to hear the message. "It is he that sitteth upon the circle of the earth, ah! And the inhabitants thereof are as grasshoppers, ah! That bringeth the princes to nothing, ah! He maketh the judges of the earth as vanity, ah! He shall blow upon them, ah!" He pretended to crumble dry leaves in his hand, opened his fingers, and blew hard. "And they shall wither, ah! And the whirlwind shall take them away as stubble, ah!"

Flailing his arms, his voice rising, he worked himself to a frenzy, jumping and dancing about the room. "Preach, Brother," Joe said.

"Thou art the God, ah! Thou alone, ah! Of *allllll* the kingdoms of the earth, ah!"

Sweat was pouring off his red face and the veins in his neck stood out like a network of rubber tubing. He shouted in rapid bursts now. "Know therefore this day, ah, and lay it, ah, to your heart, ah, that the Lord, ah, is God, ah, in heaven, ah, above, ah, and on the earth beneath, ah!" He sat down quickly and whispered the last words, the burlesque over. "There is no other."

We sat quietly for a moment. Joe, who had reached over and picked up one of the Gideon Bibles Andy Lipscomb regularly took from motel rooms began to read. "I am the Alpha and the Omega, says the Lord God, who is and who was and who is to come, the Almighty." Some of us said "Amen" again. T.J. continued to sit silently. Joe flipped the pages and read the Advent story in its entirety. Christmas was coming on, and we sang a hymn when Joe finished reading.

The year ended with the three men accused of killing Reverend James Reeb in Selma freed as Thomas Coleman had been freed.

It was a year of violence, of frustration, and of hope.

And I was strangely sad.

* * *

"Dot Stephenson, if you let them shoot that cat I'll kill you," I heard Brenda scream into the telephone. The threat seemed extreme for so gentle a woman. And to one of her best friends. We had driven to Chicago where I was to conduct a funeral. I was about to leave the apartment where we were staying when the call came. Brenda covered the mouthpiece and yelled at me. "Max is in the top of a tree at Dot's and they can't get him down!"

Maximillian was a special cat. Perhaps because he was a pedigreed Himalayan. Or perhaps because he belonged to Webb, only son and baby child. Whatever the reason, he was special. He was royalty. Beginning with Ralph, given to Bonnie by the little half-Mescalera girl, there had been a profusion of cats in the hollow. There was Ears, Magic, Circus, Cucumber, Joeboy, Cold Cream, Timothy, Kay, Juanita, Sewell, even Felix, Tabby, and Leo. A hundred or more over the years. Some were with us briefly before being adopted away, disappearing into the woods and never coming back, being crushed under the wheels of a farm tractor, or some other misfortune. Some stayed for many years. But Maximillian was different. At first he spent all his time indoors, Webb insisting that Himalayan cats should not walk on the ground, especially in cold weather. I found that strange for a breed which had evolved on the slopes of Mt. Everest, and eventually he was permitted outside. Under close supervision.

Dot and Dorris Stephenson were our closest neighbors. Dorris had noticed the cat in the top of a tall oak tree in their yard the afternoon before but thought nothing of it. When it was still there the next morning, they began to devise a scheme to get it down. Dot, a tough and assertive woman, given to jovial and sometimes excessive rendezvous with the hops on weekends, decided to call Brenda to keep her informed on the rescue operation.

I got on an extension phone and heard Dot trying to reassure Brenda. "Don't you worry, honey. I know how you feel about that cat. I told Dorris we had to get him down for you." She had summoned a team of

Dorris's hunting buddies to assist.

Brenda was vehemently resisting the plan Dot was reporting. "Now just listen to me, honey," Dot said. "Let me tell you what I've told them to do." She explained that she had six of the men standing under the tree holding a king-size blanket. Dorris was going to shoot the limb off, and the men would catch Max when he fell.

Brenda, envisioning the scene of frivolity which was inevitable when Dorris's hunting club convened in the back yard on a Sunday afternoon, was far from convinced that Dot's plan was a good one. "Dot, are you crazy!" she screamed. "You're going to kill my cat and I'm going to kill you. Tell them I said to stop!"

It was too late. VA-ROOM!! We heard the blast of the shotgun. Brenda was yelling for her to tell her what happened. Dot, still standing at the kitchen window where she could yell instructions to the men and report to Brenda on the phone, was laughing uncontrollably. "You're not going to believe this, Brenda Campbell," I heard her say when she could speak. "Dorris missed the limb and that damn cat just pissed all over Wayne Redd." Wayne Redd was a big, good-natured fellow who had once broken one of Brenda's ribs trying to "pop" her spine to cure a sprained back. The backache went away but she had to contend with a fractured rib. Apparently he was one of the blanket holders underneath the tree. I suspected that Brenda was pleased that it was he who received Max's offering.

"What's happening now, Dot? Dot! Dot! Dot!"

"Don't worry, honey. He's all right," Dot said.

"Max or Wayne Redd?" I said.

"Be cute, Will!" Brenda snapped.

"He's all right, I'm telling you. He's scared but he's all right." She said Max had jumped to another limb and the men were having a beer until she decided what they should do next. Brenda told her to call back as soon as she decided. And not to let them shoot in the tree anymore.

"Sorry to miss the next thrilling episode of the great pussy rescue," I said, "but I've got to go bury a man."

"Be cute!" Brenda said again.

The man I was to bury had died on the streets. Originally from West Virginia, he had come to Chicago to find work when he developed black lung and could no longer work in the coal mines. He did what he could to make a living but became a hopeless alcoholic. With his children grown and scattered, his estranged wife back in the coal country for whatever fate awaited her there, he took to the streets. His baby son, whom I had met when he came south with a friend who had organized what he called the White Panthers in Chicago, maintained some contact with his father. When he died, he asked me to come and conduct the service.

A terrible storm had swept through the midwest, and the temperature was fifteen below zero. The man was being buried by the county, and when I arrived at the chapel most of the children had gathered. From Kenosha, Gary, Rockford — wherever jobs, wives, husbands, or dreams had led them. My young friend told me that one daughter had not arrived but was on her way and should be there in a few minutes. At exactly two o'clock, the appointed hour, the undertaker sought me out and said that it was time to begin. I explained that we were waiting for the last member of the family to arrive. He found that no reason to delay, saying quickly, "Look, Reverend, my contract with the county is from 2:00 to 2:45. That means you gotta do your thing and I gotta do mine and have them vehicles back in forty-five minutes from right now." I was accustomed to at least a modicum of civility from his profession down home and was momentarily struck dumb by his crassness. Smarting under his insolence, a thought kindly presented itself: he doesn't know if I'm a Quaker, a Methodist, or a Druid.

"Let us observe reverence through a period of silence," I began. I stood with both my hands gripping the edge of the lecturn, while at the same time striking a trance-like pose. I waited for nearly five minutes until I saw a woman ease in and take her place beside the family. Then I did the service.

There was further contention between the two of us at the cemetery. The casket had been closed by the time the late-arriving daughter came in. She insisted that she be allowed to see her father's body before it was lowered into the ground. The undertaker, unaccustomed to the screams, moans, shouts, heavy sobbing, and swooning of traditional Appalachian funerals, was having trouble even understanding what they wanted him to do, and even more difficulty in explaining that the request was out of the question. He looked at me for assistance. I stood with my arms folded in the same fashion he had stood during my long period of silence in the chapel. When he continued to look, his eyes pleading, I slowly nodded for him to do as they asked.

"I wanna see Pappa! I wanna see Pappa!" the woman screamed over and over, falling on her knees and pawing at the cheap casket lid. The man moved in to pull her away, nodding at the same time to his assistant to begin lowering the casket. What looked like the oldest, and certainly the biggest, of the brothers stepped between the undertaker and his sister, his quick movement almost knocking the pudgy, and by then comically pathetic, little man to the ground. Simultaneously two of the brothers grabbed the assistant and pulled him away from the release lever.

"Do something, Reverend?" the frightened undertaker said, his puffing interspersed with irritated snorts. With the oldest brother awkwardly searching for the latch and two others standing guard over the lowering device, the scene was one of bedlam. The funeral director, his knowledge of Appalachian culture probably limited to Hatfield and McCoy legends, flitted about the area like a penguin. "Mercy, mercy, mercy," he said over and over as he moved. The two assistants had edged away from the fracas and were leaning against the hearse. They were trying not to look at anything at all, no discernible expressions on their faces. When the big man got the lid open and the body was exposed, an indescribable sound went up from the group as they huddled close together and gazed down at the corpse of this emaciated body which had once belonged to a man who was their father.

I had noticed at the funeral parlor that his shroud was nothing but a shirt. No coat and no necktie. Now I saw that it was not even a full shirt, just a body-fitting shirt front, the cardboard collar all one piece with it. During the fast ride to the cemetery, hitting winter potholes and jarring the casket, the molded shirt front had buckled up, exposing a wide area of skin on one side. The undertaker was looking for a place to hide.

When I returned to the apartment, I found Brenda relaxing with her friend. She calmly told me the rest of her story. Dot and Dorris had a friend who was a tree surgeon. For forty-five dollars, he would climb the tree and get Max. Brenda authorized the fee. When the man got near him, Max kept edging toward the end of the limb until it wouldn't support his weight any longer. With the blanket team in place, the man shook the limb until Max fell. In one motion he hit the blanket and scrambled to the ground, speeding toward our house, terrified all the more by seven cheering drunks trying to run him down.

"That Dot is something else," Brenda said. "We have to get her a present."

"So much for the rescue of Prince Maximillian," I said, worn-out from the pauper's burial. "Royalty is its own reward."

"Be cute, Will," Brenda said. "I couldn't just leave him up there."

"I know you couldn't, honey. I was only kidding." Then I told her all about the undertaker and the man we buried.

VII
What But Thy Grace

T.J.'S WAS NOT the only sore refusing to heal in the mid-sixties. The manifest destiny of the nineteenth century continued to lend its devious weight in our time. America accepted the bloody cudgel from the failed hands of France and attempted to do what they, the Japanese, Chinese, and English could not — conquer a tiny peasant country in Southeast Asia that most of us had never heard of. We would fail as they had. And in the failing two million human beings — American, Asian, and others — would perish. And this nation would see internal brokenness and alienation ranging from the highest level of government to the family hearth.

The whirlwind we reaped in that venture was not without warning. Despite the lofty claims of the Atlantic Charter, signed by Roosevelt and Churchill shortly before America's entry into World War II, that those nations sought no territorial aggrandizement and that we respected "the right of all peoples to choose the form of government under which they will live," we turned a deaf ear to the cries from

Indochina when that war was over.

A revolutionary leader and war hero named Ho Chi Minh, who had driven the Japanese out of Vietnam after our own cessation of hostilities with the common enemy, only to see it revert to colonization by France after a brief occupation by England and Nationalist China, sounded a warning and gave us an opportunity in the form of what must have been a demeaning plea. He wrote to President Truman eight times shortly after the war was over, recalling the words of the Atlantic Charter, stating that two million Vietnamese had recently starved because of the repressive measures of the French, and asking for help in the face of imminent catastrophe. The President did not even answer the letters. Instead, during the eight years of the new war between the French and Vietnamese, the United States was the major funding source for the French. It also remained heavily involved during the withdrawal of France. Although an international assemblage in Switzerland was charged with serving as referee, the U.S., by various political maneuvers, encouraged the establishment of a separate government in the south of Vietnam and then assisted that government in blocking the unification election scheduled by the Geneva gathering. Under those accords, the United States was allowed to have 685 military advisers in southern Vietnam. President Eisenhower secretly sent several thousand.

Even so, he sounded his own strong counsel when in his farewell address to the nation he said:

> In the councils of government we must guard against the acquisition of unwarranted influence, whether sought or not, by the military industrial complex. The potential for the disastrous rise of misplaced power exists and will persist.

Neither the pitiful begging of an Asian Communist to a rich country nor the bold warning of that nation's Republican president, both generals and heroes of the same war, was heeded.

Instead, under President Kennedy the number of military advisers increased to sixteen thousand. When some of them began to engage in actual combat, the transplant of the runny sore from the body of France to our own had been accomplished. America was at war, another civil war. But this time as third party. We had taken sides in a revolution which had begun many years earlier much like our own —

as revolt against tyranny.

The war was as disruptive in the Civil Rights Movement as it was in government and family circles. Many black leaders, and most of the whites, sought to keep it as a separate and unrelated issue. When Martin Luther King, Jr., made a strong public statement equating the carnage taking place in Southeast Asia with the continuing violence and oppression at home, many demurred. But most of the young, by then the front line troops of the Movement, cheered and agreed. That too took its toll, for it meant divided loyalties and priorities. Parallel causes were competing for the same advocates, the same passions, even the same money. Those most active in civil rights were generally first to oppose the war. Some protest marches and demonstrations sought to combine the two, but the edge of each was dulled in the process. A minor bonus was that many white youths who had not protested segregation but now saw their own freedom eroded by a war they could not support were drawn into the joint effort.

There were many casualties beyond the daily body count. I received a letter from two of them. A mother and her son. She wrote the first few pages of the handwritten letter and he typed the last two. She said that a friend she did not identify had told her I was involved in taking draft dodgers and deserters to Canada and that she might need my help. They were from a small town in the Tennessee mountains. Her son had made his final appeal to the draft board for a Conscientious Objector classification. They were camped on the Michigan border, as close to Canadian soil as they could get without leaving the country. She gave a general delivery address. If the appeal was denied, she said they were going on to Canada. If it was granted, he would return to school. She wanted names and addresses of contacts in Toronto.

Most of her letter had to do with her own childhood in Germany during the Second World War. She was from Dresden and was visiting her grandparents on the outskirts of the city on that wretched night in February, 1945, when American planes left the city an ash bed. She talked of adolescent horror as they watched wave after wave of the phosphorus inferno billowing fire and smoke into the skies, and of the pathetic and futile search during the weeks that followed for some word of the remainder of the family. Her tone was not one of outrage at the slaughter which came at a time when the war was ending, but rather it stressed that she was acquainted with the ways of war. She had, she said, taught her son the ways of peace.

His part of the letter was equally touching. "When I was ten years old," he said, "I heard my mother's story for the first time. I was so moved and frightened that I did not sleep all night, and at daybreak we knelt together beside my bed and I took a solemn oath to my mother's God that I would never shed the blood of another." He said that his own preference was to go to prison rather than leave the country, but his mother would not even discuss it.

By then I had made numerous trips to Canada and had heard many stories of young men refusing to participate in the war in Southeast Asia. This one was almost too much to believe and left me suspicious. All of us active in the resistance knew that every aspect of our work was apt to be infiltrated by the nation's intelligence apparatus. I knew that I was breaking the law when deserters stayed in the Dolan House but hoped that my low-key approach would be tolerated. I could see some value in the public and front-page news approach some were making, and I enjoyed quoting Samuel Johnson that patriotism is the last refuge of scoundrels, but it made no sense to me to put signs up pointing to the Underground Railroad station. Either something is underground or it isn't. Any effort to politicize what some of our friends were starting to call "The Church of Forty Acres and a Goat" in an effort to direct the policies of Caesar was somehow offensive to my Anabaptist genes. I had no problem with trying to rescue some of Caesar's drowning victims but, cowardly or not, I was content to leave the propagandizing to others. My mission was less ambitious and I did not want to see it ended by falling prey to a sentimental fabrication. So instead of sending names and addresses of American expatriates, I invited them to come to Tennessee. If they wished to go to Canada, I would take them there.

A few weeks after the letter came, someone called from the highway asking directions to our farm. I assumed it was the mother and the son. When they arrived a young woman, looking no more than twenty, came to the door, introduced herself, and handed me an envelope. It was a note from the mother. The note thanked me for my kindness to her son and said that the draft board had granted his conscientious objector classification. "But I want to be a part of your little network," she wrote. My visitors, she said, were a couple from their county who would tell their own story. She said she hoped I would be as kind to them as I had been to her son and to let her know if she could help.

I took them to the Dolan House and told them they were welcome to spend the night. While the woman looked too young to be involved in anything subversive, the man looked too old to be a military recruit. Thirty or so. I was still suspicious. "Don't you want to know who we are?" the man said.

"I know who you are," I said. "You're Ronnie. And she's Velma Lee. You told me who you were at the door."

"I mean, don't you want to know what we're doing here?"

"I assume you're here because you need a place to spend the night," I said, trying to sound unconcerned. "I don't ask a lot of questions."

"Do you care if we smoke?" the woman asked, unzipping a bulging knapsack.

When I nodded that I didn't mind, the man put his hand on hers, stopping her from opening the zipper completely. "She's talking about do you care if we smoke a joint," he said, faking a laugh. "We want to smoke some of the wildwood flower." He was watching my face with a cold, hard gaze. The scene made no sense. Pieces didn't fit. Two strangers arrive unannounced and uninvited. I offer them hospitality and in five minutes they ask if they can smoke dope on my property. Suddenly Jackson appeared in the doorway.

I had never tried to understand the criteria he used in deciding which guest he liked or didn't like. He generally decided quickly. They were friend or foe with little thought. Instinct and nothing else. If he liked them, he turned broadside, offering his back to rub. It made no difference if they accepted the invitation or not. If he did not like them, he bounded to the highest spot on the porch, dropped his head in a challenging position, and gave no quarter.

Although Jackson seldom came in, this time he did. He came and stood immediately between them, broadside to each. When they didn't acknowledge him, he moved closer to the man, almost touching him.

The man was still studying my every move, expression and gesture. He did not answer when I finished explaining that I was not always popular with the law and that I did not want to give them the upper hand with something so trivial as smoking marijuana. Finally the woman spoke. "What you git in trouble with the law over?" she asked, looking at the man like she didn't want to say the wrong thing.

"Oh, this and that. No big deal. I guess we all do things we had just as soon they don't know. I don't really get in trouble with the law. I just want them to leave me alone."

Suddenly it occurred to me that we were sparring, that they were as suspicious of me as I was of them. "This your goat?" the man asked, reaching down and scratching him on the side. As he did, Jackson edged slowly toward the woman, the man moving with him. When she began rubbing and scratching him too, he sank down on his front knees, then all the way down and lay at their feet. I had not seen him do that since we were first with him in Georgia.

"What's his name?" the man asked.

"Jackson. His name is Jackson."

They both began to laugh. "Jackson?" they said as one. "That's our county," the woman said, looking at him the way she had before, seeking his approval.

"It's okay, honey," he said, smiling and extending his hand to me. "This man is all right. Anybody with a goat named Jackson has got to be all right." He shook my hand, a firm, sincere grasp which he held for a long time.

"I'm in trouble, Mr. Campbell. Real bad trouble." He sank down on the couch, pulling the woman down beside him. "And oh, this is my wife."

He was a veteran of eight years in the Marine Corps and now a deserter. He spent almost a year in heavy combat in Vietnam. When he returned to California after a two-month furlough, he was immediately reassigned to a Vietnam-based combat unit. The day the ship was to leave San Diego, he boarded a bus for Tennessee and never went back. That was ten months earlier. He got married, raised a tobacco crop with his father and brother, and really didn't expect the authorities to come looking for him. But one day the sheriff of a neighboring county came to the woods where he was cutting logs and told him the FBI had been to his office looking for him and had deputized him as an agent with the assignment of bringing him in.

"Don't tell me you killed a mountain sheriff," I said, half serious.

"Aw no. Mountain sheriffs don't bring in neighbors' boys unless they're in trouble with the local law. We never had been." The sheriff said that was the second time the FBI had been there looking for him. They had the wrong county but were close. The sheriff told them the first time that he knew the boy, knew that he had jumped ship and come home, but before he could arrest him he had left. Told them he thought the boy had gone to Dayton to work in a tire factory. Then the sheriff told the boy he ought to leave. Not to Dayton but to Gary or Chicago and not come back until things cooled off.

"There's no way I'll ever go back to Vietnam," he told me. "It's unreal. All we did was get high every day and go out and find somebody with yellow skin and blow them away. It didn't matter a whet who it was. How old or young, friendly or unfriendly. I'm telling you, it's crazy. I've been saved now. And I won't ever kill anybody again. I've been forgiven. Me and my little wife both. Saved the same night. I'm happier than I've ever been. All I want to do now is go where the Lord leads me."

"And you think the Lord is leading you to Canada?" I asked, convinced now that my fears from the beginning had been unfounded.

"I don't know where He's leading," he said quickly, hugging his wife closely. "I reckon we're a lot like Abraham was in Genesis 12. The Lord told him, 'Get thee out of thy country, and from thy kindred, and from thy father's house, unto a land that I will shew thee.' That's what we're doing here. We believe the Lord will use you to show us where we're supposed to go." I was saddened by his words and uncomfortable with his confidence.

His wife began to cry. "Oh, but honey, we're still powerful sinners. Tell him what sinners we are."

I thought she was talking about the marijuana. "Well, I guess there are worse things than blowing a joint now and then," I said awkwardly, trying to speak the language I thought they spoke.

"I'm not talking about that," she said, burying her face on Jackson's side and sobbing out loud. Her husband made no move to comfort her, just let her cry. When she looked up again and dried her eyes on his shirt sleeve, her voice was calm. "It's the lying we have to do all the time. We lie everywhere we go. We lied to you. My name ain't Velma Lee and his ain't Ronnie. And we don't smoke no pot. I ain't never done it and he ain't neither since he got saved that night. Even though he'd been stoned the night we got married. We was testing you, trying to figure out if you was all right. And now we'll have to go on lying when we git to wherever it is we're going." She stood up, and when she did, Jackson stood up with her and went outside, looking back for her to follow. Instead she faced me squarely, looking at me the way her husband had earlier. "Do you think the Lord will forgive all this lying? I mean, I ain't been a Christian long but I was raised to tell the truth." I fumbled for some appropriate and comparable rhetoric. Some way to tell her that a God who would forgive the slaughter of Asian babies by her husband's gun probably could handle a few little fibs.

"I think the Lord has already forgiven us for everything," I said finally, knowing full well that answer would raise more questions in her pietistic, legalistic conversion and commitment. But she seemed relieved.

We sat far into the night talking of what life would be like for them in another country. During his Marine time he had been in many parts of the world, but she had never been outside of Tennessee. I coached them on what to say to the Canadian customs officials when they entered the country, how to look for work and apply for citizenship when their visitor's visa expired. I had them memorize the address of "The Hall," headquarters for the American Expatriates network in Toronto. The plan we decided on was that we would sell their car for the money they needed, and they would ride the bus to London, Ontario. I would fly there, rent a car in time to meet them at the bus station and drive them on to Toronto.

I wanted them to know as much about the country they were going to as possible. I told them about some things that had happened when our son, Webb, went with me. I tried to be open with the children about my work, so that if I got in trouble with the law or neighbors they would not be surprised. Yet I did not want them to live in dread and fear of the times. Childhood should be a time for joy.

"Daddy, why are you always going up to Canada?" Webb asked one summer night as the two of us sat far back in the woods listening to the whippoorwills. He was about ten years old. I explained as best I could the plight of the young men who felt that it was morally wrong for them to fight in Southeast Asia. "Will I have to go over there when I get big?" he asked, almost crying. When I was unable to speak for a moment, he continued. "When someone is over there, in the army, do they let you come home at Christmas time to open your presents and play with your new toys?"

I knew I had to control myself, try to deal with his questions, but the words didn't come. Words, but not adequate words. "Well, son," I began, pulling him closer to me, "I wouldn't worry about that ole war. You're just a little boy. By the time you're grown, that will all be over."

"I worry about it all the time," he said, trying not to cry. "Sometimes I can't go to sleep when I get in my bed for worrying about it." I asked him if he would like to go to Canada with me the next time I went. Each of the children made a trip with me each summer. He said he would. We flew to Toronto and visited with the men at The Hall. I served as cook the second night we were there, doing all the shopping and trying to make it a down-home occasion. After supper we gathered in one of the big meeting rooms and took turns playing my guitar and singing. Some of them wanted to hear the latest country songs, searching, I supposed, for some sign that they were not forgotten. Not many songs of the time took note of them, but I sang the ones that did. At one point I heard plaintive Southern sounds coming from the audience. There was no introduction and no accompaniment.

> I think I see a wagon-rutted road,
> with the weeds growing tall between the tracks.
> And along one side runs a rusty barbed wire fence
> and beyond that sits an old tar paper shack.
>
> Mississippi, you're on my mind.
> Mississippi, you're on my mind.

The group applauded and I motioned him to the microphone. A melancholy mood settled over The Hall like ground fog over the land of which he sang. He took the guitar from me, quickly dropped the top string down an octave and continued the doleful strains of his song.

> I think I hear a noisy Old John Deere
> in the fields specked with dirty cotton lint.
> And below the field runs a little shady creek.
> Down there you will find the cool, green leaves of mint.
>
> Mississippi, you're on my mind.
> Mississippi, you're on my mind.

The silence of the room was overwhelming, the contagious hurting covering every inch.

> I think I smell a honeysuckle vine,
> the heavy sweetness like to make me sick.
> And the dogs, my God, they hungry all the time,
> and the snakes are sleeping where the weeds are thick.
>
> Mississippi, Mississippi, you're on my mind.

When he finished he handed me the guitar and strolled silently into the Canadian night, a runaway soldier baring his soul to those who understood. Webb sat as quietly as the rest, even more worried, I was sure, that there might be times when he couldn't come home to play with his new toys.

The next morning we went to Montreal, rented a car and drove north into the heart of Quebec, stopping when darkness came and the road ended at almost the same time. With no radio or other distractions except the virgin forests with huge trees, standing with first limbs forty feet from the ground, forming a canopy of shade over glades, lakes, and carpets of ferns, we talked of many things. I had told Webb we would stop when the road stopped, that we would spend the night in a little frontier town uncorrupted by the civilization we were trying to escape, if only for a night. Because it was cool driving through the dense wildwoods, we had driven all day with the windows closed. When we opened the doors and stepped out, we were greeted by the reeking and unmistakable smell of a paper mill. The rustic little frontier town I had described to Webb all day existed for an American paper company. *Made in the U.S.A.* "I can't go to sleep here, Daddy," Webb said with childish candor as we entered the only inn in town. "This place stinks." I remembered Penny, a little girl of eight doing what she had learned women were supposed to do, making the beds and meticulously cleaning the room when she and I spent the night in an Atlanta hotel. And Bonnie at six, riding back with me from a speaking engagement at Tuskegee Institute where she had had a good time, asking, "Daddy, aren't you glad we're colored people?" And the smell eroding the beautiful Quebec landscape made me homesick for us all to be together, back home. And sad too that the expatriates who were our American children might have fled to a land that would soon prove no different from what they had left. Yet grateful that it was there for them.

I warned the couple that the dodgers and deserters in Canada were expecting closer scrutiny from the Ontario police. Hard drugs were becoming a problem among the Americans. "We're worried," the director of The Hall told me. "Make damned sure everyone you bring here is double clean," he pleaded. He introduced me to a deserter who had been a captain in the U.S. Army Intelligence. He told me they had reliable information that two pounds of pure heroin had been dropped in the city the week before.

"My God! Don't tell me that organized crime is exploiting this tragic situation," I said naively.

"Organized crime, my ass," he chuckled. "It's the goddam CIA." I didn't understand. "We've been getting a free ride up here. The Canadian government has been more than generous. Your government can't figure out how to get back at them. If they get enough of us hooked on the big horse, then suddenly cut off the supply, well . . . you can figure it out from there, can't you?" I told him I thought so. (It surprised me each time one of the Americans said, "*Your* government.")

"I'm sorry," I said to the young couple. "But I promised the captain I would examine every arm I send up there from now on." When they both started pulling up their sleeves, I couldn't do it. Instead we turned to singing country songs. They both played guitar and we took turns.

> Rocking chair, heavy rain
>   rapping on the shutters.
> An old man sits and taps his cane,
>   puffs his pipe and mutters,
> Sky won't give us any sun,
>   bank won't give us a loan.
> This old place needs work, but it'll all get done
>   soon as Buddy gets home.

But Buddy was at home. His last home. A telegram had come the day before but they didn't show it to the old man. Told him it was just bad news from the bank.

People staring at me
  as they wheel me down the ramp toward my plane.
The war is over for me,
  I've forgotten everything except my name.
And thank you sir, and yes sir,
  it was worth it for the old red, white, and blue.
And since I won't be walking
  I suppose I'll save some money buying shoes.

Mamma, bake a pie.
  Daddy, kill a chicken.
Your boy is coming home,
  'leven thirty-five Wednesday night.

A young soldier is on his way home from Vietnam, a blanket over his two battered legs, a bottle tucked underneath it that feels like an old friend to his touch. Before he gets home he reads in the paper "where they say the war was just a waste of time."

Kill or be killed
  just ain't much of a future for no man.
So I leave you this note, Mom,
  I'll be back some day if I can.
They'll brand me a coward,
  not knowing the values I hold.
But I can't kill nobody;
  I wonder if Canada's cold.

I watched their faces as I sang the sad songs of war. The fear, the pain and uncertainty patent in their eyes made me ashamed for whatever doubts I had about them. They were authentic. A young man and his bride, children of the soil, had made the grievous decision to leave their native land forever.

On the day they were going to catch the bus, the woman asked if she could walk with Jackson in the woods and fields. They were gone for more than an hour. When they returned his mood seemed as melancholy as hers. "She'll miss that more than anything," her husband said. "She loves animals." He talked freely of the things he would miss. His family, especially the companionship of his grandmother, was first on the list. But he talked of other things too. High school football and swimming with the boys in the bluehole. And he asked me if they grew okra in Canada. He tried to laugh as he told me he could stand almost anything if he had fried okra once in a while. "Maybe that's why I jumped ship," he grinned. "In eight years in the Marine Corps, I never had fried okra one time."

On the way to town I asked them if there was anything they wanted to see or do before they left. He said, "Mr. Campbell I hope you don't think this is silly. But I don't expect I'll ever get to come home again. There is one thing I always wanted to see. We used to listen to the Grand Old Opry every Saturday night at my grandma's house. I sure would like to see the Country Music Hall of Fame." I took them there, bought three tickets, then quickly excused myself to run some errands. I had heard a lot of last requests. This one I couldn't handle. I drove aimlessly around town and wept.

* * *

The Manifest Destiny of the age of Jackson had hit a snag. Andrew could walk out of earshot when a seventeen-year-old was being executed for refusing to clean his plate and threatening the officer who tried to make him do it during the battle against the Creek nation. But when hundreds of thousands of young soldiers lay down their guns in a battle against a nation even smaller, there was confoundment. A large number of the nomads found their way to the Dolan House. For sanctuary, rest, retreat, discussion, or way station on their journey to a foreign land. Jackson greeted them one by one. He made no distinction between Klansmen and Black Panthers, drug addicts from Nashville's music community and displaced preachers in search of rest and employment, civil rights activists or the uninvolved.

* * *

A Quaker man who had come to a planning meeting of a pacifist group from Kentucky mistook Jackson as hostile. It was Saturday morning and T.J. and I were working on a rail fence when the man arrived late for the meeting. We pointed him in the direction of the Dolan House, but he turned right instead of left and spent half an hour on a hiking trail. Again we showed him the gate and gave directions, but this time he headed for the chicken house. As he peered inside, Jackson bolted out the door. The startled man turned and ran, dropping his briefcase, Jackson right behind enjoying the game of chase. When halfway up the hill, the man tripped and fell; Jackson, too close to stop, leaped over him, turned around, and stood looking down at him. The man scrambled to his feet and ran back in our direction, Jackson still behind him. A fifty-year-old man committed to stopping a war on the other side of the world couldn't find the meeting and was afraid of a gentle goat.

T.J. and I, embarrassed but unable to stop laughing, moved out to meet him. T.J. grabbed Jackson's collar and the man stopped. "He was chasing me," he panted. "That thing was trying to kill me."

"I'll go with you," I said, and walked with him all the way to the Dolan House. He took his place on the kitchen floor, drawing posters with a magic marker.

"Will, old pal," T.J. said when I got back, "it's gonna be a long war."

* * *

"She just needs a place to spend the night," the woman on the phone said. "Maybe two. Her friend is in the hospital but she'll be going home in a few days. She's just a girl. I found her down at the bus station. She was crying and just milling around."

I told the neighbor to bring her on. "By the way, a good friend of mine at work is coming out too. Her husband beat her and she isn't going back. At least not right now. She's a black woman, and well . . . you know how that is around my house."

"Sure."

We sat around the potbelly stove eating boiled peanuts and drinking beer. The girl from the bus station said she was underage and didn't want to violate any laws. She drank Coca-Cola. Everyone talked freely. Jackson sat closest to the stove, chewing his cud. It seemed to put everyone at ease.

"It could of just as well been me," the girl said. "We was both doing it with him. Neither one of us was all that crazy about him. Me and her was best friends. I mean, he wasn't really our type. We just both liked to do it. He was a lot older than we was. 'Bout forty, I reckon. We'd meet him after school up on the side of the mountain where they pulled old wrecked cars."

"You mean, your friend knows who the father is?" I asked, trying not to act jarred at the relaxed manner in which she related things to a stranger I would not have *thought* at her age. She looked fifteen.

"Sure. She knew. We wasn't doing it with nobody but him right then. Almost every day we'd meet him up there. He'd do it with her first. I'd go sit in the back of another old car. He wouldn't do it with both of us in the same car. Said it wouldn't be right unless it was in different cars. 'Bout half an hour after they'd get through he'd come get in the car with me. Oh, he was a sport all right. And like I say, it could of just as well been me."

"Maybe you were lucky he always did it with your friend first," the black woman laughed. "Weakened his count a little, I suppose." The girl laughed with her. A blank sort of laugh.

She and her friend were from a small mountain town, not far from the home of the Marine deserter. As she talked she chewed a huge wad of bubble gum, sometimes blowing balloon-like bubbles, sometimes making little ones pop like a firecracker. She giggled each time Jackson flinched at the noise.

She said they panicked when they discovered the other girl was pregnant. Said her friend's daddy was a part-time preacher and would absolutely kill her if he found out about it. They picked up hubcaps and sold them to the junkyard, saved their lunch money, and did house-cleaning until they saved enough money to come to Nashville on the bus. They went to a free clinic but were told that the pregnancy was too far advanced for a legal abortion. Before they left, the doctor called them in his office, shut the door, and told them he knew another hospital in town where a resident would help them. He telephoned the other doctor and made the arrangements.

"We was plumb scared to death when that doctor came in the room and told her the baby was alive. I mean, he said it just like that. 'You'll have to take the baby home with you. He can't stay here.'" She appeared nervous for the first time. She snapped the gum a few times, then popped it so loud that Jackson jumped up. He didn't ask to get out, but I led him to the back door. It didn't seem appropriate for him to stay. "I bet we stayed there and cried, both of us just laying there on her bed, for more'un a hour. Just hugging one another and crying."

I had put a wet log in the stove, and when I opened the lid heavy smoke billowed into the room. I closed it quickly, opened the bottom damper and sat down. For a long time no one spoke. The neighbor, her friend, and I put our beer cans down in unison, the way men take their hats off outside when someone starts to pray or the national anthem is about to begin. The girl threw her gum in the trash, started to unwrap another piece, the kind with a riddle printed on the wrapper, then put it back in a small paper bag she held in her lap, like it would be disrespectful now to chew gum. The peanuts remained on the table. It was an uneasy silence, not the kind where people who are close can sit comfortably for long periods without talking. It had started to sleet outside and the sound of it on the tin roof seemed out of place.

The neighbor broke the silence. "What were you doing at the bus station, hon? Were you fixing to go back home?"

"I don't think so. I mean, I don't rightly know. I was just all mixed up. And I didn't have nowhere else to go. That was the only place I knew of in town that was familiar to me." Through the window I could see that the sleet was mixed with snow. I knew that by morning it would be impossible for any of the guests to get out of the hollow. For a moment the picture of a scared and tired mountain girl lying in the hospital, her baby down the hall somewhere, was fixed in my mind.

What is my responsibility? And what now is my complicity?

The girl had said there was no way they could go back home with a baby. What will happen to them? Her next words answered. She spoke as though there had been no break in the story, no lull in the conversation. "Then about two hours later that same doctor stuck his head in the door and said, 'Don't worry about a thing, sugar. The baby died.'"

"Let's talk about me!" the black woman exclaimed. It was like the ambiguities, contradictions, and obscenities of the whole thing were too much to deal with. We went back to sipping beer, the girl to chewing gum. "You know, child," she said, slapping the neighbor on the shoulder, "black husbands are lucky bastards. If your man beat you up like mine did me, you'd have something to go to the judge with. They'd say, 'Look at that poor woman's face. It's all black.' On me you can't tell a thing. I'm already black."

"The hell you can't tell a thing!" the neighbor woman screamed. "Your eye is swelled almost shut and your lips look like tomorrow's meatloaf. Let's go kill the sorry son of a bitch!"

"Naw, let's play some Rook," the woman said. "I can beat everybody in this room at Rook."

"You ought to learn to beat that no-good husband of yours," the neighbor said, dealing the Rook cards.

* * *

Wherever there is nobility, there will be gossip. It was so with Jackson. There were whispers that he was gay. In itself, that hardly weighs in as gossip any longer. But the talk about Jackson was that he was gay for *Homo Sapiens*, an inverted invert. It was intolerable and one of the few occasions when I felt that I must defend him. Jackson loved humans as he loved all creatures within his realm. But he was no Lothario. And would never have chosen a lover of lesser rank. A matter of honor.

It began when a group of Presbyterian preachers from Arkansas came for a three-day retreat at the Dolan House. Since the sixteenth century when the Calvinists persecuted my people, I have had problems with them. Well, I wasn't around in the sixteenth century. At least not in the present form. I have, however, been told by a woman who practices psychiatry in Little Rock and who claims also to be a psychic that in 1550 my name was Cecelia and I was drowned in the Amstel River outside Amsterdam for being an Anabaptist. I have no empirical basis for either believing or not believing what she says. Except that I am afraid of water and sometimes feel faint when I see a big sack.

I expect another reason for being suspicious of Presbyterians is that they generally seem so secure. And when I was growing up, the ones we knew were rich. Some of us got to talking one day about it being too bad that ethnic humor is always offensive to one person or another: Black dialect jokes to black people, Pollock jokes to people of Polish descent, and redneck jokes to me. We decided that there must be a group so confident in their heritage, holdings, and history that it would be impossible to offend them. We settled on Presbyterians. (Have you heard the one about the two old Presbyterians . . .?) I am also suspicious of fat revolutionaries and recently divorced marriage counselors. The truth is, I know quite a few Presbyterians I would classify as revolutionary. And not one recently divorced marriage counselor who is a Presbyterian. But I refuse to let the facts interfere with a favorite stereotype.

This group arrived in the middle of the night in two extravagantly outfitted vans. The kind with a lot of carpets and padding, wet bars, swivel chairs, gaudy wild West landscapes painted on the sides. One by one they alighted from the symbols of status yelling, "Soooiiiieeeee pig! Soooiiiieeeee pig!" in the same crass manner as the thousands gather in Fayetteville on autumn Saturdays and scream for the Razorback gladiators. "Soooiiiieeeee pig! Soooiiiieeeee pig!"

I knew that one of them was the son of a high-ranking Republican, and I had already decided I didn't like him. The father of another was president of a theological seminary, reason enough to approach with caution. Long before the visit was over, those two especially, and the others as well, had become highly cherished friends. But as it began, "Soooiiiieeeee pig!" from grown men and women at one o'clock in the morning was not my idea of fun.

One of the preachers had a new goosedown sleeping bag which he was proud of. The potbelly stove I had fired up for them earlier had competed well with the near zero weather outside, and he decided it was too hot for his new sleeping bag. I watched from the kitchen window with some of the others as he stretched out under the low-hanging branches of a tall cedar tree, the moon and stars giving the hillside scene an eerie van Gogh effect. Jackson approached from underneath the porch, walked around him a few times, then stood close to his uncovered head. As I left, his friends strained to hear what seemed to them a brief flirtation, seeing Jackson eventually slip close to the prone Presbyterian. Next morning the joggers (there are always the joggers; they also eat alfalfa sprouts) found them nestled side by side, the sleeping bag zipped up around them.

The gossip increased when the scene was repeated the second night and again on the third, even when light snow covered them on their last night together.

The story spread around several Presbyterian judicatories and made a lot of Calvinists laugh. I didn't think it was funny. Nor did Jackson. In my defense of him, I wrote his friend to get a first-hand account of the alleged trysts.

"I realize," he replied, "that many of the rich and famous are making money with their stories of what happened behind closed doors to titillate the perverse curiosity of their readers. But Jackson deserves better than to have his reputation damaged by such exploitation. What we shared was very special, and if he's not telling, then I'm not either. I will say that those nights were memorable, and I have no regrets."

Certainly I have no uneasiness about their friendship. But in the twisted minds of the small, the confusion of *agape* with concupiscence comes easily and bides when truth has succumbed to loose sayings.

* * *

And then there was Booger Red. That was the name I gave to Baxton Bryant, a Methodist preacher by trade who came to Tennessee from Texas with the same zeal and passion as Sam Houston and Davy Crockett had when they left Tennessee to go to their adopted Texas. When the war continued to escalate under three American Presidents, and with each escalation an increase in the number of resistors, our little organization, the Committee of Southern Churchmen, felt that we should be doing more than I could do alone. After several trips to Toronto visiting the draft dodgers and deserters, appellations they wore as badges of pride, it became clear that the greater brokenness and alienation existed among the parents on our side of the border. The men who had fled to Canada, despite physical hardships they suffered, were morally reconciled in the position they had taken. But their families, torn between patriotism and love for their young, felt shamed and disgraced in a land where fighting for one's country was established early as a cardinal virtue. We searched for ways to tell them their sons were children of honor and integrity, even a superior patriotism, but it was not easy. We enlisted Baxton Bryant to assist us in sharing that message.

He came to Tennessee shortly after the death of John F. Kennedy and had been with him just minutes before he was shot. In 1960 he ran for Congress in the conservative Dallas district on a pro-labor and pro-civil rights platform. He missed winning by ninety-seven votes. He ran again two years later but lost by a wider margin. He had established himself as an important force in Texas Democratic politics but had fallen into disfavor with the hierarchy of his Methodist denomination. We brought him to Tennessee from a life insurance salesman's job to run the Tennessee Council on Human Relations, an interracial agency concerned with civil rights. Moving about the state from Kingsport to Memphis, he soon established himself as a militant champion of black rights. The title won him esteem among black activists but suspicion and disapproval by more cautious moderate whites. He flourished on controversy, and it followed him from town to city to the most remote rural areas. In Fayette County, where planters had kicked their black tenants off the land for registering to vote and hundreds of them lived in tents on the edge of town, he was jailed for demonstrating on their behalf.

More importantly: An old woman stood crying, bareheaded in light snow, outside a tent with no heat. Inside her daughter had given birth during the night. There had been no doctor.

"Just please tell Miss Laura I'm out here. She don't know where I'm at. The menfolks ain't told her nothing about all this mess. I know they ain't. Now, Mister Gary . . . I don't know what's got into him. He know I ain't done nothing to him. I ain't been close to no courthouse. But he moved me out right along with everybody else. I been on that place since before he was born. Worked for his daddy and mamma just like I done for him and Miss Laura. Sucked him right here at these breast'es when his mamma dried up. Give him milk my own baby was sposed to git. Nursed Miss Laura when all four of hers'uns was born. And she love me. Ain't nobody ever gon' tell me she don't love me. And soons she find out where I'm at, she'll come see bout me."

"Yes ma'am. I'll tell her. I know she loves you."

But: "I don't know who you are, mister. Nor what business it is of yours. But Sara's just as bad as the rest of them. They all let some outside agitator pump their heads full of nonsense. And they all went right along with it. We've been good to her. To all of them. God knows we don't have anything against the nigras. We never mistreated them in any way. Always looked out for them. Gave them a house to live in. Lent them money. Got the doctor for them when they were sick. If she's out there now without any money and no doctor for that trifling daughter of hers, who isn't even married, well, it's her own fault. If you make your bed hard, you're the one who has to lie on it. I'm just as sorry for her as I can be, but she brought it all on herself. We can't lose everything we've worked for here on this farm because some communist Yankee tells them they can take over the country."

Next day the old black woman was handed a can of Bruton's snuff and an envelope with five ten-dollar bills in it. "Miss Laura said tell you she's not been feeling well. Said when the weather breaks she'll come to see you. Said all the children had been asking about you."

"Thank you, precious Jesus!" the old woman cried. "I know'd she musta been sick or she'd of been to see bout me. I been worried to death bout her."

"Booger Red, why'd you lie to that poor old woman?" I asked.

"For Jesus," he laughed.

"What's she going to think when the weather breaks and Miss Laura doesn't come to see about her? You know she isn't coming."

"Oh, she'll come. When the weather breaks, she'll come. This winter of hate won't last forever." Booger Red was your basic optimistic Methodist.

He was heavily involved in the Memphis Sanitation Workers' strike and was close by when Dr. King was killed there.

Following the passage of the civil rights bill in 1964, outlawing racial segregation in public places, one restaurant owner in Nashville who had been especially recalcitrant took a vindictive stance directed at a group he said was not covered by the bill. "The law says I have to serve niggers," he reasoned. "Then let'um come. But it doesn't say I have to serve hippies." It was before long hair and beards became tonsorially common. Mr. Pickens guarded the entrance of his restaurant with robust determination. Anyone wearing long hair, a beard, an African dishika, or certain kinds of sandals was turned away. The rules were arbitrary and were enforced in compliance with his changing moods. Many of the young wore salvage military garments to express disrespect for the military. Sometimes they were tolerated. Sometimes not. Not wishing to be tagged a sexist, he had trouble determining the hippie among women. They learned that if they were in the company of bearded long hairs, the rejection was automatic. But if they were alone or with other women, Mr. Pickens was often indecisive. Once a group appeared wearing identical army fatigue jackets. Two were turned away, the others admitted. They finally figured out that it was because their jackets had corporal chevrons sewed on them. Next day one of the women who had been admitted pinned captain's bars on the collar. This time she was refused entry.

For Booger Red, this was an invitation to mirth. He organized his recruits with the efficiency of a Marine drill instructor. To his massive waist-low beard and flowing shoulder-length hair, both a mixture of red and white, he added a Santa Claus suit. With a huge bag of candy and toys thrown over his shoulder, he met the Sunday lunch trade, mamma and daddy with the little children just out of church. He took the kids in his arms, gave them favors, talked with them about Christmas. Moving along with them to the door, he would try each time to enter with them. Mr. Pickins would quickly open the door for the family, then rudely push Santa back onto the sidewalk. With the children watching through the glass in distress and confusion, Baxton would pound on the door and cry, loud enough for the children and everyone else inside to hear him: "Oh, Bob. What has happened to us? When you were a little boy you used to leave cookies and milk on the table for Santa Claus when he came down the chimney. Now you're a big boy and you own this nice restaurant and Santa has come all the way from the North Pole and he's so tired and hungry. Oh, please, Bob. Why won't you let me come in and get something to eat?" With the children in hysteria, he would walk away and wait for the next unsuspecting family to arrive from Sunday church.

Once there were five couples inside, each with two or three small children all screaming at once, their parents trying to calm them and explain the unexplainable. When the owner came outside and asked the protesters to leave, Baxton said something offensive enough to goad him into losing control. Mr. Pickens went inside and called the police, exactly what Booger Red had hoped for. When the squad car roared up, siren full blast, he moved in front of the window so all the little ones could see. He refused to get in the car voluntarily, so the officers roughly and ungraciously threw him in, spilling his sack of presents in the gutter.

One dreary Monday morning I watched an incident which told me a lot about the changing mood of young blacks at the time. Baxton and his little band of picketers were walking back and forth in front of the restaurant, having been enjoined from trespassing on Mr. Picken's property. A flatbed truck stopped at a traffic light in front. A Negro boy who looked about fourteen was sitting on a thirty-gallon garbage can, elbow on his knee, chin resting in his hand, a picture of Monday morning blues. Booger Red rushed to the side of the truck. "Oh, brother, leave your truck and come and help us. When they wouldn't serve you, we left our firesides, we marched, we were jailed, our bodies bear the scars of battle."

The boy, his eyes barely open and still lowered, mumbled something like, "What the hell's goin' on?"

"They won't serve us," Baxton screamed. "They won't sell us a hamburger or a pancake. Because we have long hair and beards, they won't let us in. We need people to demonstrate with us. We need you to help us like we helped you when they wouldn't serve Negroes."

The light changed and the truck began to ease away. The boy, still as unconcerned and still showing no emotion, looked up slightly, shrugged and said, "Burn the muthafucker down."

It was a scene I never forgot. Standing on an overcast Nashville sidewalk, watching that exchange between a middle-aged white man and a black lad little more than half-grown, it was painfully clear to me that the non-violent Civil Rights Movement was in trouble. Would we ever again experience that sacrifice, that beauty, that passiveness in mass protest? I doubted it.

The issues were no longer clear to the white majority. When they saw students being clubbed, gassed, and jailed, asked them why they were doing what they were doing and they said it was because a public restaurant would not serve them, it was easy to offer to assist. But now they could go in. If two thousand people ringing a courthouse said they were there because they could not register to vote, it was easy to know their cause was just. But now they were free to register. Theaters, parks, pools, schools, jobs as airline pilots or chimney sweeps, the legal barriers were gone.

Yet niggerhood remained. And the anger and frustration could only be expressed in the fashion of the young fellow on the trash truck. "The fire next time" of James Baldwin came home to me in a visceral manner. “God gave Noah the rainbow sign.” Indeed! “Burn the muthafucker down!”

VIII
When Other Helpers Fail . . .

"THAT'S THE BIGGEST wash pot I've ever seen," T.J. said, standing back throwing a rock, trying to make it skip across the water.

"You really are country," I said, pointing to the big pot. "You know how to play ducks and drakes. Only country boys know that."

"You've been to my house. Did it look like Times Square?"

We were sitting beside a two-hundred-gallon iron pot behind my cabin office. Neighbors said Old Man Oscar Bass hauled it in on a wagon from The Hermitage. There is another one like it still there. I had put catfish in it when we first came. In one summer they grew big enough to eat, but by then the children had named each one and nothing with a name could be eaten. We compromised by catching them in a net and taking them to the lake. After that I got goldfish.

"That pot used to belong to Andrew Jackson," I said.

"Didn't everything? He must have had big britches."

"That wasn't a wash pot," I said, remembering when we used to wash our clothes in a zinc tub, scrub them on a washboard, then boil them in an open iron kettle. "That was a sugarpot."

"Well, that's a lot of sweetening," he said, still trying different size rocks to see if he could make them skip.

"Hey, did you know I'm going to be a famous sculpturer?" I asked him, gesturing around the pot to several pieces of metal junk I had welded together.

"This one here is called 'The General Confession,'" I said. We had rebuilt an old tractor and had to replace the manifold. The six protruded openings which bolted onto the cylinders, with another in the middle for the exhaust pipe, looked like a Menorah. I welded the rocker arms onto it and it formed a baroque Patriarchal cross.

"And why do we call it the General Confession?" T.J. asked, knowing that I wanted him to.

"Because it's made from a manifold."

He went into his Sambo act, scratched his head on the opposite side from the hand he was reaching with, and grinned. "Do say?"

"Yeah, hit do say," I said, doing a poor imitation of his dialect. "The General Confession, hit say, 'We acknowledge and bewail our *manifold* sins and wickedness. . . .'"

He pointed at the next one without speaking. "That's the Tower of Babel," I said. It was made of assorted sizes of augers and drill bits, welded in a zig-zag pattern and reaching twenty feet in the air. The one coming out of the ground was a heavy dirt auger, the kind used to bore post holes or plant trees. Each one going up got smaller until the top one was a short quarter-inch bit. T.J. rolled his eyes, shrugged, and grinned some more, still saying nothing. "You know. Original sin. The Tower of Babel. Trying to reach high enough to conquer God. Everytime we try to become as God, we are impaled on our own auger," I explained.

He slapped his thigh and laughed out loud. "You mean, we screw ourselves," he yelled. "Impaled, my ass. We screw ourselves!"

An antique water pump was on the far side of the pot, the downspout almost touching the water. "And that's the fountain of life," he said, no longer whimsical.

"Yep. The fountain of life."

"Don't you ever quit preaching, Will Campbell?" he asked.

"You've got your whole gospel in three rusty pieces of junk that no one else would have on their place."

"Yeah? Well, maybe so. I hadn't thought about it like that."

"Sure you do," he said, moving behind each one as he continued. "Babel Tower. First comes sin." He shook the welded augers, the shimmying metal making a swishing sound. "Then confession. Repentance." He patted the manifold cross. "We acknowledge and bewail. . . ." He moved on to the old pump, moving the handle up and down like he was pumping water. "And salvation. Man, I can preach a whole year on this trash."

Apparently when I left the structured church, I must have missed the bells more than I did the steeples. I never attempted to build a steeple but began collecting bells. Two favorites hanging on the place are matching No. 7's with similar histories. Both came from disbanded black churches, one in Tennessee, the other in Mississippi. The Tennessee one was given to me in settlement of a bad debt. I suspected that it was stolen. A friend in Mississippi rescued the other one from a junk heap. It had hung for years beside a small plantation church. He is sure it had been donated to the congregation by the plantation owner who probably got another one, for it was far too large for a country church bell. It had been rung so many times to awaken the field hands, bring them in for the noon meal, and finally at the end of the day, the eight-pound clapper was flat on each side. When farm mechanization came and there was no need for many workers to do the hoeing and picking of the cotton by hand, they were abandoned to the cities. The old church building had been similarly abandoned and rotted down. The owners had plowed up the cemetery, the bell pushed onto the heap. After failing to find any living former members of the black church, my friend removed the bell out of sentiment and respect. It was hanging near the pot.

T.J. grabbed the rope and began to ring the bell. "There's one thing after sin, repentance, and salvation," he called above the noise. "Celebration!" He laughed and did a fast buck and wing dance. He continued to ring it, dancing, laughing, and yelling loudly. "Jesus is a mess! Jesus is a mess! JESUS IS A MESS!"

When he dropped the bell rope, he sank slowly to the ground, exhausted. We sat for a long time with neither of us speaking. I wasn't sure what I was feeling. Watching a black man with a wound on his head which refused to heal inflicted by a white man, lauding a white Jesus on a bell which had once been used to preside over the slavery of his people. Jesus *is* a mess.

"We'll call this sugarpot the Pool of Siloam," he said finally, dipping his hands into the water, the water making them shine like polished ebony. T.J. knew his Bible.

The pool, as all of us called it after that, had already become a gathering place for sacramental acts. Deepwater Baptists aren't supposed to believe in sacraments. The preachers called baptism and the Lord's Supper ordinances, and they spoke often of the dangers of viewing them as anything more than symbols. To call the Lord's Supper *Communion* was papist; Eucharist was not even a word to us. Yet there was always something mysterious and mystical about it, and our daddy referred to it as "The Sacrament." He pronounced it "sakerement." When we watched our mother bake the unleavened bread, being careful not even to have baking powder, soda, or salt on the same table where the plain flour and water were being mixed and rolled thin, we knew that something holy was taking place. And when we watched the preacher unwrap it from the heavily starched white linen cloth, break it into small pieces, taking care not to drop the tiniest crumb, the deacons passing it among the congregation but only to those who had previously received the equally nonefficacious but requisite ordinance of baptism, not the Ark of the Covenant nor the Host in the hands of a Vatican priest could have been viewed with more awe.

I should not have been surprised when as pastor of a Baptist congregation I was haunted and dogged by the sacramental. And coveted sacerdotal entitlement. Similarly when I dropped out of the steeples, no longer bound by organization, structure, and the impositions of congregational whims of what it means to be Baptist and Christian, I should not have been surprised that I was less sacramentarian than when it was expected of me.

As a result, I tried again to ease back under the canopy and carried on a brief flirtation with the Episcopal Church. For faithful institutional Baptists, the notion is that unfaithful Baptists become Episcopalians for reasons of social status and sophistication. Or so they can drink whiskey in public. (I was never given to social climbing, and not having to sneak to take a drink took most of the sport out of it, and during my Anglican days I had pretty much quit anyway.)

I soon became a licensed lay reader, one who can conduct Morning or Evening Prayers from the Book of Common Prayer but who may not perform priestly duties such as administering the sacraments. If there is a sermon, the lay reader delivers one written by some staff priest at the national headquarters in New York. I declined to do that, ostensibly because it was a violation of my doctrine of the Holy Spirit but more from the sin of pride. I had been to school for eight years to learn the trade and felt I could preach as well as the priests. A more exalted level of lay reader permits him to preach sermons of his own construction. Or plagiarization. I was granted that by the Bishop. Soon, however, some of the communicants, who were also loyal to the doctrines of the John Birch Society and saw their political allegiances as a higher calling than their faith, began to appear in the audiences where I was invited to speak on race relations. When I was introduced as an ordained minister, an office I had not renounced, they would pass the word that Campbell was an imposter and a fraud, that he posed as a priest but was a mere lay reader.

I had some calling cards printed with an instant loyalty oath.

Will D. Campbell
(I am not now, nor have I ever been, an Episcopal priest)

My effort at levity did not stop them. I sent word to the Bishop that not only did I not claim to be an Episcopal priest, but knowing some of them as I did, if I were one I would be more inclined to deny it. When the year ended, my lay reader's license was not renewed. I began introducing myself as the only deposed lay reader in the history of Canterbury. A canon theologian informed me that I was in error, that a lay reader could not be deposed. He could simply have his license revoked. "You are crazy as hell," I told him, "if you think I'm going to let my children grow up thinking their father has been revoked. That's common. Being deposed has some class about it."

My career as an Anglican came to an end. Not so much because I couldn't hold the office of lay reader within the perimeter. More because the ecclesiastical gene pool, the stubborn mixture reaching back to the sixteenth century and into the twentieth — from Thomas

Hewly to Roger Williams to Grandpa Bunt Campbell — had left a spiritual birthmark I could not disguise. I resolved to be a Baptist preacher of the South until the day I die. Though never again a Southern Baptist preacher. For the first time, I knew there was a difference. And what it was.

"Why'd you drop out of the steeples?" T.J. asked one day en route to a meeting. He had asked the question before and I had several stock answers, generally frivolous. "When I accepted the call, I didn't know it was collect," was one of them. "I lost my lease," was another. I had the feeling T.J. was not going to let me off with flippancy this time.

"Don't you miss going to church?" he came back when I tried to be cute.

"I'm not sure I've ever been to church," I answered. "Church is a verb. That's what Carlyle Marney used to say."

"But don't you miss the gatherings? The singing, preaching, dinner on the grounds, the fellowship, support?"

"Sometimes I miss it all so much I think I'm going to bust." He didn't answer, just sat waiting for me to go on. "Some folks say, 'You know, every Sunday morning the old devil tempts me to stay home. Not to go to church.' Well, he tempts me to go. Yeah, old buddy, I miss it. I really do."

"Then why don't you go back?" he asked. I wasn't comfortable with the pressure.

"Well, I guess if the Lord can beckon someone to come underneath the steeples, He can beckon some folks to come out from under them."

"Yeah. Guess so," he said. "Just so we don't miss a beckon."

I motioned to a stack of church bulletins a friend in California had sent me a few days earlier. They were on the back seat with some other mail.

"Read the announcements," I said. "Go ahead." He began to read some of the scheduled events out loud. Marriage Enrichment Seminar. Weight Watchers Club. Mother's Day Out. He shuffled the bulletins like a deck of cards.

"Well now, Brother Will, don't be so cynical. What's wrong with that? A lot of marriages are in trouble, so they tell me. People shouldn't be so fat. And mamma needs some time away from the house too."

"Nothing wrong with it," I said, "but what does any of it have to do with John 3:16?"

"Let's see what the wild card says," he laughed. "We'll make this one the wild card." He flipped one of the bulletins onto the seat between us, leaving it there for a moment like it was cooling off. "Ah yeah. I'll bet you liked this on. Bible Study Ski Trip. That's *January* 3-16. For just $750, any member of the congregation can go to Aspen. Ten full days of skiing, with instruction for beginners. Bible study each evening around a cozy fire."

"Yeah. I really liked that one," I said. "Go on."

"At seven o'clock Thursday this steeple has a workshop." He put both hands to his temples. "Splitting Headaches."

"Yep, I've been there," I said. "I've had some splitting headaches under the steeples. But you're lying to me now. I don't remember that one. Don't make it worse than it is."

He threw his hands up in a gesture of, "Would I lie to you?" He pointed his finger to the line he was reading and held it up so I could see. "Splitting Headaches Seminar," he repeated. "And that's at seven on Thursday. You believe me now? Tai Chi. That's Monday at 5:30. On Wednesday it's Yoga. I thought Wednesday was prayer meeting night. What's Tai Chi, Reverend Campbell?"

"Don't know, Reverend Eaves." He reached over and honked the horn. "Something worthwhile, I'm sure. Something I don't have to go to church to get. To do. Whatever. What else do we have today for the followers of the Way?"

"Well, let's just us see what we can find here for little ole Brother Will. Gotta teach him how to hustle the program. Gotta stroke his madbone." He rummaged through the stack, pretending to pick one at random. "Ah-ha! Here's a dandy. Baptist Open. Excuse me. That's Third Annual Baptist Open Golf Tournament."

"Baptist *Open*?" I asked. "Both?"

"That's what the man says. That's out of the Bayou state. Now, let's hear it for Louisiana!" he shouted, clapping his hands and stomping his feet on the floorboard. He rolled the window down and pretended to push something outside.

"And from the great state of Texas, we have this one. It's a seven o'clock swimming party." He scratched his head from the wrong side and went into his monkey act. "Woops! Afraid I'll have to miss that one. It has an exclusionary clause: designer swim suits requested. We always went in naked, and everyone knows God didn't design black birthday suits. Anyway, black folks don't get naked." He folded the announcement sheet and put it in his pocket. "They get *neck*-ed."

"R.S.V.P.?" I asked, motioning to the pocket he was buttoning.

"No, I want to read that one again tomorrow. Today I ain't believing it. But let's hear it for Texas. Yeaaa Texas!" he cheered.

"Now who's cynical?" I said. "But you dropped one. See what it says."

"All rightie, Brother Pastor," he said, searching for the place. "Here's a goodie for you. 'Today we are introducing a new member of our church staff. Minister of Puppetry.'" He began quacking, talking like Donald Duck. " 'And we have added this week three new buses. That brings the total to ninety-one. And to encourage the kiddies. . . .'" He dropped the Donald Duck routine and read in his own voice. " '. . . to bring a friend to ride the bus to church, a dollar bill will be hidden on each bus on the trip home. Each child who brings a friend to Sunday School will be permitted to join in the search for the treasure.'" He began scrambling around the car, turning things over, jerking the glove compartment open and scattering maps and tissues on the floor, looking for the dollar. "Mamma, get the Clorox," he yelled. "And that's not all, Christian busing fans," he went on. " 'Every child who brings *two* friends gets to participate in the nickel grabbing.'" He read the rest silently, then paraphrased. "Yep! A big bucket is jam-packed with nickels, and the little kiddies get to keep all the nickels their little hands can come out of there with. Ho boy!"

He sat staring out the window, pretending to count the telephone poles as we zipped past them. I wondered if he might be thinking that his church did none of those things. If that was what he was thinking, he didn't say it. Instead he began talking about that not being the whole story, that there were some good, meaningful, helpful activities listed in the bulletins too. "Not all of it is hustling the program," he said. He mentioned soup kitchens, food banks, and tutoring classes. "What about the R.A.'s and G.A.'s?" he asked, referring to the Royal Ambassadors and Girl's Auxiliaries, church clubs for boys and girls to teach them about evangelism. His voice was like an entreaty, like he wanted very much to hear me say something kind about the steeples. "Don't you believe that's better than the kids being on the streets, taking dope or something?"

"Royal Ambassadors and Girl's Auxiliary," I said, sighing deeply. "I can tell you don't have any little girl babies to think about. The little boys are royalty. The little girls are auxiliaries. That one may be the saddest of all. At least in the long run."

"You're driving too fast," he said. "Sixty-six telephone poles in one minute."

"How many am I supposed to pass?"

"Now, tell me what you really, deep, way down deep in the bottom of your gut miss the most about it," he said, his speech more serious, more probing than it had been before. "So far you've just been trimming around the edges."

"Well," I began, not knowing what he wanted me to say, "I always liked it when the service was over and I was standing at the door and the people filed by and said, 'Mighty fine sermon, Brother Campbell.' I guess I always really liked that."

"I'd be much obliged if you would tell me the truth, Reverend Campbell," he answered, leaning back in a gesture of near resignation. Then, sitting straight up, he said, "You're still talking about show business. You didn't give a rip about all that and you know it. Mighty fine sermons, my hind leg. You weren't even listening when they filed by. Someone could have said, 'Your wife just got run over in the parking lot,' and you would have smiled and said, 'Thank you very much. I appreciate it.'"

Something took hold of me. Something strange. Almost overwhelming. For the first time I had no choice but to be serious and honest with my catechist. There was a lump in my throat. Not a sad lump and not a guilt lump. Deeper than that. I shifted nervously, but it wasn't an agitated nervousness. Some mysterious mixture of joy, melancholy, and nostalgia. I didn't try to figure it out. Without thinking, I began to speak. "In obedience to the command of our Lord and Savior Jesus Christ and upon the profession of your faith in Him, I baptize you, my sister, in the name of the Father, the Son, and the Holy Spirit. Amen."

T.J. answered quickly, like he had known what I was going to say.

"And that's what you liked the most?"

"I didn't say that's what I liked the most. I said that's what I miss the most."

"You still baptize people," he said. "You do it all the time."

"Yeah. But when I put them under the water and look up, there's not a lot of people standing on the creek bank. Or on the river bridge looking down at us. No one is singing, 'Happy day, happy day, when Jesus washed my sins away.'"

"They're not there because you went off and left them," he chided. "You plumb went off and left them standing there on the bank."

Somehow I wasn't offended, just went on feeling what I had been feeling. When I didn't answer, he began to chuckle. "Or maybe they moved inside, huh?" he said. "Say, you ever baptize folks in one of those heated tanks with a picture of the Jordan behind you?"

"Yep. I've done that too."

"You miss those crowds too?"

I didn't answer again and he didn't push me. When he saw I wasn't going to answer, he added, "I'm really sorry, Brother Will. Real sorry."

I thought I knew what he meant but I wasn't sure.

You're trouble, T.J. Trouble, man. No way white folks going to believe you happened.

* * *

How many sacraments are there?" asks the Baltimore Catechism of those receiving instruction in the Roman Catholic Church.

"There are seven sacraments," is the response. "Baptism, Confirmation, Holy Eucharist, Penance, Extreme Unction, Holy Orders, and Matrimony."

"How many Sacraments hath Christ ordained in His Church?" asks the catechist in the Anglican Book of Common Prayer.

"Two only, as generally necessary to salvation; that is to say, Baptism and the Supper of the Lord." The adjective "only" was added to avoid any confusion with the teachings of Rome. The changing of the word "sacrament" to "ordinance" in Baptist usage was for the same reason. Neither those of the Church of England nor the Baptist movement needs to have made such an issue of it. In the first place, the Christian Church existed for more than a millennium without even defining a sacrament. And when it was done at the Second Council of Lyons in 1274 and the number seven settled upon, the interpretations were never as stringent as we, who from time to time opposed the Church of Rome, supposed. Some would say there were nine, taking the ordination of deacons and the consecration of bishops as separate stages of Holy Orders. Others combined Baptism and Confirmation, and that reduced the number to six. Or eight, if one combined those two but expanded Holy Orders to three sacramental acts.

Whether nine, eight, seven, or two, most of them took place on our forty acres at some time, and in some form. And sacramentals, or sacred signs, abounded. Water in the Pool of Siloam, statues, medals, candles, and crucifixes. The outward appearances of many of them were recognizable only to us. The presence of them never bothered me. To institutionalize, ritualize, or regulate their use would have. Sacraments happened when sacraments happened.

* * *

"Daddy, will you baptize Harlan?" Bonnie asked one Christmas. Harlan was her three-year-old son, our only grandchild. I explained that I was right then writing a book about the Anabaptists and that they felt strongly about the baptism of infants. And that such Holy Orders as I could claim insisted upon it being done by immersion. Further, the person to be baptized must have reached the age of accountability.

"Since the Council of Trent," she replied, "any person, even one who hasn't been baptized, can baptize another. If you don't want to baptize your grandson, well, I'll. . . ."

"No, no, no! If it's going to be done, I'm going to be the one to do it." So on Christmas morning we gathered at the breakfast table. Even my father, who by then had been a Baptist deacon for sixty years, did not object. Years before I heard him quip, when someone asked if he believed in infant baptism, "Believe in it? I've actually seen it." I should have known he would not demur.

When I finished, Harlan, still sopping the straight-up egg with his biscuit, said, "Papa, what did you put on my head?"

"Water," I replied, hoping that would settle it. It didn't.

"Why?" His mother shifted nervously in her chair. Maybe she doesn't want her child traumatized by his granddaddy's horse and buggy theology, I remember thinking. But it was a fair question. And that he would ask it suggested that I need not worry further concerning his innocence. So I tried to talk to him in the same fashion I would to any other seeker. We talked of sin. Grace. Of guilt and forgiveness. "What's guilt, Papa?"

"Well, you know that big lump you get in your throat when you're mean to your mother?" He nodded that he did. "Well, you don't have to have that. Being mean to your mother was your sin. And the lump is feeling guilty about it. And the water was put on your head because Jesus has already forgiven you for your meanness."

Throughout the little homily he was giggling. That pleased Bonnie because she knew he wasn't being upset. When I was through, he was laughing out loud. He sopped the last bit of the runny egg, jumped down, and started to rush off to his world of play. Or reality. Then he stopped laughing, looked up at me and said, "Well, well, papa. Thank you then!" I had no further question as to the age of accountability. It was the most appropriate response to a sacrament I had ever heard. A big belly laugh. And thank you then! He was baptized.

* * *

"Look, I'm an atheist. I don't believe a goddam thing. They tell me I have five to eight months to live, and I want you to help me die." A young woman I hardly knew was lying in a Nashville hospital, just out of exploratory surgery. The lung cancer they found was already metastasized throughout her body, beyond reach of the surgeon's scalpel. They sewed her up and gave her the news. I knew that I was presiding over the second sacrament. She had made her confession. Penance was supposed to follow. But I always had trouble with that one. If the gospel, the "good news," is a message of unconditional grace, there is no place for penance. That message had become so clear to me that I didn't understand why it wasn't preached from underneath every steeple in Christendom every Sunday. Finally I figured it out. You can't build a steeple on an unconditional message. Not even unconditional grace. There *must* be a club. A threat. Something to hold over their heads. When I was a child in Mississippi the condition was, "Don't smoke cigarettes, don't drink liquor, and don't mess around on a Saturday night and you're a good Christian." I didn't see the good news in that. Even "good" and "Christian" seemed contradictory. According to the attendant teachings, Jesus had come for the bad. And what he had proved in coming was that salvation did not depend upon our own goodness.

So I went off to the theological academy where they confirmed my childhood dubiosity. They told me that such foolish legalism as don't smoke cigarettes, drink liquor, and mess around on Saturday night had nothing to do with the message of Jesus. God didn't care about such primitive trivia. What God cares about is the suffering of His people. Therefore, don't segregate, pay your workers less than minimum wages, or go to war, and you'll be a good Christian.

That worked all right for me until I realized that I had substituted one moralistic code for another. And that if the instruction of the theological academy be correct, that God cares about the suffering of His people, then my primitive ancestors were more nearly correct than they because, according to the scientists, cigarette smoking is going to cause more suffering of God's people than slavery. With drinking liquor a close second. The woman lying there smoked three packs a day.

For whatever reason, I skipped the penance with the woman who had just made her confession. Or perhaps I didn't. "Would you like to talk about this God who has damned what you don't believe?" I asked, striking my most professional posture.

"Don't give me any of your counseling shit, Reverend!" she said, trying to sit up but failing. "I just chased that fat-ass nurse out of here when she said, 'And how do you feel about what has happened to you, Millie?' How the ratfuck am I supposed to feel? Thirty-five years old and just figured out what I'm doing in this world and they tell me in six months I'll be fucking gone from it." She began to sob and I was glad. Not glad as the professional counselor; just glad that she was releasing the hurt and anger by crying. Glad because it gave me some time. Time to assign the penance. To myself. I had been temporarily more daunted by the one-sided sensitivities the culture had instilled in me — "Ladies don't say ugly words" — than by the news of her intolerable fortune. Shame on me. Shame on the culture. What makes an ugly word ugly? And for whom?

I embraced her, forgetting the incision running from her right scapula to the bottom of the rib cage. She didn't seem to care about the pain as my own whimpering blended with her sobs.

With the facade gone, I could begin. As she had begun. "Well, sugar, either I missed that course in seminary or didn't do too well in it. But I'm here." My male patronage would have bothered her in normal times, she told me later, but not on that occasion.

We spent long hours and many days together after that. We shared many things. Her anger was so furious I thought it beyond abatement. Sometimes the railing was directed at me. At other times at doctors, nurses, a mother who abandoned her at three, the great aunt who raised her, the father who drank around, slept around, and died young, two marriages which ended in disaster. But most often it was aimed solidly at God. After each harsh spasm she would catch her breath, laugh, and say, "How can I hate the son-of-a-bitch so much when he doesn't exist?"

After each out-of-town trip I made she wanted to hear every detail of what happened. She particularly savored a report of a western journey to a lavish retreat center which had once been a dude ranch. A part of the retreat was to be spent in silence. From ten at night until noon the next day, no one would speak. As we sat at breakfast, enjoying the finest Columbian coffee, English muffins, Canadian bacon, grapefruit already sectioned, pointing at platters and making ridiculous gestures, something took hold of me. "To hell with this bullshit!" I screamed, slamming my fist against the table. The startled group looked on with silent disapproval. Finally one said, "You broke the silence. Why did you break the silence?"

The words which followed were not my own. For the first time I had some brief understanding of glossolalia as I explained without even thinking of word or form. "I broke the silence because more than half the people in the world can't enjoy the luxury of worship. If this be worship. How can a mother or father maintain silence while pushing and scrounging and screaming for possession of half a cup of rice to feed their starving babies. I broke the silence because the wine and wafer which will slide down our pious gullets at the alleged altar tomorrow morning will contain more calories than that half of the world will get all day."

Millie laughed and held me close. "You know, Reverend. I just might join your church."

"I don't have a church," I said.

"No. I guess not," she said after a long pause. "You don't have a church. A church has you. Is that what you're saying?"

"I'd be afraid to get that definite about it," I said. "If I made that claim, I'd probably give it a name and put it on a bumper sticker. And then you can bet your life I'd run it. And then it wouldn't be church any longer."

As soon as the words, "bet your life," left my lips, I knew it was wrong. There was another long pause. She could no longer swallow solid foods, so she liked to sit beside the Pool of Siloam and throw bits of bread to the goldfish. The symbolism of sitting there was overwhelming. But I was trying again to be professional, to be *strong*. She threw the last of the crumbs into the pool and took my hand. I thought she was going to scold me. Instead her voice was soft and kind. "I guess somebody 'bet my life.' And according to yesterday's X-rays, the bastard is about to collect."

She loved those goldfish and had bought a little kit to measure the pH factor in the water. A few days earlier we had drained the pool and filled it with clean, clear water. All the fish were visible to the very bottom. They were swarming around the spot where she had dropped the last of the bread, begging for more. After a long time she spoke again. As gentle as before. "Will, do you think he'll parlay his winnings?"

I knew it was a cue. I had told her many times by then that I did not believe that what the clinicians call death is the end of things. She wanted to hear it again. Instead, for some reason I didn't examine, I began telling her another story about the western journey. A young schoolteacher asked me if I would baptize her. Said she grew up in a church-going family but had never been baptized. She wanted it done by immersion. I asked the director of the center if we could use their swimming pool. He said that raised certain theological questions but that he would think about it and let me know next morning. There was a Corps of Engineers lake down the road, so next morning as the sun was coming up over the mesa we climbed the fence, as close to the "No Trespassing" sign as we could get, waded into the water and, in violation of both the steeples and Mr. Caesar, buried her from the old life and resurrected her to the new. It was the most baptistic I had felt in a long time. Troublemaker. Rebel. The left wing of the Reformation. That's what we once were. But that was a long time ago. Déjà vu! Hallelujah!

Millie loved the story. She laughed and tried to dance around the pool. "I guess the next thing you know *I'll* be asking you to baptize *me*." Then, a bit embarrassed, patting me teasingly on the back, she added, "Like all those other cunts and camp followers."

"I don't push folks, sugar," I said. "But the pool is ready when you are."

"I guess we'll know when it's time," she said, laughing, lighting a cigarette, trying to pretend it was all a joke. The cigarette was marijuana. She suffered from severe nausea, and one of the doctors had prescribed cannabis capsules. When she told him she was a pot smoker and asked for a prescription for some joints so her insurance would pay for it, he said it was illegal. They would pay for capsules but not reefers. She said the capsules didn't have the same effect and she couldn't swallow them anyway. "Now you make something holy out of that, Reverend," she screamed. I was working with a country music group at the time, cooking on the bus to make some money. They called me Hop Sing, and I heard one of them say, "You know, Will Campbell is going to make some band a good wife." I told them about the cannabis capsules and Millie. They started what they called a "Joint Effort for Millie." Everyone was supposed to contribute, and after each trip they sent her a little bag of marijuana. Each time I drove home with it I was scared. One day I counted twenty-three big towering steeples as I drove along. After that the love offering of the boys in the band to a dying woman did not seem at all evil.

In the beginning she had calmly told me that she had joined the Hemlock Society, a euthanasia group which originated in England. She read all the literature they sent and started storing up the heavy drugs so that she would have enough to end her life. Instead she clung tenaciously to the last shred of it. She agreed to an experimental spinal catheter where the morphine cheated muscular and vascular waste and went straight to the nervous system. And finally to a last-ditch feeding tube where food was funneled directly into her stomach.

We sat alone in the small public housing apartment. George Barrett, the lawyer friend who had defended black demonstrators during the Sit-in Movement, had pulled some strings to get it for Millie when her money was gone. She had been nauseous all day, and I sat beside her bed with the kidney basin half-filled with the cloudy stomach fluid. She could still talk, though the esophagus was completely blocked. However, she made no verbal request, gave no oral orders. Just kept gazing at the viscid liquid, occasionally raising her eyes upward. She repeated the same movements several times. I dipped my fingertips into the basin and held them there. Her eyes accepted the offering. I slowly crossed her forehead three times, saying no words. She closed her eyes as I did. In her own way, perhaps because fate had been so cruel, she was a woman of great inner strength. It seemed proper that the sacramental came from deep within her own body. Not *ex opere operanto. Ex opere operantis.*

Baptism? Unction?

The Hospice nurse called at five next morning.

* * *

After a brief introduction, the voice on the phone said, "Dr. Billy wants to see you tonight." It sounded like T.J. He had learned to imitate any sound from Gullah to Brooklyn to Liverpool, and I was often fooled by it.

"Billy Graham or Billy Sunday?" I said. "Where the hell are you, T.J.?" I quickly added, not sure anymore.

"Sir?" the voice said. "This is Mr. Morton. I work for Dr. Graham. You know we're in a crusade here in Nashville. He wants to see you in his dressing room before the service tonight."

I had never met Dr. Graham but was not surprised to hear from someone on his staff. Marshall Frady had written a new biography of him called *Parable of American Righteousness*. As a sort of control group, I suppose, he had included a chapter on the Church of Forty Acres and a Goat. Two peas from the same pod without the same flavor. I had heard that the Graham staff was upset about it.

The man on the telephone asked me if I was planning to attend the crusade. When I told him I wasn't sure, he said, "You and Mr. Frady must be real close friends." When I asked him why, he said, "Well, he has written a book and a whole chapter is about you." When I asked him who the rest of the book was about and he said that it was about Dr. Graham, I couldn't resist saying, "Well, if one chapter about me makes us real close friends, seventeen chapters about Dr. Graham must make them bosom buddies." He didn't answer.

My elderly neighbor, who had never been in any trouble except the time he killed his wife, had died a few hours earlier, and I was supposed to give the eulogy and was going to attend the wake that evening. When I explained to the caller why I couldn't come, he said he would call back.

The next morning, Tuesday, he called again with the same word, "Dr. Billy wants to see you in his dressing room tonight before the service." I didn't want to appear unfriendly but had to tell him again that I couldn't come. I said I hoped he would understand. A young black man had been convicted of murder in our county and the sentencing trial was scheduled for the next morning, and I had been asked to testify against the death penalty. I was to see his attorney that night. He said he would call again.

Wednesday morning a woman who identified herself as a volunteer secretary called. From Crusade Director to volunteer seemed a demotion for me but I was courteous. "Mr. Morton asked me to call and say that Dr. Graham had asked him to ask you to meet with him in his dressing room tonight before the service."

"Is Mr. Morton there?" I asked. I didn't want to tell a woman I had never met why I couldn't come.

"Well, no. But I have all the information. Which gate at the stadium you're to report to. Where you are to park. Who will meet you to escort you to Dr. Graham. I have all the information."

"Well, uh, yes ma'am. I suppose you saw in the paper this morning about the man who killed his wife last night and shot her boyfriend. They think he's going to die too."

"No, I didn't read about it," she said, not seeming concerned. "Will you be able to come tonight?"

I decided to tell her the rest of the story. "Well, no ma'am. The boyfriend's mother is someone I know, and she's on her way over from East Tennessee on the bus and I'm supposed to meet her. She's a widow. Raised nine boys and none of them have ever given her any trouble. She's very upset. They're Catholic." I remember wondering why I thought it mattered that they were Catholic.

"Mr. Campbell, I'm sorry about your friend, but I have a lot of calls to make. Dr. Graham has a tight schedule."

I went on. "The man . . . I mean the husband . . . came downstairs. They say he's an epileptic, has some kind of spells or something. Anyway, he came down in the middle of the night and says he caught them performing oral sex. . . ."

"Uh. Just a moment, sir . . ."

"Hell-ooo," a sugary voice said. "This . . . is . . . Mr. Morton. May I help you?"

I was glad I had overcome my sexist timidity. The woman had not seemed upset at hearing the words about a wife dead, a man critically wounded, a mother riding a bus two hundred miles to be with her son, a husband in jail. But the words "oral sex" were too much.

After I explained to Mr. Morton why I couldn't come, I asked him to convey my regrets to Dr. Billy.

A few weeks earlier I had married an airline stewardess to a big Cherokee Indian who looked like Will Sampson in "One Flew Over the Cuckoo's Nest." On Thursday morning, an hour before Mr. Morton called again, they had called and asked if I would baptize them that evening. Said they wanted it done privately. He said that he respected Dr. Graham and had thought of making his profession of faith at the stadium, but since he was a struggling songwriter, and Johnny Cash was the honorary Chairman of the Crusade, and the service that night was to be filmed for national television, he did not want to give the impression that he was doing this for publicity. I told them that there was precedent for private, even secret, baptisms and that I would protect their privacy. I asked them to be there at five o'clock.

Jackson, T.J., and I were standing beside the fish pool when they arrived. Jackson had seen many weddings and other ceremonies on the place, but he had never seen a baptizing.

He had never shown any fear of strangers, but when this couple arrived, he appeared upset and restless. Instead of going out to greet them the way he usually did, he backed away. They tried to coax him closer but he stood back, watching. We sat by the pool for a few minutes talking about why they wanted to be baptized. T.J. joked about being glad the pot wasn't big enough for a baptism by immersion because a preacher my size would have to have a hoist to get the Big Indian out of the water. (T.J. told me later that he could call him "Big Indian" without offense but that I shouldn't try it. I didn't.) While I was asking the couple if they truly and earnestly repented of their sins and desired to follow Jesus in the rite of baptism, T.J. put a leash on Jackson's collar and led him up close. I motioned the couple to kneel down with their heads over the ledge of the pool. I held a long handled gourd dipper to pour water over their heads.

Just as I started to dip into the water, Jackson jerked loose from T.J., bounced straight up, and landed in the pool, as ungainly as I had ever seen him. I tried to continue, looked down and saw the fish darting and diving. At the same time I saw the big man's body shaking with laughter. The bride was quiet and still, pretending not to notice, the water from Jackson's splash dripping from her long hair and shoulders. I glanced at T.J., a plea for help. He was laughing too. Jackson was lunging and straining to get over the slippery sides of the pot. T.J. moved to the couple and got them to their feet. "Look," he said, still laughing. "God's got to be laughing too. He won't mind if we join Him. Just believe me. Funny things happen in church too." We all four held each other in a rollicking, dancing hug until we could control ourselves. Jackson finally succeeded in climbing out of the pool and ran into the woods as fast as I had ever seen him move, springing like a kangaroo. "Let him go! Let him go!" T.J. exclaimed, as if someone was trying to stop him. When we were done laughing, they knelt again for the sacrament of baptism.

"What was that all about?" I asked T.J. when they were gone and we were looking for Jackson.

"Don't you know?" he replied. "Don't you really know?" I said I really didn't.

"Jackson? Cherokee? Trail of tears? Come on, Preacher?" He spoke impatiently. "Tsali? Don't you remember Tsali? God, you white people are something."

Oh, yes. Tsali. He had told me about Tsali the time he, Jim Lawson, and I were in Chattanooga and went to Rossville, Georgia.

During the Indian Removal days of Andrew Jackson, there were a few Cherokees far up in the mountains the troops had a hard time rounding up. Two soldiers attacked one of the women, and she fought back with a hatchet, killing both of them. An Indian named Tsali hid the hatchet under his shirt when he heard about it so that she would not be charged. The general sent word to the Cherokees that they had to turn someone in who could be punished for the murders. The mountain resisters rejected the demand, preferring to take their chances amongst the clouds.

Tsali dissented, said that he was prepared to die for the tribe, and offered himself as propitiation. A white trader and friend of the tribe convinced them to surrender Tsali to the general with the condition that the remaining Cherokees be exempt from the removal West. The general, perhaps knowing that he would never be able to outwit the Indians in their native terrain, agreed to forward the proposal to Washington.

Tsali came down out of the mountains, accompanied by a group of his neighbors. Without indictment, arraignment, judge or jury, the Cherokees who came with Tsali were forced to execute him. Along with his brother and oldest son.

The white trader persisted in his negotiations for the pact to be honored. Perhaps because the land was both worthless and inaccessible, the state and federal governments finally agreed. The descendants of Tsali live in those mountains still. The man we baptized in a baptistry that once belonged to Andrew Jackson was one of them.

"I can't believe you've had a goat all these years and you've never read Leviticus. I can't believe it," T.J. said.

Late that night I read from Leviticus.

> And Aaron shall lay both his hands upon the head of the goat, and confess over him all the iniquities of the children of Israel, and all their transgressions in all their sins, putting them upon the head of the goat, and shall send him away by the hand of a fit man into the

> wilderness: And the goat shall bear upon him all their iniquities unto a land not inhabited: and he shall let go the goat in the wilderness.

I guess I didn't fully believe that T.J. knew what he was talking about. But it was strange, and I wondered about it for a long time. In fact, I still do.

On Friday evening of that week, with none of the Lord's work to do, I met with Billy Graham and found him to be a modest and charming gentleman.

Since 1947 when he stood in a California tent and almost equated the Communist cause with the devil, America with the Kingdom of God on earth, and William Randolph Hearst had passed the word to his newspaper empire to "pump Graham," I had thought of him as the worst of the religious and political right. But as I sat with him on a balmy summer evening thirty years later and thought of those who had replaced him, the electronic soul molesters hurling their satellites around the globe with a gospel of, "Praise the Lord and send me the money," "Take up your cross and relax," "Take up your cross and get rich," courting annihilation in the name of Jesus, while Graham had turned to denouncing nuclear proliferation, I found him a man of honor and integrity. Everything, I suppose, is relative.

* * *

"I appreciate your kindness, Preacher. Looks like they're gonna take me away this time." It was the Grand Dragon of the North Carolina Ku Klux Klan, J.R. "Bob" Jones. I'm not sure why he trusted me. He knew what I believed. Knew that a great deal of my work was promoting the cause of racial integration and that most of his was in opposition to it. I had befriended him because when Isaiah and Jesus said that they had come to proclaim release to prisoners, they said nothing of the prisoner's crime. Nothing was said about this or that ideology allowing for distinctions of our own. They were to be visited because they were prisoners. There was no condition set, no limitations fixed. It was one of the few things T.J. and I argued about. He said that visiting the Ku Klux Klan was stretching Mr. Jesus a bit too far. He generally laughed when he said it, though. Jones had not been tried for being a bigot, burning crosses, or lynching black people. His crime was that he had refused to give the House Un-American Activities Committee his membership roll. "Would you submit the names, addresses, and telephone numbers of your neighbors and friends to a hostile body?" he had asked me. I told him I hoped I would be strong and stubborn enough to resist it. He was convicted of contempt of Congress and sentenced to a year in federal prison. After the trial, an official from the Justice Department came to visit him. He told him that if he would resign from the Klan and issue a statement denouncing it, he was sure the judge would probate the sentence and he wouldn't have to spend a year in prison. The Dragon told him he would not betray his friends for twelve months, that he could hold a bear in a bathtub that long, and that furthermore, in the interest of preventing violence, he would appreciate it if he would depart his premises. The official made a hasty retreat, and soon Bob was notified to report to the U.S. Marshalls in front of the courthouse.

Though he didn't know where he was going when he left home and wasn't told where he was until he got there, he was sent to Danbury, Connecticut. I had another friend there at the time, Father Dan Berrigan. ". . . and the criminals with Him." Word circulated among the black prison population that the Grand Dragon of the Ku Klux Klan was there. Further word had it that he wouldn't be there long because he would be dead in the yard. A mutual friend in New Jersey, Pete Young, knew a Black Muslim minister who had members and numerous contacts at Danbury. The notion of separatism was about the same in both groups. The word then became that if anything happened to Bob Jones while he was in prison, the one responsible would have to answer to Muslim justice. Jones continued in good health, his best friend in prison a Black Muslim. Mysterious ways.

The night before Bob was to report, there was a party. Friends and neighbors came and went, came and stayed. We told yarns, cracked jokes, drank a lot of the grape, sang a lot of country songs, and tried to pretend it was just another long winter evening.

Before it ended, the Dragon, who had grown up a Lutheran, said he would like to have Communion. Some of the men laughed at the thought of something holy in such a setting, but when they saw that he was serious, they solemnly filled their glasses one last time. I unpacked the Gibson guitar, strummed and talked about a country song which was popular at the time called, "Anna, I'm Taking You Home." It was a song about a wayward woman and the fashion in which her man forgave her. It was the best summary of the Gospel I could think of at the time. With the homily over, I began the liturgy:

> To release the captives. Bring good news to the poor. Restore sight to the blind. Heal the brokenhearted. To preach the acceptable year of the Lord.
>
> Lord, ole Brother Bob here is going off to jail for a while.
> And we're gonna ask you to kind of keep an eye on him.
> And on us.
> Lord, you know he's not a saint.
> And you also know that we shore ain't.
> But the book tells us that's why you died;
> So that God and sinners could be reconciled.
> And we're gonna drink to that, and if it's all the same
> We'll sing our song in Jesus' name.

Then the song:

> Anna, take off that tight-fitting dress.
> Take those cheap-looking shoes from your feet.
> Wash that powder and paint from your face.
> For Anna, I'm taking you home.
>
> Turn off that scarlet light in your window.
> That tells the world what kind of girl you've become.
> I'm taking you back, where there's folks who love you.
> Anna, I'm taking you home.

And to the oblation, invocation, and invitation:

> And now, as many as believe that a man *can* find his freedom in a prison. As many as believe that no matter how blind, we can come to see. As many as believe that there is some way, somehow good news for the poor. As many as believe that the brokenhearted, those remaining at home, can be healed. Yes, as many as believe . . . that . . . Jesus . . . Christ . . . is Lord. Let them say, Hallelujah! And let them drink to, and let them drink *of* . . . *His* victory.
>
> "For Anna, I'm taking you home."

The glasses were lifted, and those who wished screamed, "HALLELUJAH!" The Eucharistic rite was over.

Some would call it heresy. Perhaps so.

In a few hours we drove J.R. Jones to the Greensboro courthouse. With the same tears which are shed when anyone leaves their family to enter the gates of captivity, we bade him good-bye.

A few years later Pete Young's house caught on fire from a faulty television set. His wife, their three-year-old daughter, and his wife's mother were killed. Pete lay in critical condition from burns he received when he tried frantically to save them. Pete was a Protestant. They were Catholic. Because the undertakers would not let the child be buried lying on the bosom of her mother, there were three caskets. That meant twenty-four pallbearers. At the front of the line was the former Grand Dragon. By then he was out of prison and *had* resigned from the Klan. But instead of denouncing his neighbors and friends, as the visitor from the Justice Department had suggested, he had denounced the war in Vietnam, because, he said, it was being fought primarily by the poor, sons of his neighbors and friends. Black and white. Beside him was his Muslim prisonmate. Others included an Australian who was editing a magazine for an organization called Clergy and Laity Concerned About the War in Vietnam, a black United Methodist preacher, another Klansman, and others young and old, black and white, Catholic, Protestant, Jewish, and nothing. All under the canopy of a Roman Catholic cathedral in Summit, New Jersey.

As we waited for the hearses to move out, Bob Jones pointed to the tall steeple and whispered to the priest, "Father McGovern, that's what I do down South." After being released from prison, he made his living selling and installing lightning rods on church steeples. The priest didn't understand. He got me aside and said, "That fellow isn't going to burn my church house down while he's up here, is he?" I told him his church house was the most secure building in the Middle Atlantic.

The priest called me when I got home and said, "Will, I just wanted to tell you that the Baptist church burned down the night of the funeral."

I said, "Well, Father, I told you nobody was going to bother *your* steeple. I didn't say the boys wouldn't get one of ours just to stay in practice." The former Dragon, of course, was back home in North Carolina. Minding his business. And his manners.

* * *

Ordination. Holy Orders. Who is a Reverend and who is more Reverend than whom? There is the Reverend, the Very Reverend, and the Right Reverend. (Why not the Left Reverend? That way we might get along better with Marxist Christians.) All of it gives me trouble, particularly since it had such a trivial beginning. It started back in New Testament days over who should put the food on the tables. Some of the Greek-speaking folk thought their widows were not getting their share. So seven men were chosen to distribute the food while the others were left to do the holy things. There was a service, the apostles laid their hands on the heads of the seven, and ordination was born.

Somehow things got complicated and turned around. Nothing seems quite as divisive as determining who can be declared Reverend. Today a lot of Christians spend more time and energy arguing over whether women should be ordained than they do opposing a nuclear end to the world.

I have tried to stay away from it. That's the way new denominations get started, and we have enough of those already. If I believe that all institutions are inherently evil, I cannot then say, "But we're going to start a pure one. We can do what they do better." It is important that no one ever take seriously, or try to perpetuate, the Church of Forty Acres and a Goat.

However. . . . There have been ordinations. Not standardized. Not institutionalized. It has never been done the same way twice, and the name for the body doing the ordaining has never been the same. Generally it has been done to subvert the State. Or expediency to fit our own schemes. Sometimes both at once. A young man who regularly visited hospitals, jails, and skid row got drafted and would have been an unhappy and useless soldier. A few of us got together and declared him a minister by the authority of the Dolan House Fellowship. Caesar asked no questions.

The next time it was a man with a Ph.D. degree in English who was assisting a Presbyterian minister in her ministry to men and women on death row. The authorities said he could not continue unless he was a duly ordained minister. She, along with some others who called ourselves on that occasion the Glad River Congregation, duly ordained him.

J. Andrew Lipscomb was ordained by the United Methodist Church when he was young. That body has what they call special appointments for preachers not serving a local congregation. Chaplains, college teachers, denominational workers, counselors, and the like have no trouble getting a special assignment. The personal advantage is that recipients can enjoy all the fringe benefits from both church and state.

Andrew's wife was the county health nurse in a poor, rural county in South Georgia. He provided his part of the family income as a carpenter. He also did priestly chores for the neighbors. After years of hedging, evasions, and embarrassed discussions, the bishop finally advised Andrew that a carpenter could not be a United Methodist minister in his Conference. Suddenly he had no authority to do the weddings and other things for his neighbors.

The Lazer Creek Congregation provided the unentitled preacher the following portfolio:

> GREETINGS:
> To all believing brothers and sisters everywhere. On this day, April 7, that being the same day as the anniversary of the resurrection of our Lord from legal execution by the state, or Easter Sunday, we of the LAZER CREEK CONGREGATION, did receive and accept Brother J. Andrew Lipscomb as a minister of that risen Lord.
>
> Brother Lipscomb, having in earlier times passed the doctrinal tests of a sister body of believers, the United Methodist Church, and we being in a fellowship and having no quarrel of essential dogma with that branch of our Lord's tree, accepts the examination as well as laying on of hands of our kindred believers upon him.
>
> We commend him to you, and by the authority vested in us by our common Savior do hereby commission him to do all priestly and prophetic duties in our, and His, name.

Several of us signed the document and Caesar has not questioned what we did. The hierarchy of the United Methodist Church chose not to comment, nor to formally transfer Mr. Lipscomb's orders to the Lazer Creek Congregation. But then, in fairness to them, it has no known address.

Certainly the structured, steepled, institutionalized church has trouble with such ecclesiastics by subterfuge. I suppose there is something wrong with it, but I haven't had time to try to figure out what it is. What the Founder thinks — well, every day I'm closer to finding out.

* * *

Why don't they get a judge, a ship's captain, or a justice of the peace? They have the same authority from the state to marry couples as I. While I would no sooner perform the seventh sacrament upon the commission of Caesar than I would baptize by that authority, the legality of what the ship's captain does and what I do are identical. I resent it. There should be a difference. And there is. Otherwise the hundreds who have stood on these acres to be joined in marriage would not have come. Even those who have not been a part of organized religion since they were children want the symbols, the ceremonial. They want holy matrimony, not matrimony.

It seemed to be Jackson's favorite rite. I think he could intuit when one was about to take place, no matter how informal or impromptu. Sometimes he would not come down to my office for weeks. But if a wedding was about to take place, especially by the pool, I could expect him. If Nell wanted to come along, he would move at her pace. If she didn't, he would come hopping, skipping like a gazelle.

A prisoner I had visited at the state penitentiary asked me to do his wedding and baptize their baby. He said the warden would not let him out twice, and he wanted to be present for both events. They were black and I told him that although I was honored to be asked, if either of them preferred a black minister to do either ceremony I would invite T.J. to come out. He said it had always been his feelings that souls didn't have color. I shouldn't have asked.

I had never done a wedding and christening at the same time and considered the theological implications and logistics of the matter. Which should I do first? I discussed it with T.J.

"Where'd this baby come from anyway?" he began. "I thought you told me this dude had been in the pokey eight years. The bull jump the fence?"

I told him as I understood it, the cow jumped the fence. The mother was in prison too. He was on some kind of minimum security work detail and was doing something near the Women's Prison. She slipped by the guards, got over the fence, and that's how it happened. After she was released, they decided to get married. Before it could go through all the legal channels, the baby was two months old.

"Well," T.J. said, "let's start with the kid. Boy or girl?"

"Does it matter?" I asked. He indicated that it did but I didn't understand.

"If you do the wedding first, that's an insult to the baby. Looks like you're trying to get them legitimate before you would consider baptizing her. 'Course, now if'en hits a little boy baby, hit don't matter so much. Little boy bastards sort of common mongst us colored folks." He switched from good grammar to dialect without a pause.

"Cut out the coon talk, T.J.," I said. "This is serious business." He scratched his head from the wrong side, grinned, and sat down.

"I know you're serious, Will. Sometimes I think you're too serious. I mean, for a Baptist. How'd you get bogged down in all this stuff about the sacraments?" I told him I didn't know. "Well, like I said, you can't very well do the wedding first. On the other hand, if you do the baptizing first it looks like you're saying you have to get rid of all the sins before you proceed. Why don't you just work it all into one service? Do it both at once."

That seemed like a good idea. They were due in half an hour, so I went to work on an appropriate ceremony. Some things had to be left out. Some things added. Not much point in asking the Lord to bless the nuptial bed when there wasn't going to be one. The groom would be in leg irons and handcuffs and had to go back to the penitentiary as soon as the wedding was over. Anyway, if there was going to be a christening, there must have been a nuptial bed already. I asked T.J. to stay, but he said he didn't think that was a good idea.

The bride and a friend arrived first with the baby. A few minutes later two prison guards came, the groom in a cage-like area in the back seat. He was wearing a new suit, and the guards, one with sidearms, the other carrying a shotgun, took the cuffs and leg irons off before he got out of the car. I asked the guards if I could be alone for a few minutes with the couple inside my cabin. "Five minutes," the one with the shotgun said. I gathered he was in charge. Most of their premarital counseling time was spent in heavy petting, with me looking out the window. I considered going in the other room but was afraid one of the guards would come in.

When we went outside to join the others by the pool, Jackson had joined the circle and was enjoying all the attention. As the couple took their place before me, the friend holding the baby to the side, Jackson stood beside her.

> Dearly beloved, we are gathered together here in the sight of God, and in the face of this company, to join together this man and this woman in holy Matrimony, and to accept this child into the household of believers. All are honorable estates. Christ adorned and beautified the first with his presence and first miracle in Cana of Galilee. And set the example for the second when John the Baptist did baptize him in the River Jordan.

I took the baby in my arms, and as I did Jackson moved and stood directly in front of me like a second sponsor, a noble godfather. I recited from Saint Mark about Jesus taking the little children in his arms and blessing them in Judea. I tried to weave a web of familyhood, moving in and out of each ceremony so that no one could say which was done first. No doubt it was all for my own benefit. Jackson's behavior was flawless. No prancing around, bleating, jumping into the pool as he had done when the big Cherokee was baptized.

When it was over, there was not the brief ritualistic embrace of groom and bride. The long, deep kiss lasted until the guard with the shotgun, who had stood at a polite military parade rest position throughout the service, cleared his throat with a loud *ugh uh* sound. I got him aside and asked him if it would be all right if the couple went inside the cabin for just ten minutes. He said his orders were to be with the prisoner at all times. "They can go inside if they want to. We're not due back in West Nashville for another hour and a half. And, preacher, they can do anything they damn well want to. They can screw like two horny minks if they want to. But I'm going to be right there with them." I didn't pursue it.

* * *

"What did you mean about me being all bogged down in the sacraments?" I asked T.J. the next time we were together. We were on a plane going to a peace rally in Washington.

"Ah, no big deal," he said, shrugging, looking out the window like he didn't want to talk about it.

"I think it is a big deal," I said. "I mean, with you. It's no big deal with me. You know, I don't set those things up. Don't ever do any of them the same way twice. Don't take them all that seriously. They just happen. People want them."

"You give people everything they want?" he said, a bit testily. "Ross Barnett wants segregation forever."

"Come on, ole friend, get off my back. Segregation isn't a sacrament."

"Then you do believe in them," he shot back.

"What the hell's going on?" I protested. "I believe in God and original sin. You told me one time you didn't believe in anything *you* do. Said you didn't believe in prayer because you might not pray right. Remember that? Well, I don't *believe in* the ceremonial things I do. People ask for them and I do them. God can take it from there."

"Why'd you baptize that little black baby? You think he would have gone to hell if you hadn't?"

"I don't *think* anything. I did it because his daddy wanted it done, wanted to be there when it was done, and for all he knows he won't ever see the damned big steel gates shut behind him."

"I don't know, Preacher. Maybe I take it more seriously than you do. I just know down in Alabama we had the Lord's Supper once a quarter and baptized folks in the river when they joined the church on their own accord."

Of course, that's the way we did it down in Mississippi too. Now it was I who didn't want to talk about it. T.J. sensed it. "Aw, don't sweat it man. You're just a good ole nigger-loving preacher. You keep doing that and the Lord won't hold all that catholic stuff against you."

Sacrament or ordinance. Two, seven, six, or nine. Despite my friend's demurral, the ceremonials of Forty Acres and a Goat continued. The Baptist genes could not standardize or institutionalize them. Yet I found myself wishing for more of them. Historically they have been divisive. Still they have a way of bringing and holding a people together. From a farm mother in Mississippi rolling unleavened dough for the "sake-ree-ment" to the splendor of the Pope at St. Peter's of Rome at high mass, there is the mystery. And mysteries will not go away.

Footwashing. What happened to it? The instruction of Jesus on washing each other's feet is as clear as the authority for Holy Communion. Even more emphatic. The remnant of footwashing remains, but only as the Pope does it at the Vatican on Maunday Thursday, and a few people who call themselves Primitive Baptist gather each spring and do it.

Snakehandling. There is Biblical authority for it. I have seen mountain men and women reach into screen cages, pull out a handful of the hissing, rattling, slithering pit vipers, their elliptical eyes foretelling death in the pale light of kerosene lamps, pass them around, hurl them over every part of their bodies, placing them finally upon the floor, running their stocking feet along their slinking spines, the evil they represented conquered. I know that I will never lift up a serpent. I'm educated. Sophisticated. I don't believe *anything* that much anymore. I was taught that Mark 16:18 is a later addition to the original text. Though they neglected to tell me that *everything* is a later addition. I know that I won't ever observe this sacrament with them. But way down deep, I wish that perhaps, someday, maybe, I just might.

The Sacrament of Friendship. Certainly when Mother Teresa takes the time to bathe the body of a dying indigent on the streets of Calcutta, rather than use that precious time to minister to the needs of the living, so that the dying one might at least depart this life with the dignity of a clean body, surely she is within the sacerdotal code. And surely she is acting as a priest, a mediator between God and human, no matter the withheld hands of the bishops.

Gordon Jennings was my friend. My buddy. The distance of years, formal education, and attitudes on social issues did not separate us. We worked the fields together, built my log cabin together, went on journeys together. His problems were mine and mine his. We shared them. When he was a young man, he tore down an old, abandoned barn and discovered that the timbers were made of wild cherry. Though he had never had a course in aesthetics, he saw the beauty through the dirt, cobwebs, cow manure, and decay. When he was old, he made beautiful sculpture from what he rescued; walking canes with four balls carved inside the staff. His vision served as my eulogy for him when he died.

"What a pair of jugs," he said of a female bank teller as we sat at her window in my pickup truck, cashing a check to get some Krystal hamburgers.

"You silly goose," I scolded as we drove away. "She heard what you said."

"Oh, hell. She couldn't hear me. There was a glass window between us."

"Well, couldn't you hear her?"

"Well, yeah. But there was a speaker on our side of the window."

"Yeah. And there's one on her side too."

He was so upset by what he had done he asked me to assign him penance. When I declined, he did it himself. He vowed he would never again make such a remark about a woman's body. For Gordon, it wasn't an easy penance.

Gordon was what the lexicon means by machismo. He had no tolerance for the slightest deviation in he-man traits. Yet when he was dying, we sat late into many nights, holding hands, expressing our love for each other. And when the end came, I quarreled with an overseer of a Methodist steeple over my right to preside, as I had promised him I would. Gordon was my friend. He was my counselor. And I was his.

Counseling. If we are going to reconvene the Council of Lyons and reconsider the number of sacraments, perhaps it should be among those considered. Counseling is often arrogant, generally presumptuous, and sometimes so professionalized as to be uncaring. But it does exist. Just as I was about to go to bed one night, a black neighbor called. He was old and illiterate. He said he had to talk to me and asked me to meet him halfway to his house. Jackson was sleeping in the back of my pickup, so I put a leash on him and let him go along. When I got to the spot we had named, I found Mr. Kilborn sitting beside the road. He got in, spoke, and began to cry.

"Oh, Mr. Campbell! My heart hurts. Mr. Campbell, my heart

hurts." He said it over. "My heart hurts just so bad."

"Mr. Kilborn, are you sick? You want to go to the doctor?" I asked.

"No, sir, I don't want to go to no doctor. No doctor can help me. My heart just hurts so bad."

I drove back to our house and we sat under one of the big oak trees. "You've got to tell me what's wrong, neighbor. Is there something you want to talk about?"

Finally he was ready. He took a blue bandana out of his pocket, blew his nose, and apologized for crying. I told him I would cry too if it would help. "Mr. Campbell, I raised six young'uns. I give up on every one of them except that baby girl. She never give me no trouble. Got one in the penitentiary. Two in California. One in Detroit. Other one I don't know where is. Up North somewhere. Think that's where he is. My baby never give me no trouble." He started to cry again.

"It's all right, Mr. Kilborn. Ain't nothing wrong with crying. Cry all you want to. But then tell me what's wrong with your baby."

"Oh, Mr. Campbell. My heart hurts just so bad."

When he could talk again, he told me that he had saved his money since she was a little girl. She always wanted to be a nurse. When she finished high school, she had enrolled in nurse's training. He was so proud of her. His baby girl was going to wear a starched uniform. Wear a white cap and take care of sick folks. That's all she ever wanted to do, he said.

"Then this morning they called me from down at the hospital. Said she was in the hospital. Scared me real bad."

He walked to the highway, caught a bus, and went to town to see about her. When he got there, she was asleep. A nurse asked him if he wanted to see the baby.

"She took me way down this hall. Pulled some blinds open and pointed to a little tiny baby lying there. That was the first thing I knew about no baby." He cried so hard this time that he went into a fit of coughing, and I was afraid he would smother.

So far as he knew, she had never had a boyfriend. When her mother left them, she was a little girl. He raised them as best he could. He had seen her a few months earlier and suspected nothing. The baby's father had no intention of marrying her, and she was going to keep the baby. The old man's heart did hurt. It was breaking.

I went in the house, got a bottle of bourbon, and we started riding the roads. I tried to get Jackson to stay, but he wanted to ride in the truck. Several miles from home I pulled over and showed Mr. Kilborn a huge, baronial house silhouetted against the bright sky. "You see that house, Enos?"

"Yessir. Used to do their yard for them."

"Did you know they have a grandbaby too?"

"Nosir. They ain't got no grandbabies. They got two girls but both of them went off to school. Doing well, so they tell me. But they ain't married. Twins, I believe they was."

"Well, they do have a grandbaby. Only it's dead. They sent one of the twin girls off to New York. She was pregnant. Just like your daughter was. Only she didn't have it. She had an abortion. Their baby never saw daylight outside the womb. Wonder why your daughter didn't do that? She knows all about that sort of thing."

"Oh, Mr. Campbell. She wouldn't never do nothing like that. She's a good girl. She wouldn't do nothing like that."

"Then be proud of her," I said, passing the bottle to him. He took a long pull, twisted the cap back on, wiped his mouth with the back of his hand, and put it on the seat between us.

"You better not be drinking none of that stuff, Mr. Campbell. Driving this old truck out here on the highway. Don't want nothing to happen to you on my account."

We drove north for a few more miles, around Old Hickory Lake and into a new development of big houses. I stopped at the driveway of one of them. By then it was well past midnight. "You know who lives there?" He said he didn't. "They have a grandson too, but they never saw him. Their daughter was about to finish college. All at once she dropped out of school. They said she was having some problems and was out West visiting an aunt. You know where she was? In a Florence Crittenton Home. You know what that is?" He said he didn't. "That's where girls go to be pregnant when they're going to give their babies away. At least most of the time. And that's what their girl did. She had the baby but didn't bring him home. Someone else took him home. She put him up for adoption."

"Oh, Mr. Campbell. What I'm going to do?" He was sipping often from the bottle.

"I'll tell you what you're going to do, Enos, if I know what kind of a man you are. And I think I do. We've been neighbors for a long time. Tomorrow's Sunday and neither one of us has anything special to do. We're going to Nashville. You're going to go up in that elevator, walk in your baby daughter's room, tell her you love her, that you're proud of her for not acting like white folks, and ask her when she and the baby will be coming home. That's what you're going to do."

He began to laugh and cry at once, tapping his fingers on his knee in cadence with the churning of the motor. We drove back to his house, a cabin not much bigger than my log house office, sat on his front porch passing the bottle back and forth until the sun came up. We talked about the crops and the weather. Listened to the whippoorwills calling that the season was here to plant corn, watched a red fox chasing a rabbit in the moonlight, and put a setting of eggs under a Dominick hen. He pulled an old car tire from underneath the porch and said it would make a fine swing for his grandson. As near as I could tell, Jackson didn't move all night. I told Mr. Kilborn I was tired of a man old enough to be my daddy calling me Mister. He tried several times to call me Will but finally gave up. Said that was the way he was raised and he was too old to do anything about it. As the morning sun streamed through his east kitchen window, we fried some thick bacon and scrambled some eggs. We laughed a lot.

That afternoon we went to Nashville.

* * *

I wonder if there is something comparable to the sacramental within the animal kingdom. I believe there is. I know there is kindness, generosity, and forgiveness. As Nell grew old, she slowly went blind. I began to notice that she always walked behind Jackson. When he moved at a smooth pace, she stayed right with him. If he walked or ran erratically, she fell behind. Got confused. As the blindness progressed, he learned that she was depending on him for guidance. When it was complete, he would walk gently along to and from the grazing area, carefully avoiding any obstacles along the way. At dusk they could be seen moving slowly and deliberately across the hillside toward the barn, Nell swinging her head from side to side a few paces behind

Jackson, close enough to follow the scent.

When she died, he grieved. We were in Louisiana for a funeral. A neighbor found Nell down, unable to stand up. He called the veterinarian. He came and examined her, as he had many times before, but said she would never get up. He recommended euthanasia. The neighbor called it putting her to sleep. They couldn't reach us and the doctor wouldn't do it unless we approved. The neighbor got five other men to help him pry and pick her up, but her paralyzed legs would not support her weight. The next day he made the decision.

It was a long time before any of them would talk about it. And when one of them did, in a mild state of drunkenness, I didn't want to hear it.

"That damn goat was just standing off to one side watching. When Bud shot that damned old mare between the eyes with that ought-thirty deer rifle, she bellowed like a bull moose. Damned if she didn't throw her front legs straight out, raise up on her hind quarters, and damn if she didn't stand up straight as a scarecrow."

I tried not to listen but he went on. Nell stood erect for a moment, Jackson quivering beside her. When she crashed to the ground with a heavy thud, he bleated in rapid bursts. As the men described the scene, I could see Jackson recoiling in horror and outrage.

They tried to coax him to the barn, but he stood beside her body and refused to leave. When they buried her the next day, he stood close and watched as the bulldozer dug the grave and pushed her into it. For two days and nights he kept the silent fast and vigil, refusing the grain and water they brought. When we returned and I led him away on a leash, he walked a few paces, bleated, turned and looked back. He did it over and over until we were out of sight.

If Jackson did not know of sacraments, he knew of mourning. Perhaps there should be the sacrament of mourning. Maybe in the animal kingdom there is.

IX
Help of the Helpless

"LET'S GO DRINK some Falstaff," T.J. said, letting the door slam shut. I was renting a fifty-dollar-a-month office in Nashville while we were doing some work on the log office in the hollow.

"You still drinking that stuff?" I asked. "I thought they signed a truce," referring to the earlier boycott of the White Citizens Councils against the Falstaff company.

"Guess they did," he said. "But even muthas like us, Toms and white liberals, have to keep up our image."

"Want to hear my White Paper No. 1?" I asked him, pulling a yellow sheet of paper from my typewriter.

"Looks like a yellow paper to me," he said. "What's a white paper?"

"You know what a white paper is. Don't give me that dumb coon bit again. I'm not up to it today."

"He grinned and scratched his head. "Naw suh, Mister Will. I jus' knows what a black paper is." Then he added in his real voice, "You redneck!"

"All right, Eaves. I won't call you boy, and don't you call me redneck. One's as bad as the other."

He sat down across from the desk, and I began reading what I had written.

SPECIAL WHITE PAPER NO. 1

FOR IMMEDIATE RELEASE TO ALL A.M. PAPERS

A committee to investigate the Los Angeles Riot was appointed by the Committee of Southern Churchmen shortly before the riot began.

The committee, composed of highly Vanderbilt degreed and skilled doctors, all of whom are experienced researchers, investigators, and profiles in courage, agreed that such a study should include not only Watts, Los Angeles, but Selma, Alabama; Americus, Georgia; Bogalusa, Louisiana; Chicago, Illinois.

PREMISE: Basic causes underlying Watts, Los Angeles, will correspond to basic causes underlying Selma, Alabama; Americus, Georgia; Bogalusa, Louisiana; Chicago, Illinois.*

The report of the committee follows:

We have done those things which
we ought not to have done and
we have left undone those things
which we ought to have done.

*(In this analysis, the scores were dichotomized at the median [25 or above; 23 below] and the chi square 2×2 test used. In the present instance $P > .01$; $df = 1$)

T.J. didn't laugh when I finished reading as I had hoped. "Well, what do you think?" I asked as he continued the same awkward pose he had taken when I started. For a moment I thought he was insulted by it. The Watts riots, the most serious of all the series of racial conflicts which gripped the nation in the mid-sixties, were still in the news, and I wondered if he thought I had not taken the suffering of Negro residents of Watts seriously. Abuse by white policemen had triggered it. Thirty-four people were killed, nearly 900 injured, more than 3500 arrested — some for no more serious offense than standing outside their homes. Certainly, I hoped, my friend knew that I didn't consider such an outrage comical.

"The old chi square, two times two test, eh?" he began, rubbing his hands briskly as if he was washing them. "P is greater than .01, huh? And df equals one. Now, what the hell does all that gibberish mean?" His voice sounded more troubled, puzzled than angry.

"Look, T.J." I started out. "I'm sorry. I hope you don't think that I think it's funny if five thousand of your people . . . uh . . . I mean . . . our people . . . God's people . . . oh, shit, T.J. I'm sorry. I didn't mean to offend you. Or anybody. Here, I'll throw the damn thing away. I was just trying to be cute. That's all." I threw it in the waste basket. He leaned over, picked it up, and began smoothing the wrinkles out of the wadded sheet, placing it flat on top of my desk.

"No, no, no," he said. "I know what you're doing. Even know why you're calling it a white paper and putting it on yellow paper. I know what the chi square two times two, p is greater than something or other, df equals one means."

"You do?!" I exclaimed. "Well, damned if you don't know more than I do. Not that there's anything new about that. I don't have the foggiest notion of what it means. I copied that footnote out of an article some sociology professor wrote about the Rochester riots. All that was actually in it. Good Lord! White cops breaking down doors of black citizens, cracking heads, rummaging dresser drawers, turning over furniture, scaring little children half to death, then having it all explained with that bullshit. Jesus! If you know what it means, I wish to hell you would enlighten me!"

"It means what you said: bullshit." His voice was calm. He handed the sheet back to me. "Yeah, I know what the chi square, df equals one means. It means you're getting about as tired of me being studied with a slide rule as I have been for a long time. It means the problem in this country is hate. And we're not going to get rid of it by spending a million dollars for one more godawful research project."

"Maybe it's just too much to expect white scholars to understand the ways of the ghetto," I said. As soon as I did it, I knew he wasn't going to let my self-righteous inanity go unchallenged.

"White *scholars* or white *people*?" he corrected. "Don't forget the truckload of tomatoes you brought us that time," he added.

Two summers earlier we had a bumper crop of tomatoes and couldn't sell them. I had to go to a meeting at a black church in town and thought I would give them away to poor people in the ghetto. I loaded the pickup truck with as many as it would hold and planned to go from door to door leaving as many as they wanted at each house.

"Would you like to have a peck or so of tomatoes? Won't cost you anything."

"No!"

Sometimes I got nothing more than a slamming of the door. After a dozen tries with the same response, I parked the truck and went to the meeting. When I returned an hour or so later, the truck was empty. Except for a few scattered on the sidewalk, dropped and stepped on in an apparent scramble, there was no sign of tomatoes. T.J. told me I should have known better.

"You see, white folks say we don't want to work. Not true. It's just that the only work some of us can find is stealing. Which can be hard work and hazardous sometimes. Those black people weren't about to have some white mutha thinking he was doing them a favor — think he was giving them something for nothing. But if they got their own bucket, walked down that hot street, maybe even have to push a bunch of other folks out of the way to get their share, well . . . that's working for a living."

Remembering that incident, I felt an uneasy kinship with those white scholars.

I began talking about a conference of Social Scientists I had attended at the Waldorf-Astoria Hotel, trying this time to keep my own self-righteous rhetoric in tow. I remembered listening to formal papers read by scholars from New York, New Haven, and Boston on, "Viewing the Civil Rights Crisis for New Research." I recalled overlooking the rich scene beneath us, thinking about the backroads and eddies of the South, the tenant farmer shacks, their often hungry occupants, occupants more concerned with survival than either new research for tenured professors or where their children went to school. I thought of separate but equal social events like watermelon cuttings, candy pulls, peanut boilings, and fish fries, and I wondered for a moment if where we were trying to go would finally be an improvement over where we had been. I thought back to integrated hog killings, log rollings, cotton picking, and barn buildings. And the houses poor people, black and white, lived in, urban and rural, which had never been segregated. But I remembered too the most blatant products of bigotry — black children walking barefoot to a school which lasted four months of the year and ended with six grades, while I rode a school bus to our nine-month school which continued for twelve grades. I heard the baying of the hounds of hate and words of the wounded fanatic, John Brown, as he was interrogated by the governor of Virginia. "You had better — all you people at the South — prepare yourselves for a settlement of this question. . . . You may dispose of me very easily — I am nearly disposed of now — but this question is still to be settled, this Negro question, I mean; the end of that is not yet." And his final written words before he was hanged: "I, John Brown, am quite certain that the crimes of this guilty land will never be purged away but with blood." The echo of three hundred children, all of us white, gathered for daily Bible reading and prayer in the East Fork Consolidated School in Amite County, Mississippi, gustily singing

> John Brown's body lies a-molding in the grave,
> John Brown's body lies a-molding in the grave,
> John Brown's body lies a-molding in the grave,
> His truth goes marching on. Glory, glory, hallelujah . . .

And of eyes that had seen the glory of the coming of the Lord. Seeing no more contradiction in what we sang and prayed, and the everyday life in the culture of which we were a part, than the chairman of the gathered scholars saw in his shushing of the black waiters preparing to feed us a hefty lunch behind the bellowsed dividing wall with the impatient yell, "You're disturbing our meeting," while we discussed their plight on our side of the wall.

I told T.J. about knowing at the time that the most honorable thing I could do would be to break wind and find the elevator that would take me to the real world. Instead I settled for the more modest witness, "My friends, we already know more than we can stand," when I was asked to respond to one of the monographs. I might have added the warning that a molting morality seemed inevitably to follow affluence and that it was being manifest at that very moment. But I didn't.

"Things do get all mixed up, don't they, Brother Will?" T.J. said. Then he told me about the time his great aunt, traveling through Virginia to care for the children of the Alabama white family she worked for, had to sit in the car while the mother and children toured Appomatox Courthouse.

"The mother?" I asked.

"Yeah. The Colonel stayed in the car drinking whiskey and trying to play with Auntie's secrets," he said. He pronounced it äuntie.

"Trying?" I said. "Why didn't he just make her let him do it. I thought that was the way that worked."

"Not him," he said. "Auntie said he was a kind man. A real good man."

"Holy Jesus," I said.

"Yeah, Brother Will. Things do get all mixed up. Auntie got freed, but she couldn't go in and see where it got done to her," he laughed.

"Gracious shit," I said.

He moved about the room, picking up ash trays, magazines, moving chairs aimlessly. He stood for a long time staring out the window, tapping on the glass with his knuckle like he was trying to scare something away.

"Will," he said when he had returned to his seat across from my desk. "There's something I've been meaning to ask you." He didn't generally call me Will. Most of the time it was Brother Will, Will Campbell, Reverend, Bro, Mutharoe, sometimes just Campbell, but seldom Will. Somehow I liked it.

"Shoot," I said, moving to a chair on his side of the desk. "I guess it's open season on bootleg preachers."

"Why do you use such dirty language?" He asked it the way a pious mother might ask a teen-age son.

"Because I'm a big boy now," I said, trying to laugh.

"No, I'm serious," he said, not even smiling. "Why do you use such dirty language? I know you weren't raised like that. And you're a preacher. At least some kind of a preacher. Me too. I slip sometimes. But you do it all the time. Anyway, among us colored folks, some words aren't considered so bad. But white preachers aren't supposed to talk that way. Why do you do it?"

I told him about a mountain mother I knew who tried hard to break her forty-year-old son, slightly retarded by our standards of measuring intelligence, from using bad language at the table. His favorite was, "Aw shit!" One day I was eating Sunday dinner with them and she was especially ruffled that he kept saying it. Finally she said, "Now, son, if you don't stop using that awful word in front of company I'm going to make you leave the table and go to your room. Can't you find another word?"

He looked a little confused and hurt. "Aw Maw, people would laugh at me. . . . I mean a big ole boy like me saying 'Aw do-do' "

T.J. still didn't laugh, just kept looking me squarely in the face. I knew he intended to make me be serious.

I tried another story. I told him about my friend Thad Garner, an iconoclastic preacher in Louisiana who was once a guest on a radio talk show in Monroe. "Don't ever make the mistake of being on one of those things," he told me. "They have a network of nuts who call in. They're all crazy. They're all fascist. And they're all mean as hell," he advised. "It's some kind of an army. A geriatric battalion of morons. They have Top Sergeants, and it's their job to locate the gonads as soon as you're introduced and alert the troops. And for the rest of the hour, you better keep you hands in your lap."

As he was driving to the studio, he listened to the callers bombarding the hostess of the show as to what she thought about Johnny Cash using a bad word on national television the night before. The woman, whose station also owned the television channel on which the program had appeared, was having a hard time placating them. Just yes or no. Did she or did she not think it was all right for Johnny Cash to pollute the airways with his foul language? Thad knew that as soon as he was introduced as being a preacher, the switchboard would light up. He had a plan.

A high-pitched voice, creaking with age and hostility, was the first caller. "Martha Lee," she began. "I want to ask your guest what he thinks about Johnny Cash using ugly language on TV. Since he's a preacher, I think I know what he'll say."

Before the hostess of the show could field the question, Thad was answering. "I don't know, ma'am. What did he say?"

The startled guest hesitated, stammered, then said, "Welllll. I can't repeat it. It was a bad word and I don't say bad words."

"I understand, ma'am," Thad said quickly. "I'm glad you don't say bad words. Now, I tell you what. I know some bad words, so I'll call them out one by one, and you just tell me yes or no if that's what he said. Okay. Here goes." He was barking like a drill sergeant.

The hostess motioned the engineer to have his finger close to the four-second-delay button. Get ready to bleep.

"Did he say 'death'?" He was speaking more softly now.

"Wellll. No," the woman said in the same grating voice.

"Very good," Thad said. "Did he say 'nuclear war'?"

"Wellll. No. That's not what he said." Her voice was showing irritation.

"Good. Okay. Did he say 'electric chair'?"

The engineer had moved away from the bleep button, watching Thad through the glass with amusement and approval. There was a long pause. Thad waited for the woman to answer. Instead there was the noise of the heavy slamming of the telephone.

"I'm sorry you left us, ma'am. Hope you're still listening. That's three of the nastiest, filthiest, ugliest, most vile words I know. If Johnny Cash didn't say any of those, and if you can't tell me what he did say, well, I guess I can't help you."

During the exchange the call-waiting lights had been going off one by one. The interviewer moved to a series of commercials, then brought on the next guest.

"Will, why do you use dirty language?" T.J. asked again when I finished the story and began filling my pipe. He spoke as though he was asking it for the first time. As if I hadn't even told the story of Thad.

"Okay, Buddyroe," I said. "The old 'hold his feet to the fire' game, eh. I'm not sure what this is about. How you suddenly got to be Mr. Purity. But you're right, I wasn't raised that way. I never heard my daddy or mamma say 'shucks,' or 'darn,' or 'heck.' On the other hand, if Mamma was especially vexed she had a preferred way of expressing it. 'Shit, and dabble in it!' she would exclaim. It was my earliest introduction to literary imagery. I could see hands, fingers with long nails, dipping, dabbling, and dripping."

T.J. had not moved. I imagined him thinking, "I'll make him squirm."

"Get it, Buddyroe?" I said. "Everything is relative."

"You going to tell me or not?" T.J. said, showing no expression. He had hit a nerve and knew it. Actually I was not at all comfortable with off-color language. Despite my mother's occasional burst of imagery, it wasn't part of my culture. Wasn't the way I was raised. But I was beginning to be annoyed by T.J.'s seeming self-righteous excursion.

A few months earlier we had watched a parade of the Free Speech of Berkeley Movement. Hundreds of young men and women, some of them almost naked, openly rolling and smoking marijuana cigarettes, flaunting their bodies along with crude and obscene posters. "FUCK THE BOMB!" was the sign most often seen. I confessed at the time that I found it offensive and wished they could find another way to protest. Yet it was T.J. who pointed out the inconsistency of a nation being outraged at the words, "Fuck the Bomb," but sitting calmly and unaffected in their living rooms watching live coverage of the bomb killing a mother's suckling baby.

I reminded him of our conversation. "So you're just trying to make a point, huh?" he said.

"Sure, I'm trying to make a point," I snapped, my voice louder than I intended. "Everytime anyone opens their mouth they're trying to make a point. Otherwise there's no use to say anything ever. You say, 'Good morning,' and you're trying to make a point."

"Maybe," he said, not convinced. "But I still think you ought to dress up your language. You're beginning to get a little following, you know. Don't mess it up trying to prove a point."

"A following?" I said, slightly shaken and surprised. "I don't *want* a following. Disciples would scare the living sh . . . uh, heck out of me. If I looked back and saw a bunch of people following me, I'd fall to pieces." He stood smiling as my voice got louder again. "I'm trying to *be* a disciple. Not attract them," I said, lowering my voice. "What's your game now, T.J. Eaves?"

"No game, Will. You have to do what you have to do. But just be sure it's what the Man wants you to do."

"Long as I love Him enough to risk going to hell for Him, I guess everything's cool."

"Hope so," he said.

I had the feeling that he wasn't finished with his pedagogy. For the first time it occurred to me that perhaps I had felt superior to him in the past. I wasn't feeling exactly inferior, but all at once I realized that there had not been real equality between us before. The thought that white people such as I were in race relations to upgrade black people, like the Yankee missionaries who had come South after the Civil War, had not hit me before either. Maybe it was recollecting the experience with the Social Scientists in New York.

For a moment I felt perplexed and downright silly. I was a graduate of two of the nation's top universities. T.J. was an off-and-on student in an unaccredited Bible college. In the past when I had considered our academic span, I had used my humble rearing to balance the academic credentials. Now I knew the span was meaningless, that wisdom does not come from class notes and lecture halls. I should have learned that from Uncle Coot. If my motivation in the struggle was to elevate a man such as T.J. Eaves, I was a fool. The sudden realization that T.J., a black man, much younger than I, far behind me in educational achievement, was my teacher and was probably smarter than I was disquieting.

"T.J., somebody ought to give you a grant," I said. "Some big foundation ought to give you a direct grant."

"A grant?" he said, starting to go into his monkey act, then deciding against it. "Man, I have a grant. I been called. I reckon that's grant enough for me."

"No, I'm serious. You know what that fuc . . . uh, that New York conference I was talking about cost?" He said he had no idea and didn't really care. "Well, I'd guess ten thousand dollars. Each presenter got five hundred to prepare and read his paper to about a dozen other presenters who got five hundred to read their paper to him."

"I believe that's called the high cost of education, Bro."

"How long could you get by on ten thousand dollars?" I asked.

"Well, that's about three times what I get by on every year now," he answered. "You figure it out. But, like I say, I got a grant."

"And the workman is worthy of his hire," I said. "You're an important man in this crisis, T.J. And you ought to get paid."

"Aw, man. Who you kidding? Important? Man, I ain't for jive." Then he did go into his hambone act. "An' say wat? Crisis? Wat crisis. I ain't seed no crisis. Ain't nothing no different to me. White folks be de one wid de crisis. Colored folks, things be de same."

"Knock if off, T.J. You do that every time you want to put me down."

He was straight again. "I'm not trying to put you down, Will Campbell. But I do get weary of white folks talking about the civil rights crisis. You know what a crisis is?" I told him I thought I did. "Well, I'm going to tell you what a crisis is. When white folks got their foot on a black neck and he just stays down, doesn't complain, that's called harmonious race relations. But let him start plucking the hair around that white cat's ankle, maybe squirming, struggling a little bit to get up, maybe look up and say, 'Hey, man, you got your foot on my neck. How 'bout letting me get up?' That's called a civil rights crisis. And that's when you start reading papers to one another about it."

I wanted to answer but couldn't think of anything to say. I knew he was still the teacher, but I was uncomfortable with the day's lesson. I thought of begging his pardon for past offenses; acts of patronage and condescension, every deigning presumption, all the random, inadvertent but real insults I knew I had committed. I knew, though, that he was not asking for that, didn't want it and would prefer that I didn't bring it up. At least not then and in that context. Finally I said, somewhat hesitantly, "Okay. I'm a white man. I can't help that."

"Now you got it," he said quickly. "You're a white man. You can't help it. And your people, white people, got a crisis. And you can help. You can be a leader. I can't. You know that. Black people have plenty of leaders now. I'm not Martin Luther King, Jr., and I'm not Ralph Bunche, and I'm not Thurgood Marshall. I'm T.J. Eaves, colored boy from Alabama."

"Now wait a frazzling minute," I broke in. "You're . . ."

"Hear me out, Will," he snapped. "I know you're not a Movement man. And I'm not either. But we're in it. Somewhere. Somehow. And we need all the friends we can get. Especially all the white friends we can get." I was confused, did not know where he was heading. "You know a lot of people call me a Tom, don't you?" I said I did. "But do you know what some good white folks are starting to call you?" I nodded that I didn't. "Well, I'm your friend, so I'm going to tell you. Don't worry about it and let it upset you, but they're calling you a self-styled anti-intellectual. That's what. My people. . . . And don't ever apologize to me again for saying 'your people.' I'm a Negro and you're white. We try to jump the ditch, and we've come closer than I ever thought we would. I never had a white buddy before. But you have people and I have people. My people call me an Uncle Tom and your people — some of them — call you an anti-intellectual." There was a long pause. "Don't you even care?" he asked in an imploring sort of way.

I was dumbfounded. Couldn't believe what I was hearing. I had never given a lot of thought to any sort of self-image. When I had it wasn't of a self-styled anti-intellectual. One has to be some kind of an intellectual to be anti-intellectual, and I didn't consider myself an egg-head. I had eight years of higher education, but that didn't make me a scholar. It had not occurred to me that I was in any way opposed to the world of scholarship, to that of which I had been a part.

"I'm just telling you," he continued, "if you let your White Paper No. 1 get around over there at Vanderbilt, you're going to lose some friends. If you don't care, well, you don't care. And I don't care."

There was another long pause as I considered what was taking place. It had begun with my thinking I had offended him. Then I learned that he knew more of what I was trying to say than I did. Now he had become my counselor, not thinking of himself at all but of what was best for me. Having a young, uneducated, black counselor was more daunting than realizing for the first time that he was smarter than I. When he continued, it was to relieve my uneasiness. "Cause I'se just a dum' nigger boy."

"Well, of course I care," I stammered, ignoring his Sambo act. "Nobody wants to lose friends. But I'm not mad at anyone. I mean, I'm not aiming at anyone in particular."

"You know that. And I know that," he said. "But they'll think you're making fun of them. And I think you are too."

"Well, hell. I'm not," I protested. "I mean, you know, I thought. . . . T.J., those guys are my friends, my cohorts. They'll know that I'm just trying to be cute." I took the paper and read through it again. "You actually think they won't know that this crap — dichotomized at the median twenty-five or above; twenty-three below and the chi square two times two test used . . . P is greater than .01; df equals one — that using that jabberwocky in a report of a reign of death in a ghetto . . . don't you think they'll see that one has to laugh at it to keep from crying?"

"Nope," he said, rubbing his hands the same way he had before. "I really don't."

"Damned if you ain't laid one on me," I said. I recalled having wondered why I didn't get as many invitations to speak, meet with classes, and such as I once had. I thought it was because race was becoming passé. I knew there had been resentment by some people at Vanderbilt when Jim Lawson was expelled from the Divinity School at the beginning of the Sit-in Movement. He and I were friends. He was married to the woman who was my secretary at the time, and it was generally known that I had strongly urged him not to resign from school. "If you've got to leave, make the bastards kick you out," I had told him. But I hadn't seen that as any big thing. There were many inside the university who took a stand with a lot more to lose than I. At one point almost the entire Divinity School faculty resigned until they were assured of concessions. The Medical School faculty threatened the same. My opposition was to the administration, the structures, the policy, not individuals who held the same views as I. I told T.J. all that.

"I'm just telling you," he repeated, "that they'll think you're making fun of them. And that I do too. Only difference is, I think they *need* making fun of. It's a religion with them. And folks don't like to have their religion made fun of."

By then I was no longer confused or surprised. I was mad. I wasn't sure at what or whom, but I knew I was mad.

"Anti-intellectual, eh? Okay. If that's the game, let's play it. If I can't remember the rules, I'll make them up."

I typed fresh copies of White Paper No. 1 on yellow sheets and together we drove to Vanderbilt University and stuck them on every bulletin board we could find.

"You know," T.J. said as we drove away, "someday I may be the only friend you'll have left. A Mississippi honky with an Alabama nigger for his only friend. Now ain't that a mess!" He slapped his knee, reached over, and held the horn on for a full block as we moved down Twenty-first Avenue.

"I'd still consider myself rich," I said when the noise of the horn stopped. And I felt strangely comforted. And freer. Though not free. Just freer.

* * *

"Is this a white dog with black spots or a black dog with white spots?" T.J. asked. Dottie, the big friendly Dalmatian, had come lumbering out to welcome him. He had gone back to Selma when most of the civil rights organizations decided to combine forces after the Pettus Bridge rout and conduct a massive Selma to Montgomery March. For the first time he had been a minor leader in the week-long activities and had stayed on for several weeks assisting in the voter registration.

Dozens of celebrities had been flown in to boost morale and entertain the participants — Tony Bennett, Sidney Poitier, Sammy Davis, Jr., James Baldwin, Eartha Kitt, Paul Newman, Marlon Brando, Harry Belafonte, and many others. T.J. served as escort, or non-violent bodyguard, to one of them but couldn't be sure if it was Brando or Newman. "All white people look alike to me," he teased.

He was not his old self but was cheerful and cordial. He gave me a day-by-day report of the march and what he had done in registering black citizens during the summer. At times he made it sound like a vacation experience. But he grew somber when he talked about the competition, friction, and hostility among the different organizations. Because of the prestige of King, SCLC got most of the publicity and consequently was able to raise a lot of money. But it was the Southern Student Coordinating Committee that had started the march and whose people had been battered at the bridge. Everyone knew it was that outrage which had generated the national attention, gained the support and protection of President Johnson, and led to the success of the march as a media event and political victory. They resented the slighting by the press and financial contributors.

"Which outfit did you work for?" I asked T.J.

"You mean, who paid me?"

"Yeah. That too."

"Nobody paid me. It never came up. I paid my own way."

"Welcome to the club," I said. "Nobody's paying me right now either."

We talked of the irony of Sheriff Jim Clark, who instead of stopping the march with his violence became the one who had inspired thousands to rally to the Selma Movement and thus was directly responsible for the passage of the Voting Rights Act. "If he hadn't turned his posse loose on us that afternoon, we would have marched across the bridge a little way, then turned around and went home."

"You mean you really didn't intend to march on to Montgomery?" I asked, remembering that he had told me the same thing earlier.

"Aw, we said we was, but we didn't even have toothbrushes. And some of the women were wearing high heels and hose. Naw, we hadn't planned no fifty-mile march. And nobody would have paid much attention to the six o'clock news that Sunday evening. As it turned out, seeing women and children run down with quarter horses, hearing them bullwhips cracking against our hide, horses running up on people's porches and them trying to run inside, I reckon it was too much even for white folks."

I thought I saw him watch to see if I flinched at his last words. When I didn't, he went on. "Yeah, man, that cracker shit in his own nest." I'm sure the word "cracker" did make me flinch. "Then before it was over, you had fifty thousand folks down there, airplanes flying up over us, army all around us, all the cameras in the world looking under every bush that moved."

"How many people do you think you would have registered to vote if the High Sheriff had stayed on his side of the bridge, had let Wilson Baker and the Selma police handle it peacefully? I asked him, ignoring the cracker reference.

"Dozen or so all told, I'd say. Give or take a few. Man, the black folks was scared. The white folks had them scared. But after they saw how they was going to be whupped up on anyhow, whether they voted or not, what they got to lose?"

"So how many will get registered before it's over?" I asked.

"John Lewis figures about twelve, maybe fifteen thousand in the county. Ain't no turning back now. Man, we carried folks to the courthouse on stretchers."

"But what about the white folks?" I said. "Won't they be voting too? Won't they just outvote you?"

"Naw. Oh, sure. They be votin' too. But their womenfolks didn't have enough babies. Ain't enough of 'em. White folks won't ever run Dallas County, Alabama, again. That day is over and done for."

His speech was neither the burlesque he used when he wanted to nor his usual perfect grammar. He seemed comfortable with it, so I didn't comment. But it wasn't the diction that concerned me. It was what I was hearing.

White dog with black spots? Black dog with white spots? Segregation? Integration? What is Dottie the Dalmatian? It didn't bother me to hear T.J. say that the violent and fatuous Sheriff Clark was the best friend black people in Alabama had. *The Lord uses even the devils to praise Him.* I was troubled to think that we had waited too late for the ruling electorate to be black and white together. If the events of Selma, Alabama, were to be the flagship of racial justice, the portent of things to come, where was the nation heading? A part of me was feeling that white people had ruled long enough; now it's the black folk's turn. Yet if I believed that all people were equally good, I had to believe that all were equally bad. Black people, if they are compelled to run it as black people, won't prove any different from white people. That was what I was feeling. But I did not suspect and would not have believed that in just two decades one of the chief organizers and participants in the Selma Movement, Bernard LaFayette, who had by then become an outstanding educator with a Harvard doctorate and an impeccable reputation, would be summarily fired by an all-black board of education. For no more explainable reason than that they had the power and authority to do it. But it happened. Three counties away.

Dottie. Not named for her spots but for Dottie West, a favorite country singer. Dalmatian. Symbol of firefighters everywhere. I had somehow associated her with what we were about. With the Movement. Neither black *nor* white. Black *and* white. The presence of all colors and the absence of all colors. Blending and combining to form a beautiful and noble sweetheart. Gentle, compassionate, loving, supportive in dependence.

Dottie was poisoned and died. We were having an early supper one evening, getting ready to take Webb to his Little League baseball game. Dottie, lying near the kitchen table, got up to go outside for her leftovers as she always did. This time she stumbled and fell. She got up but had trouble. I thought at first it was because she was so fat that she scratched and struggled on the slick floor. When she didn't touch the table scraps, I knew something was wrong. She was breathing hard and I could see she was in terrible pain.

We couldn't reach our veterinarian. Brenda remembered that we had a friend who was a vet in another county, but that was thirty miles away. We called him and when we described the symptoms, he said he was sure she had strychnine poisoning. He said we could bring her over but doubted there would be enough time, that the only hope was to get her stomach emptied and give her something to slow the seizures. He told us that a young vet had recently moved to our community, and he would try to reach him. He called back and said that Dr. George Wright, whom he recommended highly and who had fine training, was waiting at his new clinic.

Dr. Wright, a stranger to us at the time, did all the right things, including staying up with her most of the night. When he called at seven the next morning, I knew what the news would be. Her age, the amount of strychnine in her system, and the expired time were all against her. Many people-doctors could learn from the sympathy and tenderness in the young vet's voice when he told us that our beloved Dottie was dead.

I can imagine a human being doing most anything. But as I rushed the three miles with Dottie beside me, her front legs stiff, head thrown back, writhing and crying with pain, unable to stand or lie down, I could not bring into focus a neighbor taking a biscuit from the cupboard, lacing it with a lethal dose of strychnine, getting in his car, and calmly dropping it to a trusting Dalmatian waiting at the end of the lane to bring her family the evening newspaper.

Some believe that the Movement was similarly poisoned. By whom? There are many suspects. I don't know. Webb had a prime suspect when Dottie was poisoned and in his grief suggested direct and violent measures of justice and revenge. It was an opportunity to discuss whether the two can ever be related. He is a lawyer now, and I hope he remembers the lesson.

The truth was we didn't know for sure who poisoned Dottie, our neither black nor white dog. Nor do I know what happened to the Movement. Long before the murder of Dr. King, it was waning. Some think that it was cunningly and cynically sabotaged by the liberal political power structure, betrayed on the Potomac by promises unkept and programs which did little for the rank and file of black Americans. Others say that it was the anger of young blacks who fanned the flames of ancient wrongs with cries of "Black Power!" until non-violent resistance was no longer an option. Still others say that racial change in America has always operated like a sieve, that the mesh opens up where there is trouble in the streets and lets a certain number of the oppressed into the mainstream of society, and when the clamor for relief stops, the mesh closes up. Many maintain that white power and the deep-seated and intense Negrophobia which has plagued this country from its inception prevailed and took the battle.

Of one thing I am certain: It was not destroyed by hooded vigilantes and flaming crosses. Nor by chains used on school children, dynamiting of churches and homes, mass jailings. All those things were an impetus to the Movement and brought determination to the victims.

Perhaps time ran out. The vet in the next county was too far away. The strychnine of oppression too long in the belly. I don't know. I know only that at its best, it was a powerful agency for change, led and directed by black minds, but in essence neither black nor white. And there are those still around who will not succumb to all the strychnine of intolerance and hate in the world.

But a body gets weary.

* * *

"You think we ought to go in?" I asked T.J. We had stopped at a roadside cafe in northern Alabama. I was supposed to speak to a Methodist youth meeting that night in Mobile. The place was sort of a cross between bait shop, restaurant, and country store. The store area looked old, the rest of it like it might have been added later.

"You scared to go in?" T.J. asked, waiting to open the car door until I answered. A public accommodations bill had been signed by President Johnson several months earlier but was not uniformly enforced, and some eating places, particularly in the rural areas, were as segregated as they ever were.

"Not scared," I said. "Just wondering."

"The law says we can go in," he said, opening the door and getting out.

"The law said Lincoln could go in Ford Theater too," I said, getting out and following him inside.

The breakfast customers, less than twenty, appeared to be mostly local. They were all men. The waitress, an attractive medium-sized woman about thirty-five, motioned us to a table for two by the door leading to the kitchen. "What'll it be?" she called from behind the counter. Her voice was noncommital. Not hostile but not overly friendly either.

"Coffee and a plain doughnut for me," I answered.

"Could we see a menu?" T.J. asked, shifting his chair to where he could see the kitchen door as well as the front area.

"In a minute," the woman said in the same manner as before. Some of the men sitting in small groups talked in hushed tones, pretending not to notice us.

A pickup truck with "Triple Z Devon Cattle" printed on the side stopped directly in front. The first four notes of "How Dry I Am" blared from two long horns mounted on top of the club cab. It repeated three times. "Here comes crazy Delma," someone called to the waitress from across the room.

"One minute late," she said, glancing at a Double Cola clock on the far wall.

"Gooood morning, all!" the man, a short, rotund fellow who looked no more than fifty, sang out as soon as he had pushed open the door. He sang the words with the same tune as the horn. Most of the men nodded but said nothing. He stood for a few seconds surveying the room, then began whistling the same notes he and the truck horn had sounded, aiming the whistling at first one and then another of those who acknowledged his arrival. The decal on his cap had a picture of a polled red Devon bull with the inscription, "COWS COME AND GO BUT THE BULL IS ALWAYS HERE," underneath it. The blue chambray shirt he was wearing clashed furiously with his bright green corduroy pants.

"Morning, Toots," he said to the waitress, blowing a kiss as he moved to a stool at the counter. She smiled and placed a huge glass of iced tea in front of him and began dipping sugar into it from a ceramic bowl.

"The usual, Toots," the man said, blowing another kiss.

"I know," she said. "Here it is. Part of it anyway. How's your wife?"

"Oh, she's fine. Fat and sassy as ever."

"That what we trying to get me equal to?" T.J. said as the man went on flirting with the waitress.

"Watch it," I whispered, casting a quick glance around the room.

One of the customers stood at the cash register waiting for his check. "How you been, Bubba?" the fat man said. "Don't be reaching in that front pocket. Get some of that back pocket money. Get some of that folding money. I'm gonna sit here and eat all day." He looked over at us and winked, paying, I thought, no more attention to T.J. than he did to me.

"What'cha say, Delma," the customer said. "How's the cattle?"

"Fat and sassy as the old lady," the man said, laughing loudly.

The waitress still had not brought T.J. a menu. "Come back," she said to the customer as he started to walk away. "We'll see," he snipped, looking at T.J. As he passed our table, he cleared his throat harshly.

The man from the pickup truck suddenly switched to our table, pulled a chair from close by, and sat down. "Mind if I sit with you fellows?" he asked. "Hey, Gladys, how bout serving my vittles over here. You know. The usual." The waitress cast a quick, sizing-up look around the room, then back at us.

"Over there?" she said, still somewhere between friendly and unfriendly.

"Yeah. That'll be just fine. Just the usual. Three straight up and one piece of hog meat. Bring these fellows the same thing. Put it on my account." He laughed and added, "On account of they might not have any money." We tried to laugh with him. He turned and started talking to us again. "That okay? How you like your eggs? Want more than one slice of bacon? I just call it hog meat. Actually it's packing house bacon. Sliced so thin there ain't much hog meat in it. Whoever is in charge of slicing almost misses every time." He laughed the same way again, motioning to the waitress who hadn't moved. "Maybe you better bring them a menu, Toots. They might not like hen fruit staring at them this early in the morning. Let'um see what you got wrote down on paper." He turned to us again without pausing. "I just call her Toots. Name's Gladys. Known her since she was knee-high to a grasshopper. Guess you noticed I know everybody in here. Been coming in every morning for fifteen years. We're all neighbors. Farmers. Mechanics. Stuff like that. Fellow that just left paints houses." He lowered his voice and winked. "You know what they say about painters. Used to be there wouldn't be no more than four or five of us in here every morning. Before they opened the lake. Place has growed. Don't believe you fellows are from around here. Of course, this place hasn't been open but about a month. Not quite that long." We both knew what he meant by *open*. "Me, I'm glad it's open. Me and my wife talked about it a lot. Some things just ain't right. You know that?" We both nodded. "I don't care what anybody says. Some things just ain't right. My wife's in a wheelchair. Had polio. One of the last ones to get it before they started giving everybody Doctor Salk's sugar cubes. Had our last baby in an iron lung in Birmingham. He's grown now. Goes to Georgia Tech." He started singing, "He's a ramblin' wreck from Georgia Tech, and a heck of an engineer." He was looking all about the room, laughing loudly again, nodding at different ones, giving them a friendly wave when he caught their eye. Most of the people were staring at us by then.

The woman came over with two menus. "I'll just have one scrambled and some bacon," T.J. said. "And iced tea too."

"You want the grits?" she asked. "The grits go with it."

"Yeah, bring him some grits," the man said, not waiting for T.J. to answer.

"I'll have that too," I said. "But I'll still have the doughnut and coffee."

"Thank you," she said, I thought a little more relaxed. As she placed the ticket on the cook's ledge, a young man, the only one in the place wearing a coat and tie, came to the counter and began whispering to her. He handed her a dime, went back, and sat down. She hesitated briefly, then strolled casually over to the jukebox. She dropped the coin in the slot, pushed the buttons and walked away, slapping the young man playfully on the shoulder. He pulled her head down close and whispered in her ear. She went back to the jukebox, reached around it, and turned the sound up.

The room filled with the piercing sounds of a country and western band — steel guitar, banjo, drums, bass, and rhythm guitars. The tune was "Boil Them Cabbage Down." The band played through twice. Some of the men were laughing. Others seemed uneasy. Most of them were watching us. When the singing began, a booming baritone, the words were not the usual ones.

> Move them niggers north.
> Move them niggers north.
> If they don't like our southern ways,
> Move them niggers north.

As soon as the music started the man sitting with us began talking louder, trying to speak above the sound. "Yeah, that boy been working on old cars since he was no bigger than a tadpole. Put a lawn mower motor on his mamma's wheelchair when he was in high school. Won a prize for it. Got almost a full scholarship to Georgia Tech. He's going to do all right. Good boy. They're all good young'uns. God knows, they got a good mamma. Woman of steel. Never complains. Scoots around in that wheelchair and does everything she ever did. Teaches Sunday School in her Methodist Church. Makes me sing in the choir." He tried to drown out the vitriolic lyrics of the song with his laughter. "And you've heard what a great tenor I am. What you fellows do?" He didn't slow down for us to answer. "Me, I raise cows. We've been mighty blessed. Me and my wife started out with a pair of turkeys when we was first married and wound up with the best herd of registered Devons in Alabama. At least, I think so. 'Course, there ain't many herds of polled Devons in Alabama," he laughed.

When the song ended some of the men, including the one who had asked the waitress to play it, drifted away. The man with us said something to each one as they passed our table. "Don't take no wooden nickels." "Don't do nothing you can't do on a bicycle." Things like that.

When we finished eating, he paid the check and followed us to the door. "You boys be careful going to Nashville," he said loud enough for the others to hear. We had told him we were going to Mobile. "And tell Roy Acuff hello for me." He started singing as he stood at the door watching us.

> What a beautiful thought I am thinking,
> Concerning the great speckled bird.

T.J. pulled away from the restaurant and headed north. At the first exit he turned around and drove south. Neither of us had said anything.

"Yeah," I said.

"Yeah?" he said. "Yeah what?"

"Yeah, that's what we're trying to get you equal to," I said.

"Guess so," hc sighed. "I surely don't want to get equal to that fellow who played the jukebox."

"No law against playing the jukebox," I said. "At least not yet. And I hope there never will be."

"I guess I agree," he said, sighing again, deeper this time. "But it stings."

I don't believe either of us ever mentioned the song again, but I couldn't get it out of my mind. We were roaring through Alabama's proliferate black belt on a new interstate highway. In the distance, beside the old blacktop road paralleling the new one, I saw a country store with old men sitting like mannequins on the porch, their time as gone by as the road they sat beside. Their fathers farmed these fertile hills and valleys with ox teams. They with horses and mules. Now their children do it with giant diesel tractors and airplanes dropping seeds, fertilizer, and herbicides from the sky. Yet, as I watched them disappear behind us, I knew that the greatest change they had had to deal with was not technological. As they wait to die, they hear from their flag, and a lot of their preachers as well, that racial segregation is wrong. All their lives they were told, by state and church, that it was ordained of God for the common good of all. Now they have watched a new black vanguard arise and a South emerging that neither they nor their black tenants and neighbors would recognize. They watched on the television, they who laughed in disbelief when something called radio was first described to them, as their anonymous little towns became household words. Because of an upheaval as mighty as the volcanic upheaval which had formed these hills and hollows in the first place, they were noticed. In that moment I want to go and sit with them, tell them I am one of them, and they are of me. But other claims — the Movement, the Lord, claims of faith or claims of glands — have a hold on me. Have given me T.J. Yet as we rode along, the gray ghost of the Confederacy riding between us, the yellow pus from the open ulcer on his head unusually present, the parody of "Boil Them Cabbage Down," reverberating in my skull like an echo chamber, I knew their claim was still there. And somehow hoped the claim would not depart.

"Let's play 'Putting 'em in de dozens,'" T.J. said. When he explained the game, I remembered seeing Negro men play it when I was a boy, but I didn't know what it was called. It was more of a happening than a game. A group would be milling around doing nothing, maybe in front of a store, under the trees by the church house while the women, children, and older men were inside, at a fish fry, it didn't matter where. It began by one man singling out another and saying something derogatory about his mother. The challenged one responded with something a little worse, the insults mounting until one or the other broke into violence, got tickled, or walked away in defeat with derision from the group. Rhyme, rhythm, and timing were important in getting the upper hand early.

Generally it started with no greater aspersion than, "Yo' mammy is big and fat."

"Yeah? And yo' mammy lack'a bat."

As each exchange elevated to a more ribald plane, the crowd would close in, cheering, choosing a favorite, making wagers on which one would crack.

"Yo' mammy h'ists her tail lack'a cat."

"Yo' mammy crawl lack'a rat."

On occasion some vile invective like, "Yo' mammy sucked a dog an' 'nen she hatch you," would bring the swish of a knife blade or the explosion of a pistol. Most of the time, of course, the contest ended in good humor. One or another would run out of something to say, break into laughter — also a foil — and the two would jostle each other around, pound the other on the back, each good-naturedly claiming victory.

T.J. insisted I should begin the bandy since I was the oldest. Said that was one of the rules. "I thought there weren't any rules," I said.

"Just that one," he said.

"Your mother uses talcum powder from the dime store," I began.

"Your mother can't cook," T.J. replied.

"Your mother puts a lot of sugar in her coffee," I said.

"Your mother drinks Kool-Aid," T.J. rejoined. Then we both began to laugh. It was an awkward, embarrassed laugh.

"This won't work," T.J. said. "You can't do it, and I can't either." I knew he was right, and I was glad he said it first.

It didn't have to do with the incongruous ring of our precise grammar, our lack of rhythm, any deficiency in Rabelaisian skills or the inane chaff we were gently tossing. Both of us could be barnyard dirty. Either of us could have played the game with some other close friend. But we couldn't do it across the chasm of black and white. We could try to ignore that gulf, pretend it didn't exist. But when it came to white mother and black mother, we couldn't pull it off. Maybe someday we shall overcome. But not yet.

We had run into a furious thunderstorm. The rubber blade on the windshield wiper had come loose, and the metal holder made an eerie, screeching noise as it scraped along the glass. The heavy bass of the thunder was a haunting embellishment to the baritone of the singer on the jukebox. We had come to a detour on the interstate and were on a narrow state road. As the giant white oak boughs dipped low in front of us, the driving rain making it difficult for T.J. to see, I wished all the sounds would go away. Lightning struck in the distance and danced along a barbed wire fence, seeming to follow us.

The storm ended as quickly as it had begun and we had soon regained our speed and were back on dry pavement. "Everything's cool," T.J. said, sensing my mood, I supposed. He slowed down and eased around a young black man driving a wagon, an almost bizarre anachronism, whipping the team of mules to make them run down the highway as fast as they could. Thousands of wooly bears, those hairy worms of late summer someday to be tiger moths, hurried across the highway like a conveyor belt, fleeing the cotton fields in search of winter quarters, a place to hide and get grown. Or at least evolve to a more advanced state.

For an instant I thought of a gangling and retarded black adolescent who worked for Uncle Coot. We called him Skeeter. When my brother Joe got new laced boots, Skeeter wanted to borrow them to wear to his girlfriend's house nearby. The very day they arrived from Sears Roebuck. The likelihood that a colored boy would be allowed to wear a white boy's boots, new or old, was unthinkable in the closely guarded mores of Mississippi rural culture. We laughed and teased Joe about it.

"Hey, Joe. Lemme wear'ya boots." I watched the broken line of caterpillars in the side mirror, some mashed to death by the tires, hundreds of others blown off the highway by the current of the speeding automobile.

The young people at the church in Mobile had asked me to talk about the Vietnam War. They were a bright and inquiring group, most of the boys soon to be draft age. One of the adult sponsors kept changing the subject, talking about civil rights. There was no question but what his views on that issue were hostile. "How well do you know Martin Luther King? What do you think about him associating with known communists? How many times have you been in jail?" Questions like that. Finally I decided to let him make his own speech. I set him up with a remark about labor unions. He took the bait and tied race, labor organizing, and communism into one bundle.

"Now, I don't have anything against people being paid what they're worth," he said. "But if a man has worked hard all his life and has a factory, well, he ought to have the right to hire anyone he pleases. But some people don't know how to handle money. Like, we had a big strike at the plant over at Bay Minette. Some Yankees came riding into town in their big cars and big salaries, said they were for the common people. Got things all stirred up. Organized a union, and right off there was this strike. Most of those people had never made more than a dollar seventy-five in their lives. And that was all they knew how to handle."

Apparently the young people had heard it all before. They were shifting in their seats, yawning, frowning at each other when he wasn't looking. "Well, they got a big fat raise for everybody. Black and white alike. Of course, I don't have anything against that. If people know how to handle their money. But the very first payday I had some business over that way on Friday evening and stopped at this little store on the edge of town. In the colored section. Here was this old colored man sitting out on the front steps of the store. He had bought a whole stalk of bananas. Sitting there pulling one after another off a whole stalk. Do you know how many bananas are on a stalk? Do any of you know how long it would take to eat a whole stalk of bananas?" He addressed his questions to the students, looking all around the room, making sure they were hearing him. They all nodded that they didn't know.

"See. That was just poor management. See what I'm talking about? Poor judgment. Just throwing money away. Most of those bananas were wasted. Spoiled. With a lot of starving people in the world. See, they don't know how to handle money when you give it to them."

T.J. had gone to see a cousin while I was eating supper with the group and had come in after the meeting had started. He sat near the back, and I don't think the man knew he was there. "Mr. Eaves," I said with a voice of sincerity when the man finished, "what do you think about that? Do you think if you pay folks too much money they'll buy more bananas than they can eat?"

"Aw, Mr. Campbell. Ain't no question 'bout it." I knew the Methodist Youth Fellowship was about to be treated to some genuine hambone. They seemed uncomfortable when they heard his voice. "Dey'll sho buy mo'en dey can eat. Folks'll shore do it ever time. Fact is, I knowed dis man and his wife, jus' de two of 'em. Dey got fo' cars in de gayragge. Got a . . . what you call dat? A Rolls sompun 'nother. Some other kinda big ole car. Den dey got a stashum wagon an' a lil' ole truck. And she don't even drive.

"Knowed this family in town. . . . Fact is, I works fer'um. Dey got two chillun. An' how many rooms in dat house? Sixteen. Fo fo' folks. Now how dey gon' sleep in all dem rooms? Man, dey be settin' de clock, gittin' up during de night to sleep in all dem beds."

The young people were torn between being embarrassed at what they thought was a backwoods illiterate and applauding what was happening to their adult advisor.

T.J. hadn't even stood up. He continued to talk from where he sat in the back of the hall, all the students having turned to where they could see him. "And lemme tel'ya sompun else. I knows dis man, lives cross town. Like tu go fishin'. He got a houseboat haf big as dis church house. Ain't even married. Leastways not now he ain't. Hauls de thing 'round ona semi. Feller don' need sompun dat big jest to go fishin' wid. Foot, my daddy catch mo' fish dan anybody roun' jes settin' on de bank wid a cane pole an' a can of worms. Yes suh, Mr. Campbell. Dis white man sho tellin' de truf. Folks'll sho buy mo nanners dan dey need if'en you give'um too much money."

The students were stifling giggles, some of them holding their mouths to keep from exploding. The youthful president thanked me hurriedly for coming and asked one of the girls who seemed in control to give the closing prayer. In less than a minute the hall was empty.

"Who's your friend?" the man asked as he tried again to thank me for being with them.

"Said his name was Eaves," I said. "He saw my Tennessee car outside and asked if he could ride to Birmingham. He sure seems to think like you do," I added. "Of course, his grammar could stand a little touching up."

"Humph!" I heard him mutter as he rushed down the corridor.

"T.J., you crazy goose. You ought to be shot," I said when we were in the car. He was laughing too hard to answer. "A Rolls sompun 'nother! Broth-er!"

When he could talk he said, "I got him off your back, didn't I?"

"Yeah. You got him off my back. And you probably cost me my honorarium too. They promised me a hundred bucks."

"Aw, Brother Will. You probably would have just bought a whole stalk of bananas with it. You don't know how to handle money."

* * *

A heavy fog was hugging the shores of Mobile Bay, and T.J. eased the car along, heading east on U.S. Highway 90. "How far is it to Pensacola?" I asked him.

"A long way in this mess," he said. "But it'll clear up before long. That where we're going to spend the night? We can make it on to Tallahassee if you want to. Get in the back seat and sack out."

Some students at Florida State University were having a conference on the death penalty, and I had agreed to participate in what they described as a general discussion. The program was scheduled for the next afternoon.

"No, I'm not sleepy," I answered. "Got to wind down some more. That jerk and his stalk of bananas crap. I should have cut him with my knife."

"I thought you didn't believe in violence," T.J. laughed.

"I don't," I said. "Except on people who say if you pay a man what he's worth he'll buy too many bananas. Christ almighty! I really should have cut him with my knife."

"I guess there is something that'll provoke all of us to mayhem," he teased. "But I don't think ole Campbell would cripple a fellow for that."

"No. Guess not," I said. "Especially not on the way to testify against state killing."

When we arrived I found that the program was not a discussion panel as I had thought. It was a formal debate. And it was to be televised. I told the sponsors that I couldn't do a formal debate, that whatever forensic rules I might have known left me somewhere between the East Fork Consolidated High School and the Second World War. They asked me to go through with it, said it was important to get the issue in the public mind. I was more concerned when I discovered that my opponent was an internationally known philosopher, theologian, teacher, and author. I had been with him before, liked him personally, and respected his intellect and integrity, but I knew he was sure to be a formidable antagonist.

"We will ask the first speaker to come and give his opening position statement," the moderator began. The lights were on and the cameras rolling. I was scared.

For more than ten minutes the professor presented a weighty academic discourse on the nature of the state, quoting Hobbes a lot. I don't recall much of what he said because I was spending the time he was talking trying to come up with something I might peddle as an opening position. His presentation was obviously well researched and, I suspected, rehearsed. I noted that the audience was getting restless before he finished but I was sorry to see him sit down. I still had no opening position statement. The big three-legged monster was about to zero in on me, and I had always been nervous in front of TV cameras anyway. I knew I was against killing in any fashion, but I knew that wouldn't be much of an opening argument compared to what they had just heard. I wished for a power failure or some malfunction of the TV equipment. I glanced at T.J., who was sitting on the front row. He grinned, winked, and gave me an okay sign with both hands.

I heard the moderator's voice again. "And now, ladies and gentlemen, Mr. Campbell will come and give his opening position statement, on where he is coming from as he argues in opposition to capital punishment." He turned and addressed me directly. "We will ask you, Mr. Campbell, to please stay within the prescribed ten-minute limit." I was sure there would be no problem in honoring that request. As I heard the words and knew that I had to do what he said, I was sure that the greatest mercy the Lord could shower upon me would be to have me faint before I got to the microphone.

I took one deep breath, hesitated, then slowly stood up and began the few steps to the center of the stage, feeling a deep empathy with those whose plight we were there discussing. Then by some strange, some unexpected but most welcomed epiphany, I had a thought. There wasn't time to consider whether or not it was a good thought. It was the only one I had.

"I just think it's tacky," I said. I said it slowly and deliberately, rubbing my head timidly and shifting from one foot to another. I stood for a few seconds looking at the audience. Then I walked back to my chair and sat down. I recall wondering if the little bug mike attached to my necktie was relaying the pounding in my chest to the sound man.

At first there was scattered tittering about the hall. I didn't feel encouraged. Maybe I'll come back in a later round, I thought. An eight count in an early round doesn't have to be fatal. The tittering was soon followed by a continuous chattering, whispering, and giggling. Then a general outburst of laughter and applause.

I looked down at T.J. He was on his feet, cheering wildly. I knew that the ovation was not altogether spontaneous. Part of it was the herding instinct, following T.J.'s lead. But I was relieved. Not complaining.

I glanced at my opponent, tentatively pleased with my quick left jab now. He seemed confounded. Certainly not amused. Maybe he's just pitying me, I thought.

"Tacky?" the moderator asked when the audience was quiet again. He said it the way one does when nothing else seems appropriate. Repeat what the other person said and stall for time.

"Yessir," I said. "I just think it's tacky."

"Well. Is that your speech?" he said, looking more at the television director than at me.

"Yessir. I've never heard a speech criticized for being too short." Again there was a scattering of laughter. I remember thinking that I shouldn't push my luck, shouldn't appear frivolous about a matter so serious.

"Well, would you expound on it a bit?" he said, almost pleading, still looking at the director.

"Nosir. I reckon I wouldn't know how. I just think it's tacky, and that's all I think."

The director was prancing back and forth in the orchestra pit, talking hurriedly to the camera operators through his intercom, wondering perhaps how he was going to get a fifty-seven-minute program out of this seeming impasse.

"Now, come on, Will," the moderator said, his voice a little edgy. "Tacky is an old Southern word, and it means uncouth, ugly, lack of class."

"Yessir. I know what it means," I said. I wanted to shift to a more serious gear but didn't know how. "I try not to use words if I don't have some vague notion of what they mean." It seemed to be a good time to edge away from the flippant opener. "My worthy opponent chose to pitch this discussion on a philosophical level," I added, trying to act serious. "I wouldn't have done it that way myself. I'm a bootleg country preacher from the hills of Tennessee. By way of Mississippi. Don't know much about philosophy. But in my limited exposure to the subject, I do seem to recall that there was something called aesthetics." I sensed a shift in the mood of the audience and hurried on. "And if your synonyms are correct, if a thing is ugly, well, ugly means there's no beauty there. And if there is no beauty in it, there is no truth in it. And if there is no truth in it, there is no good in it. Not for the victim of the crime. Certainly not for the one being executed. Not for the executioner, the jury, the judge, the state. For no one." When there was no immediate response, I went on. "And we were enjoined by a well-known Jewish prophet to love them all."

I felt relaxed, ready, I thought, to defend my opening position. It was not long, however, until my astute adversary carefully maneuvered the discussion back to his own plain of erudition, and I spent the later rounds on the ropes.

"Triumph of the gauche!" T.J. shouted as we headed out of town with him driving.

"No triumph, I'm afraid," I said. "But it was fun for a few minutes there."

"Naw, man. You won! You won! I was proud of you. Of course, I did think you could have left off that '. . . well-known Jewish prophet' bit. Just because your opponent was Jewish. What kind of toadying bull was that?"

"Black anti-Semitic bigot," I yelled above the noise of a passing semi.

"Will Campbell, you're my best buddy in the whole wide world. And you won!"

"What did I win?" I asked, feeling uneasy with his flattery.

"You won the debate, you goose. You know you did. Get off the humble kick."

"The truth is, I didn't win," I said. "But even if I had, come sundown there'll be just as many people appointed to die."

While I had visited with the debate sponsors and made sure my opponent was still my friend, T.J. had got a beer for me and a soda for himself. "Then you're not mad at me anymore?" I said, tasting the chill of the beer as he grumbled about street signs.

"Reckon I've forgotten what I'm supposed to be mad about," he laughed. "And how could I be mad for long at a redneck mutharoe like you?" he chattered, honking the horn the way he did when he was happy and excited.

"You know, that's the first time you ever called me a redneck and I felt honored and decorated by it."

"We may be getting close to when you can call me nigger," he said, gaining speed as we moved out of town heading north.

"I hope so," I said. "I really do hope so."

"We'll know," he said softly, the exuberance gone. "We'll know." There were miles of silence after that.

* * *

"Seems like it all has to be in accordance with the program," T.J. said. "Don't you ever get sick and frigging tired of it?" Leon, the little Spitz, had suffered a stroke the day before, and T.J. had brought him from the house down to the asparagus bed I was mulching. I was glad he did. I didn't want Leon to be by himself.

"Tired of what?" I asked, helping him fold a towel for Leon to lie on. "What the devil you talking about?"

"All of it. Just all of it. Everything we ever do, sooner or later it gets back to black and white. What the heck do the Scandinavians talk about?" He gently lifted Leon onto the folded towel, pulled the edges of it on top of him, and sat down. "Like poor little Leon," he continued. "You won't even let him die without it being in accordance with the program."

"Damned if I know what you're talking about," I said. "If you want me to quit talking about him, I will. All I remember telling you is what a great little friend he's been. How we got him when we first moved here, when the children were having it rough at a new place. And I told you about the time he killed two dozen of Mrs. Dolan's laying hens and proudly placed them on our front yard, and. . . ."

"Yeah, yeah, yeah," he interrupted.

"And I told you how he gnawed through a chain link fence and dug under six inches of concrete to get to the Brandons' Weimaraner bitch in heat." I spoke as if I hadn't heard his interruption. "And how he got hung up with Dottie when the children were supposed to be watching them, keeping him inside away from her, and even though Bonnie sprayed them with the garden hose and separated them, he had sired nine puppies by then and they all looked exactly like him. That's what I've been telling you."

"Yeah. That's the words you've been telling me all right," he said, offering Leon a little piece of hamburger he had brought. "But somehow it all seemed in accordance with the program. The Movement. Black and white."

"Program? What program?"

"Like the time you were building the electric fence. Just when you called Brenda to turn the current on up at the house, Leon was checking it out. Hiked his leg and peed on it. And the jolt through his bladder knocked him five feet."

"Well, sure," I said. "I told you that. And what's it supposed to mean except if you piss on an electric fence you'll get your tail shocked halfway to glory? And short circuit the fence and let the cows out."

"Come on, Campbell," he chuckled. "And how many electric

fences been pissed on in the last few years? Just for mischief. Trying to short the circuit. But it didn't work. Blow a fuse and the Movement'll fix it. Huh? Huh?"

"Now who's talking about color?" I said, trying to find a more comfortable position for Leon.

"This here is your old buddy T.J. Eaves, Bro. He knows you like a book. Colored people always been able to read white folks. Had to."

"If you're through with the histrionic crap, Mr. Eaves, we'll go back to the asparagus," I said, putting my hand on Leon's side to see if he was still breathing.

"It ain't histrionic. And it isn't crap," he said calmly, patting my shoulder as he stood up. "Why can't Leon just be a pitiful little animal trying to die?"

"He's not trying to die," I snapped. "He's trying *not* to die." I handed him a sheet of paper I had typed that morning and put in my shirt pocket.

He walked away a few steps, turned his back, and began to read what I had written, his head casting a shadow on the paper to soften the glare of the sun.

THURSDAY: WHILE LEON WAS DYING

LEON is a dog
Who came here
about
seventeen years ago
When the children were quite young.

Penny and Bonnie and I (Webb was just a baby)
Went to the pet shop and found him — he looked rather pitiful.

We had just moved from one place to another and
the children
Were children.

Leon was their friend.

Leon got sick and
the doctor said,
"Death is mercy." But

Leon lived seventeen years after that:
romped, brought joy,
made love to DOTTIE. And

Stood guard at the front of the house.
Seventeen years before he started dying.
Leon never hurried anything. And Brenda was his wellspring.

This time he's leaving. Come the morning
we will dig a hole
in the yard he fended
and say:

HERE HE LIVED.
HERE HE DIED.
AND HERE WILL HE BE BURIED. Amen.

"Why don't you go on and cry for him like you're busting to do?" he said, handing me the paper. He walked to the far side of the asparagus bed and began throwing the leaves furiously and aimlessly.

"Thanks," I called after him, suspecting for the first time that all his talk had been a diversion, something to get my mind off Leon's leaving. Still I knew he had been serious too.

Dorris Stephenson, the neighbor who had tried to shoot the limb Maximillian was stuck on, drove up. "Brenda told me about Leon," he said, trying to be casual. "Why don't you let me put him to sleep? Got a pistol in the pickup with a silencer. Go on in the house. I'll get Bart to bury him wherever you say. No use in him having to suffer like this."

"I appreciate it, Bud," I said, "but I don't hold with mercy killing. He'll have to do it like the rest of us. He doesn't have long anyway." I remembered the time he and his buddies put Nell to sleep.

"Call me if you change your mind," he said, getting back in the truck. "He was a horny little dickens, wasn't he?" he laughed. "But I believe his rutting days are over." There's more to living than rutting and running in heat, I thought as he drove away.

T.J. went on spreading the leaves, making sure they fell where they were supposed to now. Leon was crying again and the spasms were back, so hard I thought for a moment about what Dorris had said. Suddenly the shaking stopped and I thought he was going to rally. Then there was a slight shiver, a low moan, and he was gone.

When I stood up, T.J. knew it was over. He came and placed him inside the box he had brought him to the field in. He said nothing, just carried him slowly to the end of the concrete walk in front of the house. That was where Leon always stood watch when we were gone. Next morning Brenda helped me dig the grave but went inside before I covered him up. I put the poem in the ground with him.

X
Fast Falls the Eventide

IT IS A NEAR perfect winter day. The snow is falling straight down in medium-sized flakes. There is no sign of wind to make drifts, and the snow uniformly sleeps wherever it falls, covering the ground like a cotton sheet, following the lumps and contours, not trying to disguise the earth as anything except what it is; rough in places, smooth in places. The temperature is hovering just under freezing and there will not be the slush between my cabin and the residence the way it was yesterday. The flakes seem to speed up when they near the surface, hurrying to spread the blanket, drawn by static electricity from the earth.

This morning I filled all the bird feeders and turned the switch on the bath warmer so their water won't freeze. The birdbath is one of the huge limestones Mr. Oscar Bass or some Cherokee farmer chiseled into a chicken trough many years ago. The electric warmer in it seems somehow to mock that long-gone skill.

The feeders stretch from the windowsill to the far side of the yard and into the trees. On the window platform are several sunflower heads. I planted them last summer and marvel now that each little seed I placed in the ground produced one of these hefty, twelve-inch dinner plates. When I harvested them, I did not shell the seeds off but hung them in the back room of the cabin. The bluejays, cardinals, and thrushes get needed exercise on winter days as they pick the seeds loose. And I suppose a sense of worth as they have to work for their daily bread. I remember the sight of a thousand sunrises waving in the summer breeze when the sunflowers were in full bloom.

Two slender mesh stockings are stuffed with tiny thistle seeds and dangle like summer sausage from a low-hanging hackberry tree, the titmice and grosbeaks clinging to them like leafhoppers. Two hunks of suet hang from higher limbs on a scalybark hickory tree. The snow makes the big globs of white beef fat almost invisible. Occasionally red-bellied and downy woodpeckers swing them back and forth like skilled gymnasts. Near the tree line is a hamper half-filled with black walnuts. The incredible pileated woodpeckers, large as crows with necks as strong and agile as jackhammers, will sweep in and carry them deep into the forest, where they will pierce the ironlike shells with the proficiency of a drill press. The squirrels, of course, will get their share, choosing between the nuts and the ears of corn I have hung about for their enjoyment.

I recognize a few of the towhees, warblers, and finches from earlier visits. Too bad that only the mutants can be identified. There is one of the cardinals with a bald spot on his head where the crest is supposed to be. Last year there were three of them like that, but only one returned this winter. One of the towhees with yellow sides instead of chestnut red flits and scratches on the platform feeder, and the finch with one leg dives repeatedly at the thistle stocking and hangs on. With one foot, he cannot scratch the way his playmates do. I know the increasing deformities I see each year are caused by the poisons we pour into the air and ground, and for a moment I turn to an original Mike Peters cartoon hanging on the far wall. The scene is two women and a little boy near a nuclear reactor. The caption says, "He's grown a foot since I saw him last." The boy has an ankle and foot growing out of the top of his head. I soon go back to watching the birds. I wish that the petunias which bordered the cabin all summer, their nectar drawing the needle-billed hummingbirds like magnets, were still blooming. Their little presence, I think, would complete this portrait of nature, pure and undefiled before the world. For a moment I pity the hummingbirds, wonder how ravaged are their tropical winter quarters in Central America by the guns of war.

I sit for a long time, caught up in the harmonic elegance of what God wrought on the fifth day of His creative chores. If the people of His land do not dwell safely, each under his own vine and fig tree, at least the birds of the air continue to show the way. Each on her own perch. Each feasting from the bounty of grace. Sweet peace.

Suddenly there is a sound like rushing wind. Jays, cardinals, warblers, wrens, and towhees scamper for barren timbers. It is the black plague. The scourge of starlings. Hundreds, thousands of the square-tailed devils swoop in with the fury of an unforetold hailstorm, the bane of birdlovers everywhere. Starlings!

Why couldn't one, maybe two of them come? At least at first. Let us get used to the idea, prepare for them. But no. They come all at once. They are not, of course, even native to North America. We could overlook that, forgive whoever brought them here in the first place, if only they didn't come in such droves. If they weren't so pushy. But this gluttonous avalanche, wheeling, gliding, rushing like a colony of amoeba on a microscopic slide, is disgusting. I tap the window with the handle of my cane. The dark cloud lifts, shoots off like a comet. In one instant it is back. A boomerang with a thousand beaks and bellies. I have worked long and hard to create this avian paradise. It is a certified bird sanctuary, balanced proportions arising out of years of preparation and experimentation. In the blinking of an eye, it is a wasteland, victim of unwelcome aliens.

The sunflower heads are stripped of every last seed. The platforms and chalets are empty, save for a solid layer of starling droppings mixed with empty husks. The thistle bags have been ripped apart by the yellow claws and inconsiderate bills, the seeds buried in the soft snow below. Even the suet is ravaged, nothing left of it except the stringy fiber which held the nourishing tallow together, indistinguishable now from the falling snow.

No manners and no class, the starlings. Crude, boorish, lazy, and dumb. No drive and no ambition. When they can take someone else's nest, they will. If they must build their own, it is a random pile of leaves and straw; and if you build a house for them, they will ruin it in one season. They breed like cockroaches. And they all look alike.

Last year the law sought to make them as extinct as the dodo. From low-flying aircraft, they sprayed their nocturnal ghettoes with a chemical which destroyed the waterproofing oils on their feathers. When near freezing rain hit them, they fell off the roosts in hundreds of thousands, frozen to death. Few mourned their passing. Other hundreds of thousands survived the executioners' intent and flew away. And here they are.

Look now! The food is gone. These winged desperadoes have turned a country club into a sleazy rescue mission, a glacial slum, standing bleak and still before the gathering night. From where I sit, I can see the stuffed wretches perched along a half-mile of telephone wire, whistling, sputtering, and chattering like extras on an Alfred Hitchcock film set, each one hunched like a wart hog.

Does one love birds? Or is it the harmonizing chords of red and yellow and indigo against the pure-white backdrop of winter that sends him out to brave the pneumonia elements? Compassion for creation or aesthetic lust? "Do not even the Publicans the same?" Inasmuch . . .

Bundle up. Replenish the banquet tables while it is still day. The weather channel says this is the worst storm of winter.

* * *

"Reckon ain't much changed in seventy years," T.J. Eaves said, almost yelling to be heard above the cheering and hand-clapping.

Stokely Carmichael was standing on the back of a flatbed truck near Greenwood, Mississippi. He was extolling the beauty of blackness and calling for black progress and power through a system of racial separateness. James Meredith, the man who had desegregated the University of Mississippi, had begun a solo march from Memphis to Jackson to dispel the fear which continued to plague black Mississippians. Outside Hernando, just over the stateline, he had been gunned down, and while he lay in a hospital room in Memphis, Dr. King, Carmichael (the new chairman of SNCC), Roy Wilkins, Floyd McKissick (national director of CORE), and Whitney Young of the Urban League announced they would finish the march. Almost immediately Wilkins and Young left, convinced that they could not abide the militant rhetoric of Carmichael.

"Black power!" Carmichael yelled.

"Black power!" the crowd roared in response.

"Black power!"

"Black power!" came the echo.

Dr. King stood with his arms folded, not cheering, not smiling. Those still loyal to him stood with him in silent disapproval of what was happening. When the battle hymn of the Movement, "We Shall Overcome," was sung, Carmichael's troops substituted "overrun" for "overcome" and stood mute at the line, "Black and white together."

"Guess Booker T. is back," T.J. said when the rally was over and the campers were bedding down. Television cameras and newspaper reporters and photographers were swarming around Carmichael. King was almost ignored. The cry for black power through separateness was the news event of the season.

It seemed welcomed by whites. Almost like, "Gee, what a close call. Just when we thought we had to integrate. Just when it seemed that all morality and all legality was on their side, sealed by the blessing of the god of economics, here they come chanting that they want to be separate. We really thought they had us this time. Ho boy!"

The scene was repeated in Yazoo City and again near Canton, just twenty miles from Jackson. After each noisy and ideologically fragmented rally, T.J. said the same thing. "Guess Booker T. is back." When I finally asked him why, he said, "Doesn't it sound familiar to you? All this time they've been calling me Booker T. Maybe I know why now. Stokely sounds like the speech Booker T. made in Atlanta, Georgia, in 1895. You know. The one about colored people and white people being separate as the fingers yet one like the hand."

"I don't hear Stokely saying anything about the hand though," I laughed. "He doesn't ever get past the fingers."

T.J. began to talk about W.E.B. DuBois. "But you know what? He made that speech too. A wheel ain't nothing but round. The circle goes on. I wonder why they never called me W.E.B.?" I didn't know what he was talking about but looked it up later. DuBois talked of a black colony idea. He argued that twelve million Negroes living in America had the inborn capacity to accomplish just as much as any nation of twelve million people anywhere else. (Switzerland had but half that number.) And further that Negroes who believed that they could get a quality education only in white schools were actually promoting the stigma of racial inferiority; that they were not capable of building good educational institutions.

Except for Booker T. Washington's emphasis on crafts and agriculture in Negro education, he and DuBois did seem to share the same position on racial separation. At least, closer than I had ever assumed. Things do go full circle. Go east by traveling west. Go far enough left and you wind up on the right. And the wheel goes round and round.

As far as I know, despite all that, no one ever called T.J. Eaves W.E.B.

I felt a sadness in the air. I recalled some words from an Alan Paten novel. An old African preacher said, "My greatest fear is that by the time the whites have turned to loving, my people will have turned to hating." Had my people, the white people of the South and the nation, simply waited too late? For the first time the promised land of the beloved community John Lewis continued to talk about seemed far away. I had always assumed that little by little, as the black movement edged the white majority toward an acceptance of the freedom they demanded, there was out there somewhere the distant day when black and white would sing the glad song together. Now, as the wild cheers of hundreds of young men and women, many of whom had been clubbed to the stall of death for advocating human as human continued to ring in my ears, I was not so sure. Standing in the bowels of my native land, camped between Highway 51 and the Illinois Central Railroad, South to North arteries which had carried so many of us away from home and people in our quest for something better, I was overwhelmed by a strange mood.

Are you speaking a gloomy forecast to me, T.J. Eaves, least of these? Are we beholding the celebration of some tragic mutation? Words of an idea jeered as compromise by those called militant when first spoken by Booker T. Washington in 1895, now cheered as the cutting edge of radicalism by the militants of 1966? Are we tasting the colòstrum of retreat, the first milk and strippings of a new breed of zealotry? Is the new birth of freedom being now deferred by its noblest and most promising proponents? Am I aiding and abetting the cutting of the stanchions of my own slavery? That's the Panama Limited *screaming by. Hurrying from Chicago to New Orleans so that it can hurry from New Orleans to Chicago. It will pass through McComb City in two hours, blow, slow down, even stop if anyone chooses to stop there anymore. Eleven miles from my father's house. And what would I say? What if there is not the fatted calf in waiting? No! What if there* is*? How strange and unpredictable are the ways of social movements. And how predictable is Jackson. Not predictable. Certain. I want to be with Jackson. I need some grace.*

"Let's go, Will Campbell." I didn't look around. The voice was faint and distorted, almost inaudible under the continuing raucous. As I turned, I saw T.J. about mid-point between Stokely and Martin, looking at one and then the other, the way Jackson had looked at Nell and Mr. Jenkins' goats. There was a tentativeness about his stance.

From the other side of the crowd, I heard a strident caricature of a Rebel yell. It was shrill and high-pitched, unmistakably the voice of a female. I had never heard a woman do a Rebel yell before, and to my deepest genes it seemed inappropriate, for a moment a sacrilege.

"That'll be Florence," said T.J., who had moved beside me. "She thinks she black." She was shoving her way through, charging Stokely Carmichael the way fanatical sports fans rush a victorious coach.

"Oh, baby you're beautiful!" she screamed, jumping straddle of his back, pummeling his shoulders with both hands, her legs wrapped around his waist to keep from falling. She yelled it over and over. "Oh, baby you're bee-u-tiful!" Interspersing the words was her imitation Rebel yell. "Oh, baby you're beautiful! Yaaa-hoooo! Oh, baby you're bee-u-tiful!"

Her performance seemed somehow to profane the sacrifices of Evers, Chaney, Goodman, Schwerner, and others recently martyred within those boundaries, and to accentuate the belligerent spirit which had grown to maturity during this march, stalking and threatening to dismember the civil rights coalition already foundering on the notion of non-violence. The suspicion I had always had of social movements in general reached out and encompassed this one. Total allegiance is denial. THE MOVEMENT absolutized is ersatz MOVEMENT. Left is Right, and the wheel goes round and round. Can there be a Crusade for Christ or can there be only a Crusade for Crusade? Can justice come without leaving injustice in its wake? Can death come where life never was?

When at last Stokely shook her off, jumping and bucking like a rodeo brahma, he seemed torn between kissing her in ultimate defiance of white Mississippi mores and shunning her to bolster his anti-white rhetoric. He made an unconvincing gesture at both.

Florence and four of her friends had spent two nights in the Dolan House on their way from Poughkeepsie. All of them had dropped out of Vassar to work in the Movement. She was from Newark, where her father was an investment banker. When they arrived, traveling in a fifteen-year-old Cadillac hearse, she was wearing bib overalls with no blouse and no bra underneath, cowboy boots, and a pith helmet. Her hair, cut in Buster Brown fashion, was light yellow blonde, the first half-inch from her scalp suggesting that she was blonde with frequent aid of peroxide. "I'm redneck mod," she announced soon after they arrived. I guess I didn't like her.

"What's with the fuckingmutha goat?" she asked the first morning.

You ought to learn to cuss or give it up, I thought. "Did he keep you awake?" I said.

"Didn't really keep me awake. I was already awake. I'm too excited about the Movement to sleep. But he kept banging his head into the posts on the porch. Must not be too bright. And he defe — uh shits all over the place. You all must really love that thing."

I wanted to tell her that "y'all" is one word, not two, and that it isn't used in the South to address one person. Instead I said, "Yeah, I do."

"Well now, I reckon I don't love anything that much," she said, jumping out of Jackson's way when he came close.

No, probably not.

She told me they were going to stay in Mississippi after the Meredith march to do voter registration, and someone had told her I knew all about Mississippi. As we sat in the office talking, I excused myself occasionally, explaining that I had a guinea chick at the house I had to check on. I had hatched some guinea eggs under a chicken hen and only one had lived. And it was deformed, hatched with no legs. I had built a miniature skateboard and taped it to its body. It had learned that by fluttering its wings it could scoot along the floor, moving to feed or water. The third time I left the office and started to the house, one of the students followed me outside. "Mr. Campbell," she said timidly, "I think I know what you're talking about, but every time you say *guinea chick* Florence Petrone almost faints."

"Well, tell Florence Petrone that there is nothing sexist nor ethnic about that remark. It is a *guinea*. And it is a *chick*. If I wanted to insult her, I would say I have a *wop broad* I have to check on."

I brought the little thing back with me and talked about the manner in which words are misunderstood. And about how stereotypical words might be offensive to one person and not to another. I also tried to explain, looking often at Florence, how this little imperfect guinea fowl was the paradigm of human history. And how humanity's loftiest notions — the non-violence of Martin Luther King, the lone courage of Roger Williams standing against the religious intolerance of the New England establishment, the inspiration of those who at the foundation of this democracy stood for a principle of equal rights over the prerogatives of monarchs, the raw fortitude of Harriet Tubman and those since who conducted the train on the lingering tracks of racial and sexual supremacy, the redeeming iconoclasm of our artists and their subjects from Hawthorne's Hester Prynne to Twain's Tom Sawyer to Ellison's Invisible Man to Sallinger's Holden Caulfield, the silent perseverence of those in every generation from first to now who have chosen prison to blind obedience to the State, who have espoused the individualism of Thoreau and rejected submersion in the lonely crowd — are the skateboards which keep flawed humanity human still.

But Florence went on celebrating her redneck mod. Give up, Campbell!

"Let's go," T.J. said again as Stokely moved through the crowd, accepting compliments, giving the Movement handshake to his supporters. "I don't like to watch the end of something."

"The end?" I asked.

"Yeah. The end."

We walked the half-mile to my car in silence. When we were back on the road heading in the direction of Memphis, he spoke again. "I can't watch someone applaud their own epitaph." I didn't answer.

He seemed depressed, strangely irritable as we drove north along the well-worn highway. I called out the name of each little town as we drove through. "Pickens. The man who ordained me is pastor of that Baptist Church right there."

"Let's stop and see him," T.J. said.

"No," I replied speeding up to get through the yellow of the only traffic light in town.

"But if I wasn't with you, you'd stop. Maybe eat supper. Right?"

"No. Wrong. . . . This is Goodman. There's the junior college. One of my cousins from New Orleans played football there. He was good enough to play at LSU, was offered a full scholarship and a bunch of money. But when he came here, he couldn't afford a bus ticket. Hitchhiked up here and played football for that dinky little junior college."

"Too dumb for LSU?"

"Nope. It was 1934."

"Oh," T.J. said, obviously not interested in the educational and athletic career of my cousin from New Orleans. So I didn't tell him that two beefy men wearing state trooper uniforms had knocked on Uncle Carl's door three days before his son was to leave for college, called him outside and told him that since he didn't see fit to vote for the Kingfish, the Kingfish didn't see fit for his boy to play football at LSU.

"Durant. This is where Marsh Calloway was the Presbyterian preacher." When T.J. didn't respond, I went on. "In 1955 he preached for almost a year with no one in the congregation except his wife."

"Must'a been one dull white preacher," he said. I had not heard such sarcasm from him before. I pretended not to notice.

"You ever hear of Providence Farm?" I asked.

"Can't say as I have."

"Well, they were a group of white young people who came to Mississippi in the thirties with encouragement from Sherwood Eddy, Reinhold Niebuhr, Kirby Page, folks like that. You ever hear of any of those folks?"

"Certainly have," he snapped.

"Anyway, they bought a farm over in the Delta, then moved to this county — Holmes County — for folks who had been kicked off the land for trying to organize tenant farmers. Negro folks and white folks.

You ever hear of John Rust?"

"Can't say as I have," he said, sighing and leaning his head back against the seat.

"John Rust and his brother didn't exactly invent the cotton picking machine, but they improved on it so it would work. Then worried because it would take jobs away from a lot of poor people, especially Negroes."

"You mean *blacks*?"

Something is happening. Right here in this car on the outskirts of Durant, Mississippi, something is happening.

"You know who actually invented the mechanical cotton picker? A. P. Albert. He was a Negro."

"You mean black?" he said again. The light laughter that followed had a sardonic ring to it. It crossed my mind that it could be directed at Stokely's speech. Or it could be directed at me.

"A Negro invented it and two white Socialists perfected it. And none of them ever made much money off it." We had gained the speed limit and passed one after another of the big cotton picking machines along the road being readied for the upcoming harvest, most driven by white men.

"John Rust was one of the folks who bought that farm. They did a lot of good things. Credit unions. Farm co-ops. Had a medical clinic. Lots of things. But in 1955 several hundred citizens met in the schoolhouse and voted them out of the county. Reverend Marsh Calloway stood up and told them that what they were doing was un-American and un-Christian and asked them to reconsider. He had a pretty good Calvinist congregation before that, but they all quit. His wife played the organ and she kept coming. He mimeographed the bulletin every week, worked on his sermon, the whole works."

I rounded a sharp curve, felt T.J.'s body shift, and saw that he was asleep. His thick Negroid bottom lip was curled in an offish and sullen fashion. His broad nostrils were pulsating like a blacksmith bellows, mucus from a summer cold draining over his streamlined mustache, the drainage from the tonsured wound smelling more putrid than I ever remembered. For one wicked moment white genes overcame and reigned. *You're one damned ugly, impudent nigger.* And for that fleeting moment I hated him.

"You don't know what it's like to be a nigger, Will Campbell."

"And you don't know what it's like to be a redneck. Hated by those who taught you to hate so that their own dominion might increase."

I went on talking. "From Old Miss, where I was chaplain, I once drove down to visit Reverend Calloway, admiring a preacher in Mississippi who would stand up to what was actually a mob. And who was stubborn enough to defy his racist congregation by pretending they were in their pews each Sunday. In addition, I wanted to meet a fellow liberal. After we had visited for an hour or so, and after I had assured him that I was equally as enlightened and liberated as he, Marsh asked if I had any daughters. When I told him I had two, he asked if I would want one of them to marry some blue-gummed, frizzy-headed nigger. At first I thought he was teasing. But he continued to give me the same lecture on the nature, intellect, and living habits of Negroes I had heard so many times before. He was dying for a cause he didn't even believe in. 'I don't want integration of the races any more than they do. I just thought what they were doing, running folks off from their homes, was un-Christian and un-American, and that's what I told them. If they want to stop coming to church for that, that's their problem. In Texas, I once belonged to the Ku Klux Klan.'"

T.J. didn't wake up, so I kept talking. "West. We're going through West, Mississippi, now. This is where Brenda had a wreck one time. We were coming back from Louisiana. Had a thirty-gallon garbage can full of frozen shrimp her sister had given us. She ran into the side of a big semi. Half tore the car up but didn't hurt anyone. Except the shrimp. They rotted.

"What about Constance Curry?" I asked. "Ever hear of her?" He said nothing but I knew the answer. Connie often visited the hollow, and T.J. had been with her there many times. Winifred Green and Patricia Derian, along with some other white Mississippians, had enlisted the help of the American Friends Service Committee in a program which for the first time would go public with the notion that desegregated education must come to Mississippi children too. Both Connie and Jean Fairfax, a black woman who had long been active in working to secure rights for all people, were valuable allies in their efforts. I had known both of them for many years. I had worked for Connie as consultant during four summers when she directed an integrated human relations seminar for Southern students, and we were very close. I opposed their Mississippi program to begin immediately enlisting black children to apply to white schools, perhaps primarily because I feared for her personal safety. But also because I believed any black child, no matter what age, who appeared at a white school at that time would be killed. I knew that this tough Irish woman, a Southern integrationist and feminist in the line of Angelina Grimké, was not going to pay the slightest attention to my advice. Happily, she was right. My only contribution to their organization was a twenty-five-dollar check in memory of Jim Reeves, a country superstar killed in a plane crash on the last day of July, 1964.

In the silence I reflected upon the work of those women and many others who began things on their own but soon saw it appropriated by their male colleagues. Rosa Parks in Montgomery, who refused to give up her bus seat and started a revolution. Ella Baker, a silent architect of the Montgomery Movement and later godmother to the Student Nonviolent Coordinating Committee born on Easter Sunday, 1960, in Raleigh, North Carolina, who more than any person I experienced insisted that the Southern freedom Movement be democratic. A Movement for and of the people. Artherine Lucy and Ruby Hurley in Alabama. Daisy Bates in Little Rock. The list is long.

"Winona. Okay, Brother Eaves. You have to wake up for this one. Winnona. Hey T.J.! Wake up! We're in Winona. My college roommate lives here. Preaches right over there. And no, we're not going to visit him either. Did that a few years ago. Called him from that service station right there. He told me to drive two miles south and wait for him. Slipped in the back seat of my car and we drove on back roads for half an hour. Then he said he had to do some church business.

"T.J.! Wake up! This is where the first headquarters of the White Citizens Council was. And right there in that jailhouse is where Miss Fannie Lou Hamer was beaten until her kidney was ruptured. And you know why? Because she wanted to vote and get other folks to vote."

Miss Fannie Lou was a rare, once in a lifetime character. She was a short, very fat, and very black woman in her middle years. All her life she had been a Mississippi Delta sharecropper. Over the years she had many questions about the system, but there was no one to answer them. Really no one to ask them. So she kept them to herself. Then in 1964, when the Movement came to Mississippi in force, she decided that it was her vocation to ask the questions out loud. She registered to vote, was summarily kicked off the land, and joined the Movement as singer, organizer, speaker, and leader. During those years so many people — famous and infamous and unknown — came through our hollow that our children took their presence for granted or paid them no mind. But when Miss Fannie Lou came, they always gathered around her. Late one night we were sitting around the fireplace, she in the center, her fat bottom draped over a short-legged stool, telling stories:

"One of my cousins . . . half-cousins . . . step-cousins . . . whatever your auntie's child daddied by a white man is supposed to be called . . . flat hated her daddy. I mean her real daddy. He was the overseer of the plantation. You know, they're the ones who went to Mississippi State. The plantation owners send their young'uns to Ole Miss over in Oxford, or back East somewhere. Then there's Mississippi Southern for the pulpwood hauler's kids. And then there's Itta Bena for the little darkies." She fanned her skirt, threw her head back, and laughed at her delineation of Mississippi higher education. "I mean she *hated* him. Of course, he never even acknowledged her. Him being white and all. Even though she looked just like him. He had three other daughters by his in-house wife. And they all looked like him too. I mean, he marked them like a jersey bull jumping fences and humping heifers in April. 'Course, the white girls all went to Sweet Briar, or somewhere, to learn how to be proper prissy puss'." By then Bonnie and Penny were ecstatic, holding onto every syllable. "And my cousin didn't even get to go to Itta Bena. All she did was pick cotton, wash for white folks, stuff like that. Well, when he died, we all went to the funeral in the big white Methodist church. The overseers are always Methodist. The Planters — that's the plantation owners who never hit a lick in their lives — had it all passed on from their daddies and granddaddies. They're Episcopalians. And the pulpwood haulers, they're Baptist. Just like us. Only they can't enjoy their religion like us colored folks. They can't take on and get down like we do. Well, there we were in that big Methodist church house. The three white daughters sitting on the front bench with their black dresses and lace veils, sitting there by their mamma . . . not half a tear in the bunch. And here's Cousin Ina Mae, sitting there with us on the back bench in her flour sack dress. Well, child, I'm here to tell you when that preacher — and he was some fancy dude too; been off to Texas to get fancied up to talk about the little Jesus. Child, when he started that spiel about what a solid citizen the deceased was, good family man, devoted father, faithful husband, pillow of the church — all them lies — I'm here to tell you Ina Mae done got to wailing and swooning and bellowing like a choking calf. We fanned her, wiped her face, even passed some smelling salts under her nose. Then, child, if I'm not telling you the truth I'll stick my head in that fire, be johnbrown if she didn't pass out cold. White folks looking around. Whispering among themselves. Motioning for us to quieten down so's they could listen to all them lies. Well, we picked her up and got her out of there. Took her out under a big ole water-oak tree where it was cool."

Miss Fannie Lou was laughing so hard by then she had to run to the kitchen and get a drink of water, Penny and Bonnie right behind her. "And you know what?"

"What?" both girls said.

"No sooner did we get her stretched out under that water oak than she sat straight up and commenced to giggle. We thought she had plumb lost her upper story. We said, 'Ina Mae, what the devil's got into you? All that carrying on in there? We thought you hated that old fool.' 'I did,' she said. 'But I just wanted them white bitches to know he was my daddy too!'"

As soon as the laughter from one story began to fade, she would start another. Finally she would break into a song, the melody a mixture of Gregorian chant and African dirge. "We tired. . . . We tired. . . . We sick and tired. We tired. . . . We tired. . . . We sick and tired . . . of being sick and tired."

Miss Fannie Lou Hamer was a great woman. A giant and a genius. But T.J. didn't seem impressed as I reminisced about her. All he said was, "She was married, you know. Her name was Mrs. Hamer." So I just went on talking, feeling something strange. Something unfriendly and unwelcomed. I had felt alienation from friends before, but this was different. I had never had a black best buddy. We both knew that we had not completely crossed the chasm of race which had separated his people and mine for so many centuries. But we had come close enough to feel comfortable in the company of each other. I had never felt that our friendship fed off the Movement for its success. It seemed unfair that it might be cursed by the cause we had mutually embraced. I wouldn't give up.

"And Ed King. You remember Ed King?"

"The one with half a face? What happened to the rest of his face? I've heard of two-faced folks, but I never heard of a half-faced one."

"The rest of his face was torn off in what a lot of people think was an attempted murder. He was the chaplain at a black college in Jackson. I believe Ed King has suffered more than any other white liberal I've ever known. Except the ones who got killed, I suppose."

When Ed returned to Mississippi from a Boston theological school to begin his life as a Methodist preacher in the early sixties, he got in trouble right away. He made a speech against segregation at his first annual conference, and afterward the Bishop couldn't find a congregation that would have him. And the Conference wouldn't accept him as a full member, entitled to all rights and privileges of a fully ordained minister of the Methodist Church. He took a low-paying job at Tougaloo College, and since his communicants were black, their problems became his problems. He was an activist in the Civil Rights Movement in a fashion no other white person I know of could match. Of course, he was considered a fanatic, a radical, and a Communist by the white people who were running the state at the time. Wherever there was trouble, he went. When he was arrested in Montgomery, a Jackson newspaper carried his picture wearing striped clothes on a road gang. When the four little black girls were murdered in the Sixteenth Street Baptist Church bombing in the fall of 1963, he attended the funeral. When the funeral was over and the large crowd of mourners, left behind when the important figures of the Movement left for the cemetery in limousines, were about to become a leaderless mob facing police machine guns mounted on surrounding buildings, Ed quieted the crowd so that Diane Nash, the black woman who came into prominence in the Nashville Sit-in Movement, could address them and convince them to disperse.

Some white clergymen from Chicago came to Jackson and attempted to attend a white church on Worldwide Communion Sunday with some black students. They were put in jail and not even Dr. Ralph Bunche, undersecretary of the United Nations at the time, was allowed to see them when he appeared at the jail. The Methodist Bishop declined to go to the jail and give them the Communion they had missed at church. Ed managed to get in, and with a steel bunk as an altar, a rusty prison drinking cup as chalice, a cold prison biscuit as the host, he sang the Psalms with them and gave them Communion.

A drifting young folksinger named Robert Zimmerman used to hang around the Movement haunts in Greenwood and other Delta towns. No one knew who he was and many considered him a nuisance, his songs pure Midwestern corn ("The Times, They Are A-Changing," "A Hard Rain's A-Gonna Fall"). Ed encouraged him, used him wherever he could. The unknown minstrel later emerged on the national scene as Bob Dylan.

"And you know what?" I said to T.J. When he didn't respond, I went on. "Late one night, not far from the place we just left, a car driven by the son of a judge and well-known segregationist forced Ed to plow into another vehicle. The rest of his face was left in the exploding wreckage."

T.J. shrugged, mumbled that he was sorry but said nothing else.

I told him about twenty-eight other young white Methodist preachers who, about the same time, signed a joint statement questioning the racial policies of the state. Threats of violence, late night telephone calls, cross burnings, and other harrassment forced most of them out of the state, some within a matter of days. They are scattered now throughout the country. One is dean of a prestigious theological seminary. Others teach in colleges or pastor large congregations. But their much-needed leadership was lost forever to the church of Mississippi. Unwilling exiles.

As I talked, I realized that it had been a long time since I had felt like a self-conscious, defensive white Southerner. I knew that white sacrifice and suffering had been minor compared to the centuries of injury black people had known. But there had been a presence. I wanted T.J. to know it the way I knew it. Not so much for self-justification. Just so he would know it too. He had often exaggerated and praised my own petty efforts. Sometimes to the point of embarrassment. Now he seemed unconcerned as I related far more laudable offerings.

"And not far away," I went on, "is the jail Mickey Schwerner, Andy Goodman, and James Chaney were locked up in, then turned loose to be chased down like wild rabbits, caught, beaten, killed, and buried in the red clay dam of a Neshoba County pond."

I could tell that he was awake now, listening. "Aren't you interested in any of this?" I asked, somewhat pleadingly.

"Maybe Mr. Carmichael is right," he said, sitting up and stretching, bluffing that he was relaxed and at ease.

"Duck Hill. This little piece of geography is called Duck Hill, Mississippi. A friend of mine almost got killed here one time. I didn't know him then, though. About 1937, I think it was. I would have been thirteen years old, but I guess it wasn't considered news at the time. Least I didn't hear about it then. Two Negro men were supposed to have killed a white merchant. As they were being brought out of the courthouse in Winona, twelve men — that's how many disciples Jesus had, you remember — grabbed the two prisoners, brought them up here to Duck Hill, chained them to two big pine trees, and burned them up with blow torches. They hung there until a preacher begged a Winona undertaker to cut them down. They put both of them, what was left of them, in one pine box, had a funeral in the back of the funeral parlor, you know, where they embalm bodies and store the coffins, and buried them around here somewhere. My friend, Buck Kester is his name, came down from Tennessee and investigated it for the NAACP. The local white folks found out who he was, and he crawled across the state line on his belly, just did get away from the lynch mob."

T.J. had been gazing out the window as I talked, occasionally munching from a sack supper they had given us at the marchers' camp. He wadded the paper sack, threw it in the back, stretched again and repeated, "Maybe Mr. Carmichael was right."

"About what?" I said, seeing that he wasn't going to change bait until I took the one he offered.

"About white folks," he said, loudly and emphatically.

"Buck Kester was white folks," I said. "And Mickey Schwerner, and Andy Goodman too. Viola Liuzzo. And the preacher in Winona who did the funeral for Roosevelt Townes and 'Bootjack' McDaniels. James Reeb and Jonathan Daniels. They were white folks too. And so is Ed King. Walking around with half his head torn off. Jesus, brother! What's eating you?"

"But white folks don't get lynched," he said, reaching over and turning the radio on for the hourly news of what was happening at that moment back in Canton.

"Tell Mickey and Andy that," I yelled above the sound of the radio, my voice showing the confusion and impatience I had felt since we left the camp site. "Dammit to hell, T.J., tell Mickey and Andy that."

"But they were Jews." He quickly snapped the radio off and waved his hands back and forth in a gesture of cancellation. "I didn't mean to say that! I mean, I didn't mean it the way it came out. I mean, I never did think about Jews as being white people. What I mean is, if Jesus had been white, he never would have been crucified. You know what I mean? I mean, we always prayed like Jesus was one of us. O Jesus, Will. Ain't no way you can understand what I mean."

Something is happening. Right here in this car in the middle of Mississippi, something is happening.

I wanted to will it not to happen. It had a nightmarish déjà vu quality. I wanted to tell him that my people had bet on that horse and that it had brought us to that moment. When the War was over, a war in which the poor whites had no vested interest but were deceived into fighting, and the gentry class had no more use for them and they had nothing except the color of their skin of which to boast, they had said "white is beautiful." I wanted to try to explain something of that burden. Not the "white man's burden," as defined and discussed by the aristocracy, but the burden of having to live with the consequences of their devilment. But I said none of that. Knowing that so much of what Stokely, Malcolm X, and others said about white wickedness was historically true, I felt I had no right to say it. If I had given my life for the civil rights cause as Goodman, Schwerner, Reeb, Jonathan Daniels and other whites had, perhaps I could scream it from my rotting bones. But I had been little more than a sympathetic observer. So I said, "Are you putting me on, Thomas Jefferson Eaves?" pretending that I was going to ram the car into a bridge railing, jerking it back just in time. "Or is it that speech back there?"

"I don't know, Brother," he said. He whispered it. "I really don't know." He quickly seemed asleep and snored loudly as we moved along.

"*Were* Jesus white?" he said when he sat up again. He stretched, yawned, and scratched his head.

"I guess I always thought so," I said.

"But I don't know." I tried to whisper it just the way he had whispered. Tried to sound just the way he sounded. "I don't know," I said again.

"Then was He lynched?" he asked.

"No," I said. "It was all quite legal. But so was segregation."

* * *

In 1969 James Forman interrupted a communion service in New York's prestigious Riverside Church and read a document called the Black Manifesto. I had first met Mr. Forman at Tent City in Fayette County, Tennessee, where he was working with the people who had been driven off the farms and plantations for registering to vote. He had also been active in SNCC, the Southern Christian Leadership Council, and other groups and was considered one of the most articulate and aggressive young leaders. Among the demands contained in the Manifesto was that white churches and synagogues pay $500 million in reparations to black Americans for past injustices. That was the gauntlet. Liberal white Christians from the North who had marched in Selma, been jailed for trying to integrate white churches in Mississippi, or signed numerous petitions censuring Southern mores never expected to be put to such a test. Had the die been cast in the First Baptist Church of Birmingham, they would have been pleased. But to hear the words from underneath America's most enlightened, liberal, and influential steeple was stunning and beyond belief.

The Manifesto represented more than the thinking of one individual. It was the findings of a meeting of an organization called the Black Economic Development Conference. Its members included many of the finest black intellectuals and activists. It was not some cynical or contemptuous joke they were playing on white religionists. They really were demanding that the white religious establishment spend $500 million of its vast wealth as expiation of its sins against black people. If it could have worked, it would have been a small price to pay. Unfortunately judgment cannot be bought off. (But for Grace!)

The interruption of the Service of Holy Communion at Riverside Church was the clearest signal that the Movement of black and white, together we shall overcome, was winding down.

In a way it was depressing to experience the waning of the social and political movements of the sixties and seventies. Many of us had found a home there. Meaning, fulfillment, purpose. Flesh and blood activity to express the things we believed. But causes and movements come and go. Tom T. Hall, noted entertainer, storyteller and novelist, marks the ending of the Hippie era at the occasion of the Democratic National Convention in Miami Beach in 1972.

Four years earlier in Chicago, the young had rioted, been gassed, beaten, and arrested en masse while protesting the Vietnam War in particular and the state of the world in general. Instead of being met in Miami by helmeted police officers with riot equipment, they were greeted by paid entertainers and allowed free run of Flamingo Park. Hall, an astute observer of human behavior and politics as well as gifted artist, sensed a drastic shift in the mood of the audiences he faced from the park stage from those of earlier days. There were efforts at disruption but the passion was not there. The crowds seemed to be on an emotional hangover, content to yell an occasional secondhand slogan, wave an old placard. Mostly they sipped their beer, flaunted their joints and bodies, the major concern being that no one cared or tried to stop them.

Tom T. found it a gloomy picture. While he would not have approved or applauded the violence of four years earlier, he said the absence of previous exuberance gave him pause. He knew where they were coming from but couldn't guess where they were headed. When his last song had been sung, about the time of the last gavel and *"sine die"* from Larry O'Brien inside Convention Center, he was too drained by it all to do anything except walk away. "You can have it," he said of the stand-up amplifiers, guitars, and valuable sound equipment. The nearest thing to a riot during the week was the scramble for pieces of what he was leaving.

Tom T. went to the bar of his hotel where he drank blended whiskey and, reflecting on the experience of providing the dirge for one of the most potent political leagues ever put together by the nation's unfledged and some words of an old black man cleaning up the lounge, wrote a country song which has become a classic.

> There ain't but three things in this world
> That's worth a solitary dime;
> That's old dogs, and children, and watermelon wine.

Those three remain. All else passes away.

XI
And Tears No Bitterness

"THE MOVEMENT HAS finally made its way to Talbot County, Georgia," Joe Hendricks told me on the phone.

"Come to die?" I asked. It had been six years since Dr. King's death. The Southern Christian Leadership Conference had not had a really successful organizing campaign in all those years. The organization, with Reverend Ralph Abernathy as president, had remained active but flawed by internal dissent and lagging interest as more and more surface concessions were made by government and society.

"Maybe," he said. "But right now it's pretty much alive. All hell's breaking loose down here. Why don't you and Jackson come down and take a look? Jackson needs to see Talbot County one more time."

Jackson loved to ride. Occasionally he went to town or to the store with me, but he hadn't made a long trip since we brought him here. He was getting old and one more trip to the land of his birth did seem proper. In addition, he had not been well. Had been badly hurt by one of his closest friends.

"It was Gordon," Brenda told me when I returned from a trip to Detroit. "Gordon hurt Jackson." She walked me to a nearby shed where she had put him. He struggled to get up and bleated softly as we approached.

"Gordon?" I said. "That's hard to believe." Gordon was the son of Heather, an Irish Setter a friend in New York had given us. The other half of him was Golden Retriever. He had always been a gentle, well-mannered dog and, from the time he was born, a close friend to Jackson.

Gordon was celibate. He had had many temptations of the flesh but had never yielded. Even when packs chasing a female in heat came through the hollow, he never joined in. Once we tried to breed him to a neighbor's Retriever, and for two days he discreetly ignored her.

He had never been off the farm except the day he was born, when I took him to the veterinarian because he was premature and I thought he was going to die.

Brenda told me how it happened. A friend from town had come to visit and had brought her spaniel. The little dog started circling Jackson, barking and leaping at him. Jackson turned round and round in place, head and horns down, ready to exert himself if necessary. In the past, when Nell was alive, Jackson would have darted under her belly and she would have shielded him. But the protective old black mare was gone. Jackson, who had led her around danger in her time of blindness, had to fend for himself. Suddenly Gordon entered the fracas, and before Brenda and her friend could get outside, Jackson had been knocked to the ground and a deep wound was ripped in his flank.

"I ought to whip you, Gordon," I said as we stood beside Jackson. But he seemed as concerned as we, licking the wound, making no effort to harm him.

"I think it was the influence of the city," I said to Brenda as she continued to scold Gordon. "He had to show off for his new friend. Show her how the big tough boys in the country do those things."

"He could have killed him," Brenda said.

"How could you do that to your best neighbor?" I asked Gordon.

"It happens all the time," she answered for him. Then she added, "But it works both ways." I thought of Nell. The Movement. And the old woman in the Woolworth store with the egg poacher. Jackson recovered but he never seemed to get his old spirit back. There is no hurt like a hurt inflicted by one's own.

Yes, I thought Jackson and I should go to Talbot County. We went in the pickup truck. The Mercedes-Benz he came in was long gone.

When we arrived in late afternoon at the Hendricks place, we found that the Movement had in fact arrived. And in the same form as it had gone to Montgomery, Albany, Selma, St. Augustine, Birmingham, and scores of other towns, cities, and counties. It was there with the same tactics and strategy — marches, mass meetings, and economic boycotts. But too late to save the life of at least one black citizen, Willie Gene Carreker. He had been killed by a white policeman following a traffic violation. That was why Joe had called.

During the decades of its heyday, the Civil Rights Movement bypassed Talbot County, Georgia, and in many ways it was a surprising oversight. The Southern Leadership Conference was born a hundred miles to the west and was headquartered ninety miles to the north. In addition, Talbot County had the third highest proportion of blacks of any county in the state.

In many ways the symbols and message of Jackson paralleled the history of Talbot County. It was born if not of royalty then certainly of aristocracy, and its history since its earliest days had been inextricably tied to the institutions of race, slavery, and betrayal of the Indians. In 1825 the Treaty of Indian Springs was signed. However culpable Andrew Jackson might have been in other transgressions heaped upon those earlier owners of this land, apparently he washes clean on that one. He considered it a fictitious document, arranged by deception, signed by but one or two of the tribal chiefs, and said that if he had been on the Senate floor instead of at home attending his ailing wife, he would have voted for its deferment.

Shortly after the shaky and controversial treaty the General Assembly of Georgia created Talbot County from a part of the land. It proved ideal for growing cotton. And if cotton, then slaves. Twenty-three years after its creation as a county, almost nine thousand slaves were listed out of a total population of slightly more than sixteen thousand.

The county was the namesake of Matthew Talbot, direct descendent of the Earl of Shrewsbury. Matthew's father, John Talbot (also the name of the first Earl), had bought fifty thousand acres of land from the Lower Creek Indians. An Englishman brought over to survey it, George Walton, later became a signer of the Declaration of Independence. Eli Whitney, a teacher of Talbot's children, invented the cotton gin in a little shop near the schoolhouse. Though his father's plantation was not within the boundaries of the newly created county, Matthew Talbot had been governor of the state for a short time, and the new county was given his name.

Lazarus Straus, who later founded Macy's Department Store, had been an early freedom fighter in his native Bavaria. When that revolutionary movement failed, he fled to America and through a series of circumstances settled with his family in Talbotton, the county seat. While he had actively opposed European tyranny, he prospered in the new country and apparently was offended by neither the oppression of the Indians nor the tyranny of American slavery. (Everyone is for freedom until he gets it for himself.) The three sons of Lazarus Straus — Isidor, Nathan, and Oscar — became famous sons of Talbot County. They went on to take their places in the fame and prominence of American history in the fields of commerce, medicine, and diplomacy.

Within two decades, Talbot County became one of the most cultured and prosperous counties in the state. The aristocracy would see that their issue were educated. So private academies, institutes, and colleges sprang up and served the wealthy of several states.

But with the Civil War and the end of slavery, the advent of the boll weevil and the demise of a cotton economy, the beginning of public schools and the bankruptcy and closing of the private academies and colleges, the ravishing of the pine timbers between the two world wars which had rapidly taken over the uncultivated cotton fields, Talbot County declined to today's skeleton of former wealth and splendor. It has approximately one-third as many people today as it had in 1850.

It is, of course, a familiar Southern story. What makes it different is that it was one of the last spots to be challenged by the Civil Rights Movement.

Four individuals, two with the same name, one with no name at all, the other with one of the most distinguished names in the county, can be mentioned as landmarks in the long journey from the Jackson era to the coming of the movement in the days of Jackson A'Goat.

In the spring of 1909, an elderly black man dressed in seersucker pants, black silk coat, red vest, and red derby hat was the only passenger arriving on the train from Atlanta. Almost totally blind, he carried a well-polished walking cane, and the gold watch chain across his chest made him something of an unusual sight for those at the depot in Talbotton, Georgia, that day. Though he was known by no one in the town, black or white, he was taken in by a prominent black farmer named William Carreker, a great-uncle of the young man killed six days before Jackson and I arrived.

It was not long until the white planters noticed a deteriorating attitude on the part of their colored people, and having just gone through the scare of the populist movement, the aristocracy put its spies in the black community to work. It was said that the old preacher was preaching to the local blacks about their continued state of slavery to the white man, telling them that if they would declare their independence they would be "free" as he was free and could wear a gold watch and diamond ring even as he did. That was radical talk in 1909 in South Georgia. In 1974, it was still radical.

The whites decided that some corrective measure was called for. A Committee of the People, which today would be called a mob, formed on Sunday afternoon on the grounds of the Methodist Church. (What would John Wesley have thought? He wrote and published his first hymn book not far away.) About fifty men on horseback called at Carreker's farm and informed him that they were afraid of insurrection and that they were there to flog the old preacher and make him leave the county. Only one spokesman, a wealthy landowner named Will Leonard, had approached the door. The others remained in the shadows of early evening. Carreker asked that the old man not be hurt, explaining that he "didn't mean no harm. He just ain't got all his wits about him." When Leonard persisted and motioned for the group to move in closer, a shotgun blast from just inside the door dropped Leonard to the ground, his head blown off his shoulders.

The Committee on horseback quickly adjourned, leaving their spokesman where he fell. William Carreker was known as a gentle colored man. They had not expected such a development. The next afternoon they regrouped, with numerous additions from several counties. The body of Will Leonard had already been found at the Carreker front door, the hogs rooting and feeding on his brains.

Within a matter of hours, the nameless "old preacher" had also been found hiding in a nearby barn. He was hurriedly bound and weighted down and taken to a bridge spanning the Big Lazer Creek. Whether he was shot before, during, or after his plunge into the water is not certain. His body was found four days later a half-mile downstream, the gold watch chain glistening in the sun.

Two days later the befriender of the mysterious preacher turned himself in. That night he was taken from the jail by a mob and next morning the body of William Carreker, who had never been in trouble before and meant only to entertain a stranger in the manner his white Jesus had instructed his followers to do, was found swinging from the cross arm of a telephone pole on the courthouse square.

A brief account of the lynching was reported in the June 24, 1909, issue of the Atlanta *Constitution*, concluding with the statement that ". . . when the doors were opened it was the work of but a few minutes to get the negro. It was all done quietly and in perfect order."

William Carreker was given a Christian burial by his family and neighbors. The blind preacher who had come proclaiming justice and freedom left neither name nor shrine. The place and manner of his interment are not known.

Sixty-five years later, Joe Hendricks asked me to serve as a consultant to an interracial committee which had been formed following the death of the young black man and the subsequent unrest. To get a feeling for the present climate, I asked Joe to take me to the Big Lazer bridge where the preacher had met death, to the courthouse square where William Carreker had been hanged, and to the spot where his grandnephew and namesake had been shot. Jackson stood between us in the cab of the truck, and we made the rounds. I had expected some sort of reaction from Jackson, some sign of recollection at being back where he had come from, but there was none. He seemed to enjoy the ride, conversation, and excitement but showed no awareness of covering old ground. When we left the last spot, I told Joe there was one other place in the county I wanted to see — the birthplace of Clarence Jordan.

Clarence, a white preacher, proclaimed the same message of justice and freedom as the nameless black one. And came close to sharing his fate. The Jordan family was one of the most prominent ones in the county. His father was a banker and merchant. His brothers are important figures in local industry, agriculture, commerce, and law. His cousin, Hamilton, was an important aide to President Jimmy Carter. One brother, State Supreme Court Judge Robert H. Jordan, wrote and privately published a history of the county. I have drawn upon it in the description of the dual lynching of 1909. Clarence rated nothing more than a listing in the book.

Clarence went from Talbot County schools to the University of Georgia and studied agriculture. He decided early that he wanted to be a preacher and just as early felt that there was something terribly wrong and un-Christian about the system of segregation and discrimination in his native land. At the Southern Baptist Theological Seminary, he learned to read the Bible in Hebrew and Greek, probably the first of his county to be able to do so since Lazarus Straus read it in his store and living room to visiting Methodist and Baptist preachers who could barely read English.

Jordan earned a doctorate in New Testament, became an ardent pacifist in the midst of World War II, and returned to a neighboring county to establish a communal and interracial community called Koinonia Farm. While at first he gained some acceptance as his contribution to improved agricultural methods in the area was realized, his community later became a center of controversy and violence. Barns, stores, and smokehouses were burned, residents were fired upon, and exclusion from local churches soon developed into a total economic boycott during which those who lived at Koinonia could purchase absolutely nothing in the county and the town of Americus, not even the services of a physician.

I spent many days and nights at Koinonia Farm during the boycott and seige, sometimes joining the unarmed night watch to ward off the shootings, sometimes just listening to this fascinating man telling stories or translating the New Testament directly from the Greek text into what he called the Cotton Patch Version.

Clarence preached total integration of every facet of society, opposed war in any form, and through the example of communal ownership of property confronted the entire American economic system with his understanding of the Biblical Faith. He received few accolades from his papers in the white community, and when he died in 1969, his body had to be hauled to Americus because it was illegal to bury someone not pronounced dead by a physician, and the coroner honored the boycott. He was buried on the Farm in a pine box made by members of the commune, wearing his faded khakis. Though he left many converts throughout the world, and even in life was counted a prophet, he was without honor in his own town and among his own people.

As we drove back to the Hendricks place, Joe pointed out a landmark of another important and famous Jordan, this one a black man. "You might want to level off the feeling with this one," he said, motioning for me to pull over. It was a common latter-day Talbot County scene. An old house, roof caved in, the standing walls covered with kudzu vines, cattle grazing in what was once a dirt yard swept clean with dogwood brooms. "That's where Vernon Jordan used to visit his auntie," he said as we climbed through a barbed wire fence, Jackson remaining patiently in the truck.

When I first met Vernon Jordan, he was just out of law school, a field secretary for the NAACP. He would later be head of the Negro College Fund and then the National Urban League, a position he held when he was gunned down by a sniper's bullet in Fort Wayne, Indiana. He survived to become a prestigious Washington attorney.

"I guess some things have changed," he said as we drove past the cemetery where Willie Gene Carreker was buried the day before, a week after he was killed. The casket containing his body had been carried from Talbotton to Woodland, seven miles, in a procession of several hundred protestors singing freedom songs in the July Georgia sun.

"Yeah, I guess some things have changed," I said. "William Carreker died at the end of a rope. Sixty-five years later his nephew dies at the end of a gun. What's changed? Except the mob didn't get paid and the lawman did."

"Don't write your story yet, Will Davis," he said, not commenting on my cynicism. "Let's go to the store. I want you to talk to John Goolsby."

Goolsby, owner of the largest market in the little town of Woodland, talked freely and easily about the shooting, the protest demonstrations which had escalated each night, and about the economic boycott.

He told me there were several versions of exactly what happened. He gave bits of each one. Then his own. Two police officers, the entire force of the town, were seated in their patrol car slightly after midnight when they heard what sounded like a crash on the other end of town. When they arrived at the vicinity of the noise, they found nothing except tire marks and a damaged electric pole. They assumed that the driver had entered a housing project less than a block away and would have to come out the same way. When he did, they pulled him over, gave him the balloon test for alcohol content, and arrested him. When he resisted, they radioed for a state trooper to come help them. When Carreker agreed to go to jail, they canceled the call. Mr. Goolsby said that from that point on there were inconsistent reports. The officers said that Carreker had jumped from the car and run into a corn field. One of them chased him and said that about twenty feet into the field, Carreker shoved or wrestled him to the ground, that they had tussled and his gun had gone off. He later admitted that he had drawn his gun when he ran into the field. He consistently denied that he had fired the shot on purpose.

"What we know for sure," John Goolsby continued, "is that a human being is dead. And that's bad." He told me that the boycott was a hundred percent effective. He also said blacks were right in the demands they were making. "The first person I hired twenty-two years ago was black. And they have always been treated fair. A lot of the folks doing the picketing and leading the boycott hated to boycott me. Some of them called and said they could arrange it so my store wouldn't be picketed. I told them I was white too.

"Now, I could have sold a lot of stuff out the back door. But I never asked anyone to come in my back door and I'm not going to do it now. You know, my kids still go to the public schools. There's only nineteen whites in that school of eight hundred, and two of them are mine. But I don't send them there because I have black trade. I send them there because it's right. And I'm proud of my church in this thing. You know there was a meeting to form the biracial meetings, and it was held at the Methodist Church. My little daughter got up and said, 'Maybe I'm out of order, but my daddy always taught us not to hate anybody, and I'd like to nominate my daddy to serve on the committee.'"

His voice broke and he drifted away, losing himself in the counters of his near empty supermarket. When he regained his composure, he came back and continued to talk.

"And some folks, black and white, criticize me about Waterboy there." Waterboy, an elderly black man who couldn't talk, stood just outside the door, occasionally drifting in and out, giving the impression that he didn't understand what was happening. "Waterboy has worked for me for twenty-two years. I've taken care of him ever since I've been in business. You know what he did before that? White folks would give him a half-dollar on Saturday evening to holler, just to make a bloodcurdling noise in his throat, and folks would cheer all over town because they could hear him — like a fog horn, you know. I can't pay him much, but it's better than a human being hollering for a living. He had a stroke or something that left him like that, and he doesn't have much mind. And that's the only thing that I really disagree with the demonstrators on. When the picketing first started, some of them would tap on the window and try to get him to come outside and join them. I called the leaders and told them Waterboy didn't understand all that and they had to leave him alone."

John Goolsby stood for a long time, just looking at a sixty-year-old man whose only known name in the community was "Waterboy." I thought of Mr. Charlie Hendricks, who told the social worker years before that they weren't going to uproot "Dummy" and put him in a home in Atlanta. Like Mr. Charlie, it was obvious that Mr. Goolsby was content to let others judge this *noblesse oblige* of a bygone era. And within the wretched system, he would offer a more humane solution for the likes of "Dummy" and "Waterboy."

Jackson and I stayed for another week, watched the boycott pickets by day and the mass meetings and marches by night, attended negotiation sessions of the biracial committee and strategy meetings of the black protestors, witnessed the signing of truces and pacts.

As we drove home, I felt depressed. Jackson sat on the floor most of the way, occasionally nibbling from a box of grain Joe had given him for the return trip. He was not the playful, exuberant fledgling of springtide, ever alert, fearful of missing one bit of the action, who had ridden those roads years before. He was getting old. As was I. As was the Movement. Though the activities of the past two weeks in Talbot County had some of the spirit of "We Shall Overcome," the fire never sparkled as it had in Birmingham, Selma, Albany, Montgomery, Memphis, and Nashville.

I reflected upon each one, my mulling approaching brooding. In earlier campaigns the important ingredients for successful organizing and protest seemed always available. To succeed there had to be a national press coverage and a visible enemy. In earlier years when a black person was killed in the civil rights struggle, the nation was reminded of it by the hourly news. Reporters, live microphones, and camera crews filled the villages, small towns, and cities. The death of Willie Gene Carreker got no such coverage. An executive producer of NBC News summed it up when I asked why his network took no notice of the death and the activities that followed: "A white officer shooting a black man is not news," he said. "It wasn't news twenty years ago. Then it *was* news for a decade when the movement was big. Now it is *not* news again. It has lost its sexiness. In the first place, we didn't even hear about it." Even the lynching of the great uncle got better coverage. "It was all done quietly and in perfect order."

The other necessary ingredient for a mass protest movement is a visible and identifiable enemy. People will march when the cameras are rolling. They will march more readily in combat with a bigoted elected official or vicious Southern sheriff or police chief, knocking heads, violating the most elementary civil rights. Bull Conner, Ross Barnett, and Orvil Faubus fit. Sheriff Jeff Hendricks of Talbot County didn't. Yet he had to be used as the visible symbol.

> No more Sheriff Hendricks.
>   No more Sheriff Hendricks.
> No more Sheriff Hendricks over me,
>   Over me.
> Before I'll be a slave, I'll be buried in my grave,
>   And go home to my Lord and be free.
>
> Freedom! O, freedom!
>   O, freedom over me.
> Over me. . . .

He did carry a gun and he did wear a badge. But the gun had not been used during the ten years he was in office, and the badge looked more like the kind that used to come in Post cereal boxes than one belonging to the stereotype of a "redneck" lawman.

The mother of Willie Carreker said that she considered the sheriff "good and kind" when she was held in his jail awaiting trial for the murder of her husband's paramour. And when her son was killed, it was Sheriff Hendricks who sent his brother to the women's prison to bring her home and arranged with the state officials to give her an extended furlough during the time of mourning.

As I drove over the mountain, not far from where Tsali, his son, and brother were executed by their friends, the futility and seeming impossibility of revolution ever completing its mission continued to pester me. Why did the Movement organizers have to pick on Sheriff Hendricks, son of Mr. Charlie, brother of Joe? I knew the answer but it didn't seem fair. I knew, and certainly they knew, that the real enemy of poor black, and poor white as well, those whose lives and fates have been tied to the land from their earliest beginnings, was not Jeff Hendricks. I knew, and am certain that they knew, that a greater enemy is the corporate structures. And agribusiness, with its callous disregard for their ties or their needs. But try substituting "military-industrial complex," "corporate structure," or "agribusiness" for "Sheriff Hendricks," in the lyrics of the freedom song. Try singing it to the tune of "O Freedom Over Me." It doesn't work. It throws the meter off.

The Civil Rights Movement of Dr. King was an emollient the South had long needed and should not be scorned. But the notion making the rounds in the early sixties that the movement had to do with the redistribution of America's wealth and not with buying a hamburger and a cup of coffee never got off the ground. A large landowner in Talbot County told me that ". . . it's pretty much a matter between the colored people and the crackers. It really doesn't concern us." He was probably saying more than he meant to. He was saying that all that was going on and had gone on was not a threat to the corporate structures of which he was a part, did not deal with the powers and principalities of this present age. That the struggle was really still over who gets the hamburger. It was not, and never has been, over who gets the filet. He was saying that it was largely a matter between the store and the trade, the pulpwood hauler and the pulpwood broker, the sheriff and the blacks in the street, none of whom are wielders of much power.

Or maybe that is the only power that will ever be up for negotiation.

The rich indulge the poor to fight so long as it is among themselves. Whatever, the blacks and second-echelon whites of Talbot County, Georgia, in the last mass campaign of the Movement, worked the things out that were theirs to work out.

The nameless blind preacher and Clarence Jordan would have been proud that they did. Unfortunately, so would the Earl of Shrewsbury.

"Cheer up, Jackson. We're almost home."

XII
The Darkness Deepens

THERE IS A CEDAR thicket at the end of our driveway. It runs along the road for half a mile. A heavy growth of honeysuckle has trellised itself on a barbed wire fence. Honeysuckle is a redolent blessing in early spring when the morning dew combines with the little orchid-like blossoms to grace the air but is a wretched enemy to farmers the rest of the time. Over the years the vines have followed the sun southward, backing through the cedars to the spring branch fifty feet in the direction of the house, the tight overlay discouraging all but the most nimble-footed from encroachment.

For several weeks I had noticed a wallowed-out area underneath one of the trees. Each morning when I went for the newspaper, Gordon and Heather sniffed the air when we came close, Gordon sometimes bouncing his way over the tight maze to check it out. Twice he came back with an empty potted meat can, and I assumed some neighborhood children were hiding in the underbrush to play picnic. It was summer, and when the flattened area did not spring back and it was obvious that it was used often, I wondered if a tramp might be sleeping there.

In rural Mississippi during the 1930's, tramps stopped often at our house. They asked for food and water, offered to do some minor chore, and were on their way. I was intrigued and tempted by their way of life. There was always a backpack, usually a ragged quilt fashioned into a mysterious roll, the unkempt beard and long hair, the weatherbeaten skin, and in each one I thought I could see an impish twinkle in squinted eyes. Tramps were not to be confused with bums, who were trash, often criminals, and did not want to work and were never to be trusted. Nor with the hoboes, who rode freight trains by choice, went North in the summer and South in the winter as sort of a profession. There was a romance about what they did, even beyond that of tramps, but freight trains and hoboes were of the cities, foreign to my experiences at the time. And one did not confuse tramps with beggars. They were also of the city, often blind or crippled, and since they asked for money and not leftovers, we didn't see them as our responsibility. Tramps were harmless, innocent, and strangely our friends. I hadn't thought about them for a long time. In the mid-eighties, though we are told often that the economy is booming, I see many more people tramping the roads again. Not many rails are left, so there are fewer hoboes.

When I went for the newspaper or to the mailbox at the end of the lane, I checked the area around the wallowed-out place in the cedar thicket to see if a tramp was there.

Then one day I saw him. I had gone to get the mail in early afternoon and sat under a tree near the road reading a magazine. A passing car honked and swerved, and when I looked up he was standing about fifteen feet down the road looking directly at me. Gordon and Heather were inside the house, and I had not sensed the presence of another as one sometimes does. For a long time we stared at each other, neither of us giving ground or acknowledging the other. He was obviously one of patience, standing as still as the fence which separated us. He seemed neither annoyed nor curious that I was there. More like, "Well, I've been expecting you to show up."

"Okay, boy," I said, seeing that he wasn't going to make the first move. "If you're going to sleep under my tree, you have to say howdy to me." But he didn't. When I moved toward him, he turned and edged back, keeping the same distance, looking over his shoulder to gauge how far he had to move, stopping when I stopped, moving again when I moved. I could tell that even the slow walking pained him. The trouble appeared to be in his hips. His legs hardly bent at the knees, and when he was standing still, there was a swiveling in his midsection. He was drawn and emaciated. His eyes were pale and sad. His overall countenance was not one of despair, more like, "If you will just leave me alone, I can make it. I won't bother you if you don't bother me." As I began gaining on him, he hurriedly crossed the road and disappeared in a field of heavy broom sedge.

"Now where in the hell did you come from?"

He was a medium-sized German Shepherd, old, darker than most shepherds but not the long-haired strain and not big. What I took to have been name and vaccination tags had been removed from two hooks still attached to a sequined leather collar. There was also a flea collar, the end of it pulled from the loop and dragging the ground.

"Well, maybe we can work something out. One thing is certain: Somebody has done you wrong. But have you done somebody wrong as well? I doubt it. If you had, you would probably be a dead dog. They wouldn't have dumped you out here in the country with no identification. Yeah, you would be a dead dog by now."

It had been two months since I first noticed the mashed-down area in the grass and weeds. Despite his gaunt appearance, he had to be finding a little food somewhere. Several things were puzzling. One, why had he picked that particular spot as his reference point? It was a common occurrence for city people to dump unwanted animals on our road. Grown dogs, puppies, mother cats with a litter of kittens, even Easter chicks and ducks, generally by Pentecost Sunday. Day-old ducklings waddling about the house with colored down are cute; at seven weeks they are rather a nuisance. Generally the abandoned animals — three Shetland ponies one time — would make their way to the door in search of people shortly after they were left, and it was our job to find them a home or make other decisions for them. This one had asked for nothing. And why was he so aloof? Most dropped animals were unusually friendly, compensating for their lost plight, assuring us that they meant us no harm.

Brenda said this one was smarter than most, that he knew that was where he was left and assumed that his former friends would return to that spot to get him. Most of the day was spent foraging but the rest of the time he waited.

We made some gruel from table scraps and left it near his hideout. Next morning it was gone. For more than two weeks we didn't see him. Each evening when we left the food, I had the feeling he was not far away, watching through the brush or from the top of the hill. We did not thicken the consistency of his food, fearing the months of starvation. One morning we found the first of several messages from him. He had turned the bowl upside down, let the water trickle down the hill, and eaten the solid pieces from the ground. Brenda said he was saying he preferred dry dog food. That night we fixed two bowls. In one we put the chunks as they came from the sack. In the other we fixed the usual gruel. That one was turned over. The other one was still upright, the food gone. He was willing to accept our favors but he wanted to set the terms. A bit uppity.

He began showing up at feeding time, taking a stand about fifty feet away and moving toward the food only as we moved away. I tried waiting him out. "I know you're hungry and I'm not. I'll stand here all night unless you come and eat in my presence." It didn't work. He was determined, defiant, and gave no quarter. I even gave him a name. Toby. "Here, Toby, come on boy. Come on, Toby."

"Don't call me boy!"

We tried moving the bowl closer to the house, thinking that eventually we could toll him to the yard. Sometimes he would drag the dish back to his territory and sometimes he didn't come near it. Once I tried dropping one piece at a time in a trail leading from his bowl to the house. He ate what was on his side of the spring branch but stopped there. That seemed to be the line he had drawn. "This side is mine. That side is yours."

Winter was approaching. While he was partly sheltered from heavy rain and snow by the cedar boughs, the temperature sometimes drops to minus fifteen degrees in the hollow. We borrowed a large doghouse from a neighbor and pulled it on a groundslide behind the tractor and put it over the fence near his spot. On the coldest nights he ignored it, sleeping in his usual place under the trees. "Who needs your help?" The alienation continued.

(When we were just yearling boys, we used to go swimming in Mr. Marshall Purdy's pasture on Saturday afternoons. Boys and girls were not allowed to swim together. No one had swimming trunks, or as the girls called them, bathing suits. We always met at Miss Retha Mayfield's store. One time Skippy Graves bought a vanilla ice cream cone. His aunt, visiting from New Orleans on some kind of government pension because her dead husband had been in the Spanish-American War, had given him a nickel. It was the Great Depression and nickels were rare.

As we made our way down the country dirt road, then over the fences and through the dense swamps to the river, we began to ask Skippy for a lick off his ice cream cone. It's hard to imagine in these days just how badly a young fellow can crave bought ice cream. We had homemade ice cream several times during a summer, but most of the time the cows had eaten bitterweeds. Even when the ice cream wasn't bitter, it never tasted like the bought kind.

So ice cream cones were not eaten, just licked and savored and enjoyed as long as they lasted. At first we asked Skippy gently. "Hey, Skippy, good buddy, how's about a tiny little taste of your vanilla there, ole pal. Whadda ya say?" Things like that. But Skippy held the ice cream cone with both hands. Some of the bigger boys threatened to beat him up if he didn't share it. He said if anybody touched him he would throw it in a pile of cow dung and stomp it.

Eventually we tired of aggravating him and ran on ahead, stripped off, and jumped in. We splashed and played water tag, pretended we were baptizing each other and just all sorts of things. Skippy was way behind, holding onto his ice cream. We knew he could hear us laughing and hollering and having a good time. He was so occupied with defending his ice cream, he missed the path and wandered around far up the river. He was so lonely and frightened by then that he started yelling through the woods for us to come and get some of his ice cream.

"Yey y'all. I've changed my mind. Come help me eat this ice cream. Boy, is it good! Come help me eat it." But the truth was it had pretty much all melted in the hot August sun. The flies from Mr. Marshall's barn had lighted on it, and what was left was filled with grime and fly specks.

On our way out of the woods, we found him sitting on a log by the path crying, clutching the last bit of the soggy, dirty piece of cone, his hands covered with flies swarming on the melted ice cream.)

During the decade of the sixties, black people, generally in the company of white friends, sought to attend all white churches. In city after city they were turned away, sometimes under threat of serious violence, often by arrest and imprisonment.

Today many of those same congregations have evangelism committees fervidly trying to recruit black members and wonder why they meet with almost total failure. Like a pear tree blooming in September, it's just too late.

Toby was a challenge to me. I was determined that we would somehow become friends.

He was not a tramp dog, however. We have had those come by also. They are trying to make it back to where they came from, generally in a hurry. They'd stop, get a drink of water, and ask for food. Then they move on. Toby stayed for almost a year, and during all that time we never broke through to him. A few times I thought we were close, but then he would back off. Eventually he did cross the creek, come to our side. And a few times he drifted into the yard. Heather and Gordon, almost always hostile to animals not a part of the household, were liberal and sympathetic. They had their personal food bowls and guarded them from each other with human-like fervor. They said nothing when Toby came close. But he never attempted to eat with them. And never responded to occasional overtures of friendship. Eventually they gave up and ignored him entirely.

Only once did he let me come close enough to touch him. I had noticed that there was one thing on which he would reveal a weakness to the point of offering a temporary compromise. One thing terrified him out of control: He was afraid of thunderstorms. When one approached, he could feel it in his diseased joints, and long before the first burst sounded he became anxious and jittery, running this way and that seeking shelter in one of the outbuildings. On this occasion I was working in the small garden near my cabin office. I had noticed a cloud moving slowly from the west and felt a slight breeze but had heard no sound of thunder. I saw Toby running and stumbling, sometimes falling in his haste, in the direction of the office. I watched as he hurried through the door of a small greenhouse attached to the cabin. Within five minutes, the first bolt of lightning struck in the distance and was followed by an almost continuous rumble of thunder. I made my way to the greenhouse and found Toby standing in a far corner, whimpering and trembling. I talked to him gently and reassuringly for a few moments, then edged slowly toward him. The old flea collar he still wore had stretched, and the loops which held the end piece in place had come off, letting it drag between his front legs when he walked. He often tripped on it, making it even more difficult for him to move about. When I was close enough, I opened my pocketknife and without touching him cut the collar off and let it drop to the floor. When he made no effort to move away as he always had, I placed my hand lightly on his head. He stopped whimpering and the shivering eased off. I thought we were about to come to terms as he stood still and calm, considering. The rain and a strong west wind beat against the oval plexiglass roof, dulling the thunder. Lightning flashed and cracked continuously, striking often in the distance. A huge limb from a scaly bark hickory tree plunged thirty feet to the ground, narrowly missing the house. We were in the midst of a full-blown electrical storm. I continued to stand with my hand on his head, gratified that he was not resisting.

"So. You need me. Only an eighth of an inch of synthetic glass separates us from the mightiest tempest we have had since you came, and you need me. Well, like I told you all along, we're pretty decent folks. We never meant you any harm. We wanted to be your friend all this time. Now you see how mistaken you really were. But that's okay. I won't remind you of what a fool you've been. I forgive you. And you know what else? I guess I need you too. I'm scared all to hell of a storm. Was in a hurricane once in the South Pacific and damn near got washed into the ocean. Had to help pick up the drowned bodies a week later. Bloated, swelled three times their natural size. And, Jesus, I can still smell them. Yeah, I'm glad you're here with me. I had nightmares about that hurricane for years after the war ended and I was back home. This stupid captain had stationed four of us on each corner of a pyramidal tent and told us not to let go of the ropes. The force of the wind got under it and blew it straight up like a kite. One scared little

private had wrapped the rope around his wrist and couldn't turn loose. 'Let go! Let go, you little fool!' the captain kept screaming. By the time he could unwind the rope, he was way up in the air. He broke both of his ankles, and when we had to move inland, I carried him on my back. The weight helped keep me from blowing away. In two weeks he was dead. Got what they called a fat embolism from the fracture and died. I remember I went to see his girlfriend in Chicago a couple of years after the war. By then she was married, though, and didn't want to talk about him. Even asked me to leave before her husband came home from work. Folks are a mess, Toby. I'll bet you're glad you're a dog. That what makes you so distant? You afraid you'll act like people? Well, I guess I don't blame you. But I'm glad you're here with me. That damn tent. Just about the size of this greenhouse.

Suddenly Toby turned his head and moved out of reach. He looked up and our eyes met. It was the first time we had looked each other squarely in the eyes. I thought of Buber's words about animal eyes. I started to pat him on the head, but he moved to the door and I heard a faint but emphatic growl from deep in his throat. I reached toward him, tentatively. This time it was a brief honest snarl, and I could see the hair along his spine starting to stand. I pushed the door open with my foot and stepped back. Without further comment, Toby raced into the raging storm. And I was alone.

* * *

Not much later I was a guest at a dinner party in the home of some old friends in a large Midwestern city. It was a couple I had known since the early days of the Civil Rights Movement. They were old now but still deeply committed to all forms of human rights. Both are well educated, cultured, and intelligent. He has been a champion and leader of the American Civil Liberties Union, Chairman of his state Civil Rights Commission, and has received many awards for his humanitarian activities. She was well known as a fundraiser for cultural, interracial, and interreligious organizations. She has been in extremely poor health for several years and now suffers from mild loss of mental faculties.

"Will, you remember it used to be there were always Negroes at our dinner parties. And other Gentiles. We simply would not have had a dinner party without them and at all our Seders. We brought Martin Luther King, Jr., here long before he was nationally known. Gave him a prestigious award. The first one he ever received, he told us later. What happened, Will? Where are they now? It wasn't just a cliché when we said some of our best friends were Negroes. Lord knows, we wouldn't use that expression unless it was the truth. For obvious reasons. They really were our friends. And we were theirs. At least, that's what we believed. And still believe. But what happened? We kept on inviting them. At least for several years. But they would decline. Make one excuse or another. We don't ever see our Negro friends anymore. Even when I was so sick in the hospital, not one of them came. Well, Pearl Louise, but she works for us. It hurts, Will. It really hurts. We tried, Will. We really tried."

There was a lengthy silence around the table. The other guests, though most were somewhat younger, had been almost as involved in what was once called liberal causes, but none of us knew how to respond. Eventually she broke the silence.

"They just act like children now. Rebellious children. Want everything at once. But we tried. Didn't we, Karl?" Karl nodded that they had.

Late that night, when only he and I were left, we sat in the library and discussed what his wife had said. Ever the liberal and analyst, he wanted to approach the subject from every angle. First he apologized and explained that his wife had not meant it the way it had sounded. "You know, age affects each one differently. With me it's these damn cataracts. I can't half see. With Anne. Well, as you can tell it has done a little something to her mind. She's all right. She just gets things confused sometimes. Like, well, for instance, she knows that black people don't like to be called Negroes now. But she forgets."

"For God sakes, Karl. We've been friends too long to apologize for a little blockage in a blood vessel. Not only that, what did she say that isn't true?"

"I know, Will. But I think some of our guests didn't understand what she meant when she said black people act like rebellious children. She doesn't mean to be discourteous to black people . . . critical of them. It is more of a judgment upon us."

He began a long review of the history of race relations in America, comparing it often to the growth and development of his family.

"Anne was referring to the relationship between the two cultures. The sad fact is that from the beginning of this country we have had a white society and a black society. That was what the effort toward integration was all about. So far we haven't pulled it off. We still have a segregated country. Her analogy has some hazards, but it isn't far off. The major weakness of it is that it puts whites in the role of parents and blacks as their offsprings. But even that holds up historically. I'm not saying it was right or just. Not even fair. It was none of those things. But it is historical fact. The power was held by whites, and they doled it out to black people as they saw fit. The same way parents do to their children."

I began to see his point. When our children are very young, we control them totally. We decide how much freedom they will have. What they eat, wear. We read what we want to read to them. Tell them when to get up, when to go to sleep, when to go to school, when they can spend the night with a friend. We are the dictators. The slavemasters. And not always benevolent. Some parents abuse their children. Many are killed with violence. Always it is their effort to control them. Other parents are kind and gentle. But in either case, we are the decision makers.

He used the metaphor of the adolescent's use of the family car. "I remember one of our daughters. When she was fourteen, she wanted to drive the car. Now, there was no rational reason why she shouldn't. She was big for her age and unusually careful and responsible. But we hid behind the law, like the South did with legal segregation, you see. We know there is no reason why you can't eat here, go to school here, but the law says you can't and we are law-abiding people. Used to be a boy or a girl had to be sixteen to get a driver's license. Then the law changed in our state, and a fifteen-year-old could drive. But we still didn't think it was a good idea for Sarah to take the car out alone. Too dangerous. She was ready for the change but we weren't. Pretty soon there was tension. We couldn't understand what had happened to our sweet and docile little girl. She was rude and inconsiderate. Sometimes she would go for days without speaking to us, or she'd fly into a fit of pique at almost nothing. One night Anne and I came home from a friend's house, and both Sarah and the car were gone. We panicked. It was a many faceted crisis. There was concern for her safety. She was breaking the law because she was not a licensed driver. But more than that we felt betrayed. The moral code of the family had been violated. She had disobeyed those who knew what was best for her. Or thought they did. She had been disloyal to those who were the best friends she had in the world. Or so we told ourselves. She came back shortly, had gone no farther than the next block to get a book she needed to complete her homework. This brought different values into conflict. 'Yes, of course we want you to do well in school. And no, we don't want your friends to make fun of you because they are allowed to drive and you aren't. But you have committed a serious breach of trust. An offense against this family. Your behavior is a threat to the structures which hold it together.' We punished her in the same manner as we had on other occasions: no allowance next week, no Sunday afternoon bowling for a month, and if it happens again, no trip to the beach with the rest of us next summer."

"Did it work?" I asked. Karl had crossed the room and was warming himself by the fire. He stood swirling a small amount of brandy around in a large snifter. He laughed heartily at my question, turned and threw the remainder of his drink into the fireplace. As the brandy ignited and flamed brightly, he came and sat down, still laughing.

"There's your answer," he said, pointing to the blaze. We sat silently as the flare died away and the fire became a comfortable, peaceful glow again. "And there's your answer too," he said, motioning toward the amiable logs quietly warming the room with goodwill again.

"Of course it didn't work. Things got worse and worse and worse. Sarah didn't go to the beach that summer. Nobody went to the beach that summer. We had the wildest, most belligerent female adolescent you can imagine. Oh, it wasn't hopeless, and we kept trying. We gave some. Knew we had to. We sent her to driver training school, though she didn't take it seriously at all. Said she already knew how to drive. No thanks to us, was the way she put it. We gradually eased back. You know, said she could use the car but she had to be in by nine o'clock. And how long do you think that lasted? Not long, I can tell you that. It helped at first. But pretty soon she started tugging at the leash again.

Nine-fifteen. Nine-thirty. One night after midnight she came in drunk as Cooter Jones. Hair all disheveled. Blouse rumpled and half unbuttoned. Oh, Will . . . God . . . dammit. . . ."

He put both hands over his eyes, and I thought he was crying. He sat for a minute and then got up and began stoking the fire. When he turned around, I could see his moist eyes glisten, tired but ready to continue. "Will, we almost lost her. She left us, ran away. There should be a euphemism for that wretched term, but there isn't. She ran away from home like trash. For three months we didn't know where she was. If she was dead or alive. We're family people, Will. A proud, upper-middleclass Jewish family. That sort of thing just doesn't happen to us. But it did. Oh, did it ever happen to us."

Unexpectedly, we heard Anne's voice from the door behind us. "And that's what I meant, Will, when I said the Negroes are acting like rebellious children. I didn't mean it literally." She was in her nightclothes. I had not heard her come in and did not know how long she had been there. "I couldn't sleep," she said to Karl. He poured a finger of brandy and handed it to her. She took the chair closest to the fire, lit a cigarette, then immediately snuffed it out. "Have I quit smoking?" she asked, looking at Karl.

"Almost," he said, lighting one of his own and handing it to her. "But almost is not quite. Enjoy your brandy. And your nicotine."

"The Supreme Court said they could use the car," she laughed. "But the white folks told them they had to be in by nine. And that's where we are now."

"Speaking of now," I said, "where is Sarah?"

Karl went to the library shelves behind us and removed a silver-framed picture and handed it to me. The woman appeared to be in her mid-forties. A handsome, casually dressed man of about the same age sat beside her. On the floor in front were three smiling children, two girls and a boy. I guessed them to be in their early teens.

"Sarah is a clinical psychologist in Baltimore. Chuck teaches history in high school." Anne reached over and took the picture, looked at it for a long time before slipping it out of the frame, turning it over, and handing it back to me. On the back of the photograph was inscribed: TO THE REST OF OUR FAMILY IN PITTSBURGH. It was signed, "Sarah, Chuck, and three little half-Jews."

"I noticed she didn't say, 'Three little half-Gentiles,'" I said.

"First things first, huh, Daddy," Anne said, reaching over and patting Karl on the knee. "You can't have everything."

"But she did come back," I said, not as a question.

"Yes. Thank God. She did come back," Karl said. "We couldn't have lived if she hadn't. For we drove her off. We didn't mean to, but we did."

"So there is hope," I said, pouring a little brandy for myself and moving closer to the fire.

"There is always hope," he said.

I couldn't sleep when I finally went to my room. Children. They act like children. I had trouble with the statement even after the metaphorical explanation. I thought of the cold and violent February of 1960, the beginning to the sit-ins in Nashville, and of Kelly Miller Smith. James Lawson. Diane Nash. John Lewis. Vivian Henderson. No children they. Moral and intellectual grown-ups. I thought of the early days of the Southern Christian Leadership Conference, listening in strategy sessions to the wise counsel of Bayard Rustin, Ella Baker, Andrew Young, C. K. Steel of Tallahassee, Joe Lowery of Mobile, counsel which would have been a credit to any discussion of foreign policy among diplomats of the highest rank. And one of the number would attain such rank. I heard the sage words of Herman Long of the Fisk University Race Relations Department, Jean Fairfax of the American Friends Service Committee, Dorothy Cotton of the Southern Christian Leadership Conference. I saw a fifteen-year-old woman named Dorothy Counts spit upon by a mob in Charlotte, North Carolina, as she approached the school she was determined to attend, her father, a saintly Presbyterian minister and professor by her side, whispering as they walked through the angry throng, "Remember who you are. Don't answer back. Remember who you are."

I remembered another fifteen-year-old, Elizabeth Eckford, sitting on a park bench outside Central High School in Little Rock crying all alone from both fear and a broken heart. The rulers and warriors of her state, along with a raucous mob, had met her at the schoolhouse door, the warriors with tanks and automatic weapons, the assemblage from the citizenry cheering their efficiency. I talked again with her seventy-four-year-old father, who had told me that night that if anyone harmed his baby he would kill them, still not asking how one old man with a rusty twenty-five-calibre pistol tucked behind the bib of his overalls could effect such revenge against the force of armies.

Medger Evers, amiable civil rights leader of Mississippi, killed in his driveway by a Delta Compson. Denise McNair, Carol Robertson, Addie Mae Collins, Cynthia Wesley. Children? Yes. But grown enough to pray. And grown enough to die at the site of their Birmingham altar.

I walked along the balcony of the Lorraine Hotel in Memphis, and as I approached room 306, where Martin Luther King, Jr., had been shot dead two hours earlier, I saw again the vapors rising from his blood still puddled on the floor, vapors looking like fog hovering over a Louisiana bayou on a summer night. The whirling blue and red lights of the police cars and standby fire engines combined to throw a strobic pattern against the window, reflecting downward to the ghostly claret of the martyred chieftain.

I thought of T.J. and wondered where he was.

A few months earlier he had driven into the yard early Saturday morning. Brenda and I were sitting at the kitchen table, barely awake. Usually he simply opened the door and walked in. This time he knocked. It was warm and only the screen door was closed.

"Come on in, T.J.," Brenda called, moving to greet him. By then I was in the den, pretending a rage because I couldn't find my socks. It was for his benefit. He always enjoyed seeing Brenda end such antics with a firm, "Be cute, Will!"

"I don't have much time," I heard him say. "Is your husband home?"

"Come on in," she said again, holding the screen door open. "Don't you want some coffee?"

I really don't have much time, Miss Brenda. Thank you very much."

When I got my boots on, I went outside. He was squatting underneath one of the big pin-oak trees. There was a strange awkwardness in the air, a dull formality. Instead of the ceremonial Movement handshake we generally went through, he reached out and shook my hand quickly. Except for the Vick's salve on his fingertips, it was almost the way we shook hands the first time we met.

"How you been, Brother?" I said, motioning him to some benches nearby.

"Pretty good, Will," he said, not looking at me. And that was all he said.

"Well . . . uh . . . where you off to? Don't you want some coffee? I mean . . . what's the big rush?"

He began tossing acorns at the big plantation bell hanging not far from where we sat. Each one landed with a flat ping sound. I felt an urge to ask him if he didn't want to ring the bell, pull the rope and hear the rich melodious pealing that would fill every inch of the hollow, the way he had done so many times before. The day Dr. King was being buried in Atlanta, he rang it so hard it turned all the way over in the brackets.

I began throwing acorns the way he was doing, the alternating sluggish sounds the only conversation between us for what seemed a long time.

"Will, I'm moving back to Alabama," he said finally, still throwing or thumping the acorns at the bell.

"Running to or running from?" I said, hearing his words but not really considering what I was saying in response.

He stopped throwing the acorns and gazed in the distance. "That's a strange little word," he said. He spoke each word slowly, deliberately. "There's running to, and running from. Running to and fro. Run about. Run for. Run of the mill. Run into. Run out of. And then there's the back door runs." He threw another acorn hard against the bell, the sound more like that of a rock. "Yeah, that's a strange little word. Takes up almost two columns in the dictionary. Three letters, but it means almost a whole page in Mr. Webster's book."

I knew that it was my move, knew that I was behind in whatever was taking place. I suggested again that we go in the house and have some coffee. I began carving little figures from the larger acorns, placing them in a row on the bench beside me.

"Say good-bye to Jackson," he said, standing up and moving toward the car.

"He's up at the Dolan House," I said. "You want to go and tell him yourself?"

"No. Just tell him I said good-bye." He turned and walked back toward me. "And by the way. Tell him I said thanks."

He shook my hand, firmer, but still not the Movement grip. We embraced, each with bumbling restraint. He rushed to his car and I stood watching him maneuver it out of the muddy lane and head south.

"Well, we almost made it," I said aloud when he was out of sight. I thought I heard him answer but didn't understand exactly what he said. It sounded like, "Don't eat no yellow snow."

"You look like you're mad," Brenda said when I went back inside. "Like you've just been hit in the face with a wet possum."

I was mad. But I wasn't sure at whom. Or what.

William Snelgrave, prototype of the slave trade. Chieftains of the Mande, the Susu, peoples of Dahomey, and other African nations who violated blood and alliances to capture and deliver brothers and sisters to the barracoons for plantations and mines. Eli Whitney, whose invention sent the ships on hurried expeditions to the coastal waters of Africa for further raw material of shame. I was mad at them. Yet without any one of them, T.J. Eaves would not have been to me. I would not have been to him.

And Ben Tillman, Hoke Smith, W. K. Vardaman, pursuing the passions of Negrophobia with rhetoric so extravagant and original as to merit the rank of literature had it not been so real. Tom Watson, who had a chance to slow the flood tide of hate but chose instead to mount the podium of intolerance. Fuel which surely powered the little car T.J. steered onto the road and into the morning sun. At least there was the sun.

Andrew Jackson, who might have led us better.

Huey Newton, Bobby Seale, Stokeley Carmichael, who tattooed "Black Power" onto the fringes of American history. Ross Barnett, George Wallace, and Leander Perez, who made their judgment inevitable.

"There ain't no revolution, Mutharoe," T.J. would say when he saw the Movement appropriating the things it claimed to detest. No revolution? No evolution! Caucasoid . . . Negroid . . . Mongoloid . . . race . . . race . . . race . . . race. What hath God wrought? What have we wrought. T.J., turn around.

And mad at myself. For thinking that in one lifetime of good intentions and carefully placed good deeds the canyon of tragedy would be bridged.

I couldn't sleep that night. Nor could I sleep now as I lay in the home of a Yankee friend and wondered about "the children."

Where are the children in this company of giants? Still I felt the truth in what my hostess had said. There *is* estrangement in the air. And anger. There is more social segregation today than there was fifteen years ago. The conscious effort to have black and white together in every endeavor and occasion is gone. Certainly much of it was strained, some even counterfeit quotas to meet prescribed guidelines. There were jokes about "Rent-a-black" agencies. And worse. But at least people were getting together.

"The civil rights gains we have made are largely cosmetic," my old friend, Kelly Miller Smith, told me just before he died. One would have expected to hear those words in earlier times, when the gains of black people had been more modest than it seemed to me they had been during his lifetime and mine. He had been a pivotal figure in it all. Buses and taxicabs, schools, restaurants, theaters, parks, swimming pools, as well as participation in the political process had all been desegregated since he and I had come to Tennessee from Mississippi in the rigidly segregated decade of the fifties. He from a black church in Vicksburg, I from a white university in Oxford. His little daughter had been one of the nine brave children who faced the violent mobs to begin the slow and painful process of integrated education. The church he pastored for thirty-four years was headquarters for the massive sit-in movement. Quietly or obstreperously, whatever the situation indicated, he negotiated with mayors, governors, merchants, and owners such issues as employment, housing, fairness, and decency in general.

All that he had been party to and more. Yet here he lay, a few weeks from death, saying that all his efforts had produced no more than a cosmetic coating over an inveterate malignancy as socially lethal as the one claiming his life. I protested with a roll call of the improvements he had presided over. He listened in his usual smiling, affable manner as I listed them one by one, beginning with public transportation in 1956 and concluding with his being a dean and teacher in one of the most prestigious universities in the South where he could not have been more than janitor not many years earlier.

"But they still don't respect us," he said sadly. After a long pause for needed oxygen, he continued. "Look at the television shows. Listen to the rhetoric on the streets. They still don't respect us."

His words were a startling awakening. How far I had missed the point of it all. How dissimilar the promised lands two Mississippi men had envisioned. To grant the truth of his words would be to acknowledge that the years of both of us had been wasted. He spoke with approval and gratefulness for the things I recited, but as he did it became clear to me that the one thing which was behind all else was never his. Respect.

Freedom is respect.

I recalled another conversation with an activist of equal vigor but different orientation in which I was told, "I don't give a damn if I make them sick. I don't care if they vomit in their plate when I'm eating in that restaurant. Just so they don't try to stop me from being there." Were too many of us partly persuaded by that era of anger? And by our own academic platitudes of, "We're not trying to change attitudes, just behavior"? If so, black and white together must now share in the responsibility. Both should have known better. Watching without daunt a neighbor vomit in a plate because of one's presence is not part of the human make-up. For surely we are created to love one another. It has to be all right that the other is there, or old attitudes will some way, some time recapitulate old behavior.

Freedom is reconciliation.

"They still don't love me." That was what my dying friend was telling me. *Freedom* is love.

When our last tearful embrace was over and I was about to leave his hospital room, I could think of but one thing to say. "I thank you, Kelly. You gave me my freedom. I'm sorry I couldn't do more to give you yours." Though the words were spontaneous and cumbersome, they might have been a brief summary of the Civil Rights Movement of the sixties. I know I am more free than when it began, but I do listen to the rhetoric on the streets as Kelly advised me, and I know that he spoke the truth. The Civil Rights Movement may be over for black people. It is far from over for whites.

As I drove alone back to our hollow, I thought of the day the starlings came. "Does one love birds?" I had asked as I looked out upon the bird world I had created rent asunder. Or is it one's own sense of beauty and balance that made him strive?

Black Americans would never again accept an assigned place.

Federal court decisions and national legislation had finally heard the call and had joined forces with the Movement. Halting, timid, and tentative as it was, the rigid pattern of segregation which had prevailed for so long was being dismantled. Local and state sanctions which had held it in place crumbled, and black people were at least free enough to act like the rest of us. As they did, many a dedicated white liberal fell by the wayside. Disillusionment set in. Old stereotypes were renewed and the question, "What do they want now?" was the one most frequently heard. What *they* wanted, of course, was to cease being *they*, just to be birds, not *the starlings*. Yet a large part of the liberal community could not appropriate their arrival. Their behavior seemed ungrateful. A few on the block, in the school, in commerce and industry were desirable. But the flock was threatening and disquieting. What was the basis of the fear? No one seemed to know. Yet alliances which had held firm for two decades began to come apart. Merchants and industrialists who had been generous in their financial and political support of the Movement began to be taunted by many urban blacks as "Jew exploiters." "What meaneth this bleating of the sheep and the lowing of the oxen?" Would the victors yet again accept the gods of the vanquished? Was the beloved community destined to become a tankard of hate, choosing wrong enemies, spewing invectives learned from former captors? Philanthropic foundations which had funneled millions of dollars to race relations agencies in the South and nation began to search for new causes. Federal programs of the New Frontier and the Great Society began to vanish in a whirlwind of reaction.

Where is the beloved community, Thomas Jefferson Eaves? You were an old fashioned integrationist. So was I. Black and white together. And we were not alone. But we are losing, T.J. Or have we lost already?

Certainly no one can say there have not been changes, that all our efforts were in vain. It is presumptuous for me to say our *efforts. It was you thrown bodily into the back of the paddy wagon in Nashville on a cold February day twenty-six years ago. I went home to my family while you and almost a hundred others stayed in jail. Most of you were just children. How many long and tortuous nights did you spend in Southern jails, T.J.? And how many times were you beaten, once left for dead? Too many.*

And things did change. Sometimes I wonder in which direction. In 1963 Mississippi State University had not one black student enrolled. That year their basketball team won the Southeastern Conference and was invited to play in the NCAA tournament. The first game would be against Loyola of Chicago, a team that would start black players. A furor developed and an injunction was issued prohibiting the team from leaving the state, despite the university president's approval. Before the injunction, later vacated, could be served, the coach's staff literally slipped the team out of the state under cover of darkness. The state's largest newspaper editorialized that, "harping over a chance at a mythical national championship isn't worth subjecting young Mississippians to the switch-blade society that integration inevitably spawns." This year I watched the NCAA tournament. Several Southern teams were in the finals. I looked in vain for one white face on the starting lineup of any of the teams. I guess that bothers me too. Is that integration? Or is it black folks dancing fo de man?

Yes, things have changed, T.J., John Lewis, Diane Nash, Bernard LaFayette, Jim Lawson. But where is that for which you suffered so passionately? And that which I came within one long distance phone call of dying for? And you know, and certainly I know, that I wasn't that important in the Movement. Some folks had simply got that desperate.

Last night I went to the City Club with my son and a friend. The Club has a fancy restaurant overlooking the area of the city you knew as a battleground for equality. My son is a brand new practicing attorney in Nashville now. He was one year old when you were arrested for ordering a hamburger and a cherry Coke at the Woolworth lunch counter. And got a wound which has never healed. When he was a little older, and you and I more secure in our friendship, you took him fishing and had your picture made with him holding a ten-pound carp. He was so proud of that big fish. When the two of you got back from the lake and I tried to explain why we didn't eat carp, he didn't understand. You had already told him that in Alabama carp was a favorite with Negroes. "What are Negroes, Daddy?" he asked. "I want to be a Negro so I can eat my fish." Last night we ordered blackened redfish, a specialty of the chef.

George Barrett was the friend who took Webb and me to the Club.

He's a member now. When he, as a young lawyer not much older than Webb is now, stood beside Mr. Looby to defend you and the other criminals who marched downtown that day and sat beside white folks at the lunch counter, he couldn't afford to belong. It took a lot of courage for a young white lawyer to be assistant counsel to a black one in a civil rights case in 1960. But he survived it. And prospered. I hope my son will have similar mettle. But can he? Is it possible? Have the years of alleged progress, the manipulation of issues, computerized politics and human relations by technology so eroded the genes of spunk as to render the young professionals moral geldings?

I wonder in retrospect why the Movement didn't picket the City Club and the Belle Meade Country Club instead of F.W. Woolworth. Why didn't we know that it was they who could make a difference, who would finally decide? Why did we incur the wrath of the boys who had come to town to get their hair cut at the Barber College for a quarter and who, finally, would not even be a party to the truce? Why didn't we go to the clubs and tell them that we had come to break bread with them? And when they refused tell them that we were Lazarus there to gather the crumbs from the table of Dives? Would the settlement have come any sooner? Or would the certain defeat have been for a long time? Were we demanding of the patricians that they force the plebians of all colors to eat together while they remained unaffected behind the dividing wall of affluence? I fear the frail truce. Where are you, T.J.? Where am I? Are we distanced by the cunning of the gentry who continue to profit from our disunion? Is the second reconstruction over and done with? And is the report of the Kerner Commission that we are moving toward two societies in America, one white, one black, separate and unequal, destined to become reality? Or is it already reality?

* * *

The day following the thunderstorm and our conversation in the greenhouse, Toby disappeared. None of the neighbors saw him. No trace of his body has been found. I wonder if I will ever see him again.

XIII
Swift To Its Close

"JACKSON, WHAT ARE you doing standing in my door?" When I returned to my cabin office from lunch with Brenda, he was just outside. He had not been here for many months. When he first came from Georgia, he liked to come down and watch me work. But he developed some bad habits. He nibbled the flowers, ate seeds from the bird feeders he could reach, and on several occasions jumped on top of my desk, pulled paper from my typewriter, and ate it. All of it combined got to be a nuisance, not funny anymore. When other things failed to keep him away, I stretched an electric fence around the building. I watched through the window when he came down to join me next morning. Always suspicious of anything new, he eyed it carefully, considered leaping over it, then reached out and touched it with the tip of his nose. Instead of stepping back, he bounced straight up, danced about for a moment, then touched it again. I had walked out in the yard, and he saw that I was standing there, watching him. This time he didn't jump, tried not even to flinch when the charge hit him. He stood very still, eyeing me stoically, then turned and walked toward the Dolan House. After about fifty feet, he turned and looked at me again. This time I thought there was a look of hurt and disappointment in his expression. "Why did you do that to me? I trusted you." I went with him on up to the Dolan House and we sat on the porch for a few minutes.

After that he came only for special occasions or when I invited him. Now here he was, standing in the door waiting for me. He knew what I didn't. That it was an extraordinarily special occasion. I spoke, asked him what he was doing there, and started inside. He bleated softly but didn't try to follow me. When I closed the door, I heard his whining cry again. I went back to him and he let me rub his horns, something he would never allow before. I assumed that the horns were his only claim to masculinity after the fraternity boys had finished their shame upon him. He seemed to have trouble breathing, and occasionally there was a hacking cough. I offered some oatmeal which I sometimes fed the goldfish. He ate some from my hand, then followed me inside. He lay down halfway across the room and I called the doctor, forgetting that it was his day off. I pulled the paper from the roller of my typewriter and offered it to him. He acknowledged the offer but didn't take it. He seemed uncomfortable but didn't move while I worked on a speech.

We had to drive to Huntsville, Alabama, later in the afternoon, and as I left the office he got up and went with me to the house. When I went inside, he tried to go with me. I told Brenda how he was acting, and she said it was almost time for her to feed him, that she would take him up to the Dolan House. Monika Rusch, a young Swiss woman who spent several summer vactions working on the farm and who loved Jackson as much as anyone, went with her. He didn't want to go, so they put his leash on him, something we seldom did unless he rode with one of us to a neighbor's house. With one pulling gently on the leash and the other coaxing him with the bucket of feed, I watched from the kitchen window as they disappeared through the gate and made their way up the hill to the Dolan House. Brenda said they put his feed on the same big flat rock as she had done over the years. He lay down beside it but didn't eat. He watched them all the way down the hill, bleating faintly. He didn't want to be alone.

When we returned the next day, we found him underneath the back porch of the Dolan House. He was lying in the exact spot he had spent his first freezing night when we arrived from Georgia. He was dead. I am sorry that Jackson A'Goat died alone.

The next day was the Fourth of July. I ring the big bells on the Fourth of July. Some of the neighbors used to think I was the most patriotic citizen in the valley. And I do love my country. We have the title, a clear and unencumbered title to forty acres of it. It is home. It is ours. But my patriotism is not a virtue. It is my sin. It is something of which I repent, not something I celebrate. So when I ring the big bells on July 4, first the one by the log house office, move on to the smaller No. 4 halfway to the house, then walk the two hundred yards to the other big one and ring it, it is a lamentation. It is to remember the Dolans and the Youngs, the Mescalera and the blacks who held clear and unencumbered title before we came. It is to lament the results of the doctrines of Manifest Destiny, the Jackson Harvest, the roll call of the Iroquois and Sioux, the Cherokee and the Navaho, Hopi and the Crow. It is to confess the ideas of racial and sexual supremacy which continue to dominate this land, the roll of generations of slaves. It is to acknowledge and bewail our manifold sins and wickedness, the patterns of greed, conformity and blind obedience to witless authority that would spell doom if left, like genocide, to follow their own grim logic. Grieve for the soldiers on both sides of a war that was to be a new birth of freedom, and the casualties of great Social Movements, like the ones which have claimed all of my own adult life, dedicated to somehow alter the legacy of original sin. Vietnam, and the mining of Nicaraguan harbors. The execution of our mentally ill, and such contradictions as the condemnation of Nestle's formula which would claim the lives of fifty thousand a year in what we pridefully call Third World countries, while accepting in an almost cavalier fashion the termination of the lives of two million of the unborn in our own nation.

And yet, save a little of the tolling, if not for celebration then at least for thanksgiving. Thanksgiving for the great counter-ideas: tolerance, helpfulness, the notion of community, and the greatest idea of all — that there be worship of no other gods than One who said to Moses from the burning bush, "I am Who I am."

And thanksgiving for Jackson, so long alive, now lying dead. Ring the bells for him.

I thought of T.J. as we rang them, wished that he were there to ring the one by the Pool of Siloam the way he had the day we stood there talking of metal sculpture theology. "Jesus is a mess! Jesus is a mess!" he had screamed, his head still bandaged from the billy club of a Nashville policeman. I remembered years after that, an Easter morning, when our little grandson, barely able to pull the big rope, had rung one bell while I rang another, yelling to the full extent of his tiny lungs, "Jesus is risen! Jesus is risen! JESUS IS RISEN!," his high tenor voice echoing in the distance, his laughter blending with the pealing of the bells. Two No. 7 bells, each one cast in Ohio more than a hundred years earlier, one for a black church in Tennessee, the other to regulate the lives of black field hands on a Delta plantation, now calling in unison that the One each had confessed as Lord, along with their white masters, had conquored death.

"Will, it's time to bury him." Monika Rusch said as she came into the kitchen where Brenda and I were sitting in silence. She had dug a grave beside the grave of Blind Nell and had somehow managed to get his body from the Dolan House to the grove of trees where he would lie. All was in readiness when she came for me.

It seemed appropriate that Monika was the one to help bury him. She was somehow summary and quintessence of all the hundreds who had touched and been touched by him as they passed through this hollow. An alien who called a Tennessee valley *home*. She had come as others had come. Now a phantom everyone, paradigm of the congregation. *Let's all bury Jackson*.

I looked down at his bloated body, little yellow eyes still beautiful, freckles on his nose flirting even in death.

"The age of Jackson is over, Will," Monika said as she rolled the little fellow into his final resting place. She knew well his history and ours.

"Yes, I know."

"Your brother was buried on Valentine's Day," she said, handing me a shovel. "And today is your country's Fourth of July."

"Yep," I said, leaning momentarily on the shovel handle, taking one last look. I did not trust myself to say more.

Together we shoveled the earth upon him, sweating in the summer sun. I mumbled some words as she leveled the heaped up mound and drew a cross in the fresh ground. Time, distance, space, geography melded to pronounce a nourishing benediction as an American man approaching the Biblical allocation of years and a European woman barely grown stood together in somber support.

"It's done," Monika said, her voice sounding more soft and gentle than a Swiss German accent generally does to deep South ears. "It's done," she said again when I didn't move. "Let's go to the house." When I still didn't move, she began walking away, leaving me alone, with and without Jackson. She looked back twice to see if I was all right.

I sat on the ground between the graves of these two sweethearts. A cloud came between me and the sun, hesitated briefly, moved away. A formation of giant C-130 airplanes, used by the Tennessee Air National Guard, moved northward, drowning the sound of a big earth mover clearing land on a nearby farm for a subdivision. The sounds, place, and occasion seemed reason enough to cry out loud. Old hurts returned and I gave each one a moment of the grief.

My brother had been dead for more than ten years and I still missed him. Weep.

I relived our childhood; picking cotton to buy our own school books, wearing clothes handed down to us by New Orleans cousins, hearing our father's anguish on Christmas Eve night because the rains had not come in time to save his crops and there would be a slim Santa Claus for his children — injuries the Great Depression inflicted upon its young, wounds I thought had long since healed. Weep.

I heard the breaking of my sister's heart as I stood in her kitchen and told her that her twelve-year-old son was dead. I made no effort to stay the tears. Sitting there in the broiling sun, I seemed almost to revel in their flow.

Suddenly I realized that I was weeping for none of that. I was crying because I loved Jackson. And he was gone.

I was grieving for a goat. And it was all right. All at once I knew that it was all right. Like a little boy whose doll has been smashed by a speeding car, shamed by his father for playing with a doll in the first place, then for not being a man about it when it is destroyed, somehow knowing when his father walks away that if his sister can cry, well . . . so can he.

Weep for a goat. Go ahead. It's all right.

A kaleidoscope of his years filled my mind. I saw him staring out the back window of a Mercedes-Benz on a Georgia highway on a Sunday afternoon and spending the night in a Holiday Inn. I watched him choosing between spending his life with an old black mare or a herd of his own kind, then leading her gently in her final years of darkness and grieving for two days beside her fallen body. I smiled as he played king of the mountain on the high porches of the Dolan House and scared many an unsuspecting guest in the middle of the night. I defended him again from gossip and ridicule as he climbed timidly into the sleeping bag of an Arkansas Calvinist preacher. I thanked him when he brought me comfort and welcomed me home at the end of many a sad and weary journey. I scooped bushels of his pill-like droppings to feed the tomatoes, the zinnias, and petunias that brought the hummingbirds in summer.

Something fine, something of essence, hopeful and elegant, gauge of civility and a more excellent way, something of us at our best was gone. I sobbed some more. Then when I had cried enough, I got up, blew my nose, and went to the house. Jackson was laid to rest.

In life, in death, O Lord, abide with me!

* * *

Brenda, never one for funerals, was sitting at the kitchen table when I walked in, pretending to wrestle with a difficult crossword puzzle. She didn't look up. "I forgot to tell you that T.J. called this morning," she said over the noise of the radio.

"T.J. Eaves called?" I exclaimed, my grief delayed. I had not heard from him for almost two years. Not since the morning he came by and told me he was moving back to Alabama. I knew that he was married and someone told me they had twin girls and one of them was named Willene.

"Yes. You were in the field."

"Well, great! Where was he? Is he coming out? Where's his number?"

"He didn't leave a number," she said, snapping the radio off. "Said he'd call back."

"Call back! Lord Jesus, when? Why didn't you get the number? I need to talk to him! *I have something to tell him*. When is he calling back?"

"He didn't say."